The authors illustrate the multiple dimensions of democracy in education, from classroom practices and classroom interactions, to ideologies underlying the curriculum and educational policy. This book combines in an excellent way reflection and practice, and therefore it is relevant reading for teachers and prospective teachers. This volume is based on shared expertise of scholars from two countries, discussing intensively and systematically, not only the opportunities and significance, but also the challenges of democratic education.

Arja Virta, Professor of History and Social Science Education, Department of Teacher Education, the University of Turku, Finland

Educating for Democracy in England and Finland

With the growth of terrorism, instability in the EU following recession and the acceleration of support for right-wing political parties in Europe, discussions on the nature of democracy and democratic citizenship have never been more important. Exploring the relationship between democratic values, classroom practices and neo-liberalist ideology in England and in Finland, *Educating for Democracy* argues that it is the role of governments and the education systems they support to create teachers and students who can voice critically appraised judgements to guide their citizenship.

With chapters co-written by English and Finnish authors, this book analyses the history and current state of education systems in England and Finland, with reference to other European countries, in order to establish whether they are effective in creating democratically minded citizens. Recent years have seen decreasing control of educator professionalism as governments have become more concerned about economic growth, and in some cases, survival. The contributors to this volume question whether educators are becoming less effectual as a result, exploring the idea that democracy is a dying concept, and asking whether educators are now simply creating cogs for the neo-liberalistic/capitalist machine.

This book will be essential reading for academics and researchers in the fields of teacher education, education studies and comparative education. It will also be of great interest to those concerned with issues surrounding citizenship, democracy and the role of the government in education.

Andrea Raiker is an independent consultant and researcher in higher education in the UK and internationally.

Matti Rautiainen is Vice Head of the Department of Teacher Education at the University of Jyväskylä, Finland.

Routledge Research in International and Comparative Education

This is a series that offers a global platform to engage scholars in continuous academic debate on key challenges and the latest thinking on issues in the fast growing field of International and Comparative Education.

Books in the series include:

Educating for Democracy in England and Finland
Principles and culture
Edited by Andrea Raiker and Matti Rautiainen

Transformative Learning through International Service-Learning
Towards an ethical ecology of education
Phillip Bamber

The Critical Global Educator
Global citizenship education as sustainable development
Maureen Ellis

Investigating Education in Germany
Historical studies from a British perspective
David Phillips

Knowledge Hierarchies in Transnational Education
Staging dissensus
Jing Qi

Global Identity in Multicultural and International Educational Contexts
Student identity formation in international schools
Nigel Bagnall

Teaching in Primary Schools in China and India
Contexts of learning
Nirmala Rao, Emma Pearson and Kai-ming Cheng with Margaret Taplin

Educating for Democracy in England and Finland

Principles and culture

Edited by Andrea Raiker
and Matti Rautiainen

LONDON AND NEW YORK

First published 2017
by Routledge
2 Park Square, Milton Park, Abingdon, Oxon OX14 4RN

and by Routledge
711 Third Avenue, New York, NY 10017

Routledge is an imprint of the Taylor & Francis Group, an informa business

© 2017 selection and editorial matter, A. Raiker and M. Rautiainen; individual chapters, the contributors

The right of the editors to be identified as the authors of the editorial material, and of the authors for their individual chapters, has been asserted in accordance with sections 77 and 78 of the Copyright, Designs and Patents Act 1988.

All rights reserved. No part of this book may be reprinted or reproduced or utilised in any form or by any electronic, mechanical, or other means, now known or hereafter invented, including photocopying and recording, or in any information storage or retrieval system, without permission in writing from the publishers.

Trademark notice: Product or corporate names may be trademarks or registered trademarks, and are used only for identification and explanation without intent to infringe.

British Library Cataloguing in Publication Data
A catalogue record for this book is available from the British Library

Library of Congress Cataloging-in-Publication Data
Names: Raiker, Andrea, editor. | Rautiainen, Matti, editor.
Title: Educating for democracy in England and Finland : principles and
 culture / edited by Andrea Raiker and Matti Rautiainen.
Description: New York, NY : Routledge, 2016. | Includes
 bibliographical references.
Identifiers: LCCN 2016020642 | ISBN 9781138640825 (hardcover) |
 ISBN 9781315630915 (electronic)
Subjects: LCSH: Citizenship—Study and teaching—England. |
 Citizenship—Study and teaching—Finland. | Civics—Study and
 teaching—England. | Civics—Study and teaching—Finland. |
 Democracy—Study and teaching—England. | Democracy—Study and
 teaching—Finland. | Education and state—England. | Education and
 state—Finland.
Classification: LCC LC1091 .E38414 2016 | DDC 370.11/5—dc23
LC record available at https://lccn.loc.gov/2016020642

ISBN: 978-1-138-64082-5 (hbk)
ISBN: 978-1-315-63091-5 (ebk)

Typeset in Bembo
by Apex CoVantage, LLC

Printed and bound in Great Britain by
TJ International Ltd, Padstow, Cornwall

Contents

List of contributors		ix

1 **Education for democracy in England and Finland: insights for consideration beyond the two nations** 1
ANDREA RAIKER & MATTI RAUTIAINEN

2 **Living between two education systems** 17
JOSEPHINE MOATE

3 **The role of the teacher in educating for democracy** 27
ANDREA RAIKER, MARJA MÄENSIVU & TIINA NIKKOLA

4 **Democracy, classroom practices and pre-service teachers' conceptions of excellence** 42
ANDREA RAIKER & MATTI RAUTIAINEN

5 **Searching for the roots of democracy: collaborative intervention in teacher education** 54
EMMA KOSTIAINEN, ULLA KLEMOLA & UVANNEY MAYLOR

6 **Democracy and the curriculum: English and Finnish perspectives** 69
NEIL HOPKINS & MIRJA TARNANEN

7 **Power, democracy and progressive schools** 81
SAKARI SAUKKONEN, PENTTI MOILANEN, DAVID MATHEW & EVE RAPLEY

8 **Perspectives on accountability in education: local democracy versus national regulation** 93
JENNY GILBERT, PENTTI MOILANEN & SAKARI SAUKKONEN

viii *Contents*

9 Inclusion and democracy in England and Finland 109

CATHAL BUTLER & AIMO NAUKKARINEN

10 Educational research for democracy 127

JOSEPHINE MOATE, SARAH COUSINS, WENDY CUNNAH & MARIA
RUOHOTIE-LYHTY

11 Fighting against the flow in theorizing education 140

OLLI-PEKKA MOISIO, ANDREA RAIKER & MATTI RAUTIAINEN

12 Towards the future 154

MATTI RAUTIAINEN & ANDREA RAIKER

Index 163

Contributors

Dr Cathal Butler is Senior Lecturer in Special Educational Needs at the University of Bedfordshire, England.

Dr Sarah Cousins is Director of the Early Years Programmes, Centre for Lifelong Learning, at the University of Warwick, England.

Dr Wendy Cunnah has recently retired as Principal Lecturer in Education at the University of Bedfordshire, England.

Dr Jenny Gilbert is an independent reviewer for the Quality Assurance Agency for Higher Education, UK.

Dr Neil Hopkins is Senior Lecturer in Education at the University of Bedfordshire, England.

Dr Ulla Klemola is a lecturer in the pedagogy of physical education at the University of Jyväskylä, Finland.

Dr Emma Kostiainen is a lecturer in interpersonal communication at the University of Jyväskylä, Finland.

Marja Mäensivu is a doctoral student at the University of Jyväskylä, Finland.

David Mathew is an educational developer at the University of Bedfordshire, England.

Professor Uvanney Maylor is Professor of Education at the University of Bedfordshire, England.

Dr Josephine Moate is a post-doctoral researcher at the University of Jyväskylä, Finland.

Dr Pentti Moilanen has recently retired as Professor of Education at the University of Jyväskylä, Finland.

Adjunct Professor Dr Olli-Pekka Moisio is Senior Lecturer in Philosophy at the University of Jyväskylä, Finland.

Adjunct Professor Dr Aimo Naukkarinen is a lecturer in inclusive education at the University of Jyväskylä, Finland.

x   *Contributors*

Dr Tiina Nikkola is a post-doctoral researcher at the University of Jyväskylä, Finland.

Dr Andrea Raiker is an independent consultant and researcher in higher education in the UK and internationally.

Eve Rapley is Curriculum Enhancement Co-ordinator at the University of Bedfordshire, England.

Dr Matti Rautiainen is Vice Head of the Department of Teacher Education at the University of Jyväskylä, Finland.

Dr Maria Ruohotie-Lyhty is a post-doctoral researcher at the University of Jyväskylä, Finland.

Dr Sakari Saukkonen is a project manager at the University of Jyväskylä, Finland.

Dr Mirja Tarnanen is Professor of Language Education at the University of Jyväskylä, Finland.

1 Education for democracy in England and Finland

Insights for consideration beyond the two nations

Andrea Raiker & Matti Rautiainen

Introduction

According to Dewey (1939), the aim of education is to unite individual citizens and their society through an approach based on democratic values and practices. The purpose of education is the achievement of progress through giving voice to all sectors of the community. Dewey's perception of democracy is based on a philosophic perspective that has:

> ... faith in the capacity of human beings for intelligent judgment and action ... so that they can fully take part in democratic life ... to respond with common sense to the free play of facts and ideas which are secured by effective guarantees of free inquiry, free assembly and free communication?
> (*Ibid.*:3)

Although written nearly 75 years ago, Dewey's conception of education for and through democracy still has persuasive power when today's issues are considered. Progress in the key global issues identified by the United Nations (see, e.g., 2015) of peace and security, human rights and development, humanitarian affairs and international law, global warming and sustainability are all predicated on contributions from an educated, knowledgeable and critically reflective governance and citizenship. We argue that it is the role of governments and the education systems they support to create teachers and students who can voice critically appraised judgements to guide their citizenship.

We also argue that teacher education, as a principal developer of students' higher-order thinking skills of critical reflection, analysis, evaluation and synthesis (Raiker, 2010), has an essential role in creating educated, knowledgeable and critically reflective citizens. This process, beginning in schools, culminates in teacher education based in universities, and is focused on research. Research in universities creates new knowledge; the new knowledge created informs practices and content embedded in tertiary curricula. However, the ability of teacher education to do this is being curtailed by '... the hegemony of globalised knowledge economies in which knowledge is a prime commodity' (Boden & Epstein, 2006:224). The phrase 'knowledge as a commodity' defines neo-liberalism, a

2 Andrea Raiker & Matti Rautiainen

global ideology that aims to combine liberal politics with economic growth and profit. Neo-liberalist nations regard knowledge as a product and aim to control it to be consumed in increasingly competitive educational institutions. This determination of teacher and school education as knowledge production to be consumed by citizens as a 'value-for-money' commodity, controlled through the bio-power of the neo-liberalist state (Foucault, 1984), does not resonate with Dewey's conceptions of the democratising power of education or of faith in the capacity of human beings for intelligent judgment and action (Dewey, 1939:3).

In Europe, governance and hence the education systems they support are based on democratic ideals. However, all have developed differently over time from unique socio-economic, historic and political factors, factors that have also resulted in warfare. It is not surprising that the European Union (EU) stresses education for democracy as a basis for the well-being of Europe (e.g., EU, 2013). Member States of the EU share similar values and aims for democracy, but also varying degrees of adherence to neo-liberalist principles. To explore the relationship between democratic and neo-liberalistic approaches to education, we focus on two countries, England and Finland, with reference to other countries to place our arguments in a wider context.

England, as part of Great Britain, has been a colonial power and has introduced its education system worldwide. Finland is a member of the Nordic states and has developed a unique system that has been contained within its national boundaries. Both countries are well-known democracies within Europe. Their education systems have been shown to be currently successful by international assessments such as the Programme for International Student Assessment (PISA) and the Pearson analysis. However, the British government has and is using Finland's greater success and England's declining achievement in PISA as an example and driver for change in teacher education. But in Finland, teachers are considered of paramount importance in education and for promoting and developing democracy. In England, teachers are regarded as instruments to achieve neo-liberalistic ideals, a perception that Dewey would regard as undemocratic. In Finland, the teacher's level of autonomy and pedagogical freedom, indicators of Dewey's conceptions of faith in democracy, is one of the highest in the world; in England, the teacher's autonomy and pedagogical freedom is constrained by league tables, examinations and government inspection. Nevertheless, according to an *International Civic and Citizenship Education Study* (ICCS; Kerr et al, 2010), English students have more opportunities to participate in democratic processes, such as collaborative school activities and decision-making, than their Finnish counterparts. This is surprising, as the *National Core Curriculum for Basic Education* in Finland states:

> Basic education must provide an opportunity for diversified growth, learning, and the development of a healthy sense of self-esteem, so that the pupils can obtain the knowledge and skills they need in life, become capable of further study, and, as involved citizens, develop a democratic society.
> (2004:12)

Education for democracy in England and Finland 3

It appears democracy is acknowledged but not actioned in Finnish classrooms, even when the teacher has autonomy to choose activities according to personal pedagogic principles (Rautiainen & Räihä, 2012).

The complexity inherent in the word 'democracy' and how it is manifested in English and Finnish educational processes and practices is becoming apparent. This is due in part because education systems arise from socio- political conditions, all of which have historical roots, resulting in unique national systems. The process to establish current systems in England, Finland and all European countries has been lengthy, going back centuries in some cases. However, all are being orientated by the current international political climate that is tending towards neo-liberalism. This has revealed itself in decreasing control of educator professionalism as governments are becoming more concerned about economic growth, and in some cases, survival. If the trend continues, there are implications for teacher education and classroom practice in nation states. It could be argued that educators, whose own democracy in the seminar room and classroom has been undermined, will become increasingly ineffectual in creating democratically minded citizens. The impact of this could be that national education systems will create future citizens who have no concept of European and global democracy. Furthermore, they may be content for nation states to be forced apart, as currently could happen in the United Kingdom and Greece with regard to Europe. It may even be possible that democracy is a dying concept, and what educators do is to create cogs for the neo-liberalistic/capitalist machine in a way recognizable by Marx in the nineteenth century, or by Weber in the early twentieth as 'birds in an iron cage'.

At the heart of these issues are two fundamental questions which we will explore in this book:

> What are the similarities and differences in educating for democracy in England and Finland that could be used as a basis for developing shared understanding and an agreed direction for Europe and beyond?
> What are the key elements in developing democratic practices and how might these be achieved?

The concept of democracy

The concept of democracy is complex and multidimensional, with a long history and large content. Peters (1958) provides an overarching definition of democracy as a specific form of social structure, even of control. Western democracy has its roots in the ancient city-states, particularly Athens. However, Athenian conceptions of democracy were based upon certain formal rights, such as freedom of speech, to ensure that all designated citizens had the same opportunity to express and gain support for their opinions (Sinclair, 1988). The present-day usage of the term 'democracy' refers more to the political system – which may be left, center or right-wing – and includes a wide-ranging electorate, free elections and a free press (Moyn, 2006:1). We will argue that this is too narrow a definition and that a fundamental element has been omitted: the responsibility of a democracy to establish environments where citizens' abilities to engage effectively with democracy and its processes could be developed.

This was not required in the city state of Athens. The etymology of 'democracy' is from the Greek *demos*, meaning the people, and *kratia*, power or rule. In Athenian democracy, 'the people' (i.e., men, not women or slaves) were all citizens. They had the right to speak at the monthly Assembly, the supreme legislative body, and in the courts where justice was administered. Their engagement with democracy was direct: citizens were aware of their responsibilities. No doubt, some citizens concerned themselves more assiduously in the preparation of perspectives and their delivery at the Assembly than others. Nevertheless, their views and arguments were delivered face-to-face with the presiding executive committee and issues were debated in the immediacy. This is very different from the current situation where the number of citizens in a nation can be counted in millions. For the two countries that are the foci of this book, the Finnish population stands at just over 5.47 million (Statistics Finland, 2015) compared with approximately 53.9 million living in England (ONS, 2014). Representative democracies have developed as pragmatic solutions for nations believing that citizens should contribute to debates on finding solutions to social concerns. Additionally, there are many issues, both inside and beyond the frontiers of nations, and all have the potential of, to a greater or lesser extent, impacting on citizens' day-to-day lives. Examples affecting Europeans include the rise of Islamic fundamentalism, the success of left-wing political parties in Greece and Spain with anti-austerity policies and the high levels of carbon emissions affecting climate. How can an individual among millions in Estonia, Italy, Finland or England convey his analysis and evaluation of situations that could affect his family, present and future? Furthermore, how can that individual acquire the knowledge, understanding and critical thinking to give reasoned, nuanced judgments on such issues?

In this, the Athenian experience can help us. For Socrates, Plato and Aristotle, citizens should strive for the 'good life', by which was meant the virtuous life. According to Aristotle (1981), the good life included political participation and taking care of public affairs. Democracy was not something separate from a citizen's day-to-day life, but an essential part of human life and humanity. The conception of democracy as an essential part of human life has caused debate on the role of education for democracy since the Enlightenment: how much power and participatory citizenship can and should be given to a child in a society or in a school? Locke argues this question from the viewpoint of freedom. According to Locke, a child should not be given right and freedom for decision-making too early, but on the other hand, a child's education should not be excessively patronized. Education's fundamental task, according to Locke, is to promote autonomous thinking and activity which are keys for an autonomous citizenship in society (Locke, 1880:105).

For Dewey (1966), the underlying principle underpinning education for democracy is simple: just begin living democratically, because education is life and not merely a preparation for it. In the same way, schools should be constructed as miniature societies whose activities are directed by democratic ideals. Through their actions, Dewey believes that schools should be able to offer genuine social living rather than cutting themselves off from society, for example, as a place for doing homework or for bringing parents, students and teachers together. Democracy is a way of life, not a form of organization or administration. On this basis, Dewey defines one of schools' fundamental tasks as being the development of communality and communal life: democratic living (Dewey, 1966: 94–95, 120). The school represents an integrated entity where the taste of real life – something Dewey demands for schools – is constantly present in the everyday life of the school. The communality of school is thus not separated from, for example, the teaching of school subjects, but the total activity of the school. Therefore, this activity, including school subjects, should be organized in such a way that the study of communality and communal life is possible as a natural part of the activities of human communities.

The teacher's role in this process of creating schools that are miniature democratic societies is important. Teachers can create a culture where participatory democracy is possible in classrooms and in school, but they can also create a superficial democracy that shows something about democracy in practice without the vision of democracy. In fact, the school can also become a community which is no longer a representative democracy, but more like an aristocracy or even a dictatorship.

This is how democracy came to be viewed in all Western democracies by the 1800s, with consequent negative connotations of the majority terrorizing the minority: for example, in England's perception of the people *versus* the aristocracy in France during the latter's revolutionary years. Literally in the event, a new conception of democracy in Europe came with the French Revolution. Liberalism was one of Revolution's 'children' and stressed the individual's freedom. According to Herbert Spencer:

> Every man has freedom to do all that he wills, provided he infringes not the equal freedom of any other man.
>
> (Spencer, 1954:95)

Today, 'neo-liberalism' is more commonly used than 'liberalism'. Neo-liberalism as a term became widely used in public debate after World War II. Originally associated with principles of liberalism combined with neo-classical economics and the free market economy (Harvey, 2005), the term now has different meanings depending on the speaker and the situation. For many, neo-liberalism represents social, economic and political inequality and the development of society into and for two groups: the ruling elite of the rich, and the poor (e.g., Bourdieu, 1999). According to Oravakangas (2005), this is reflected in a change in school ethos as schools respond to demands concerning international competitiveness. The aim of education is no longer Dewey's vision of individual citizens united in their humanity and with their society through an approach

6 Andrea Raiker & Matti Rautiainen

based on democratic values and practices. It appears to lie in the production of measurable objectives with learners reduced to figures on a spreadsheet in a master plan to produce wealth on a national level, with the many serving the interests of the few privileged and rich, and with scant regard for sustainability and the well-being of undeveloped nations.

England and Finland in the context of democracy

Despite its complexities, democracy is essentially about how a society relates to an individual, and how that individual relates to society. In England, the principles determining British democracy were laid down in Magna Carta, the discussions leading to its first iteration being agreed between King John and his barons on June 15, 1215. The barons demanded the re-establishment of ancient personal liberties they had enjoyed since Anglo-Saxon times. Its clauses laid down the responsibilities of the King, the ruling body and towards the barony in terms of life, liberty and property. The agreement was to be implemented through a council of 25 barons, working with the King. John and his successor, Henry III, both challenged Magna Carta. It was cancelled, reinstated and changed on several occasions, but on January 20, 1265, the first Parliament was held to discuss reforms to taxation and the law. It consisted not only of the barons, but also of the county knights and the burgesses from the major English towns. So the social, or class, divide in English democracy was enshrined in two embryonic institutions that became the House of Lords, consisting of the barons or landed aristocracy, and the House of Commons for the 'common' people.

There were no clauses in Magna Carta dealing with education. Nevertheless, over the centuries, reforms in education in England and the rest of the UK have followed the extension of suffrage, though not necessarily being the direct result of it. Rather, at certain times, the will of the people culminating in social unrest demanded change, and this manifested itself in various ways, including reforms to suffrage and to access to education. This, in turn, can be connected with the growth of capitalism and the need for a literate and numerate population to work in industry, business and commerce.

For example, suffrage for all men and women aged 21 and over in the UK was established by the Representation of the People (Equal Franchise) Act in 1928. This was at a time when the country was far from recovered from the impact of World War I and just before the beginning of the Great Depression in 1929. No sooner were some parts of the country returning to relative prosperity when global war again broke out in 1939. Before World War II had ended, it had become obvious that the pre-war system of universal primary education supplemented by secondary education for those who could pay for it was unfair and would not support an impoverished nation struggling to reassert itself in a post-war world. The Education Act of 1944 established a tripartite system of education for secondary schools in England and Wales and made all school education free for all pupils. However, the class system that had framed democratic

Education for democracy in England and Finland   7

processes and was evident in Magna Carta and De Montfort's first Parliament underpinned the 1944 Act. Three different types of secondary schools were established: grammar schools, secondary technical schools and secondary modern schools. Success in taking a test, taken at age 11 and known as the 11 plus, determined which type of school a child would attend, and hence to a great extent decide his future. Though not recognized at the time, the test was biased towards children from middle-class backgrounds in that it used language and question contexts more familiar to that class. Those that passed the 11 plus, predominantly the children of middle-class parents, went to academic grammar schools whose focus was on university entrance and professional careers; those who failed, who were predominantly working class, went to secondary modern or technical schools, destined principally for blue-collar work in trades and industry. Nevertheless, the act brought more girls and children from working-class families into secondary education and subsequently into higher education. However the greater number of young people educated brought awareness to the working class of their lower social position, causing great bitterness, particularly between the working and middle classes. Expanding educational environments had been created where citizens' abilities to engage effectively with democracy and its processes had been developed, but these raised fears of impending social instability.

At the same time, teacher education became a graduate profession. Teaching and learning was considered the business of teachers. The 1960s were a period of experimentation, with Local Education Authorities working with universities and schools. An example is the secondary Humanities Curriculum project, aspects of which are still in evidence today in the form of dialogic teaching and the use of philosophy for children to explore problematic social and emotional issues. But 'progressive' education had powerful detractors. The Black Papers One and Two were published in 1969, attacking what the authors saw as the excess of progressive education. The William Tyndale affair of 1975 promoted rumours of anarchy in the education system. As a result, in 1976, the Labourite Prime Minister James Callaghan launched his 'Big Debate' on education in a speech given at Oxford University's Ruskin College. This was the beginning of the end for teacher and teacher educator autonomy in England and Wales. Public respect for teaching as a profession decreased. In 1983, Margaret Thatcher's Conservative Government published *The Content of Initial Training*. This signaled the end of university control of teacher education. With the *Education Act* of 1988 prescribing the curriculum and the 1994 Education Act establishing the Teacher Training Agency to control teacher-training supply, funding and content, teacher and school education became manifestations of government ideology. That ideology was and is neo-liberalism, defined by performativity. According to Ball (2003:216) 'performativity is a technology, culture and mode of regulation that employs judgments, comparisons and displays as means of incentive, control, attrition and change . . . [representing] the worth, quality or value of an individual or organisation'. Levels of performativity were overseen and maintained by a new regulatory body, the Office of Standards in Education.

8   Andrea Raiker & Matti Rautiainen

The quality assurance/audit-driven approach established by Thatcher of prescribed curriculum and assessment, league tables and inspection of schools and teacher training providers was not tempered by the ascendancy of the Labour Party in 1997. Tony Blair's rhetoric of putting emphasis on education and of 'raising the bar and closing the gap' was researched by Thomson et al. (2010) during the final years of his government. They concluded their research by stating:

> We showed that the policy mantra of raising the bar AND closing the gap is an ideological construct which sutures together these two goals in conceived policy space, then mandates a technology of targets and tests. This translates into everyday educational practices geared to the transmogrification of students into data, and their teachers into alchemists, in the perceived space of contemporary English schooling.
>
> (2010:653)

The deprofessionalization of teaching and curricula tied to testing was and is not conducive to creating educational environments where future citizens' abilities to engage effectively with democracy and its processes can be developed. Dewey's (1966) assertion, that schools should be constructed as miniature societies reflecting the wider society's democratically driven activities, is not being advanced. The 2010 White Paper *The Importance of Teaching* has not improved the situation. In England and Wales, greater emphasis is to be placed on school-led and school-centred initial teacher education, with the possible endowment of teacher accreditation by providers other than universities. What is more, the Foreword to the White Paper (2010:3), signed by the Prime Minister David Cameron and the Deputy Prime Minister Nick Clegg, states the following:

> So much of the education debate in this country is backward looking: have standards fallen? Have exams got easier? These debates will continue, but what really matters is how we're doing compared with our international competitors. That is what will define our economic growth and our country's future.

It is clear that the ideology driving democracy in the UK is not democratic at heart but neo-liberalistic, defined by competition, compliance and political control. This is supported by the current *Teachers' Standards* (TS, 2012:10) requirements which state that teachers will demonstrate high standards by:

> '... ensuring that personal beliefs are *not* [our italics] expressed in ways that exploit pupils' vulnerability or might exhort them to lead the law' and that teachers will demonstrate high standards of ethics ... by *not* [our italics] undermining fundamental British values, including democracy, the rule of law, individual liberty and mutual respect, and tolerance of those with different faiths and beliefs'.

Education for democracy in England and Finland 9

Individual liberty and respect for the rule of law were explicit in Magna Carta. The establishment of Parliament was to promote tolerance through debate – that is implicit within the word 'Parliament'. Not only does this statement suggest the writers of the *Teachers' Standards*, who are government officials, do not understand the concept of democracy themselves; they have no faith that pre-service and practicing teachers do. Furthermore, as teachers are a subset of the population, it suggests that the population as a whole does not have a clear conception of democracy. If this is the case, the fault must lie in some part with school practices and curriculum content which are mandated and controlled by government. It appears that the British government will be more concerned with engineering schools to improve school and teacher education for competitive reasons, such as improved performance in international tests, e.g., PISA, than developing environments where citizens' abilities to engage effectively with democracy and its processes will be developed.

In contrast, during the past decade, Finland has risen at the top of the world in surveys measuring the state of democracy. According to Economist Intelligence Unit metrics, Finland has been one of the most democratic countries in the world for many years. In comparisons made by Transparency International, Finland was consistently the world's least corrupt country until 2013, when its ranking fell to third place. According to a survey made by United Nations (Helliwell et al, 2015), Finland is also one of the world's happiest nations at present. These results have driven debate in Finnish society because Finland is not used to seeing itself at the top of such surveys: traditionally, Finns have held feelings of inferiority in relation to other nations. Because Finns do not believe themselves capable of such high rankings, doubts have been raised about the reliability and validity of the surveys' methodologies.

Historically, the position of Finland as a Western democracy is interesting. As did many other European countries, Finland gained its independence after World War I following a century under the Czarist Russian Empire as an autonomous Grand Duchy, which in turn was preceded by a 700-year history as a part of the Kingdom of Sweden. In the 1600s, governance and the establishment of law were organized through the four-estate parliament known as the 'Diet for Estates'. Particularly in the 1700s, the Diet had considerable power, compared to that held by the Swedish King. Participation in the rule of his kingdom was a fundamental right for estates. The Finnish estates were fully involved in the activities of the Diet, and by doing so, created the basis for the Finnish system which survived when the country became part of Russia in 1809. At the beginning of 1800s, Finns were accustomed to live in a system where representation ensured their views could be heard and they could participate in the decision-making process. Though this was not democratic in the Athenian sense, even peasants could gain access to the King through the Diet. Because these processes were so engrained in the Finnish tradition of governance, it was possible to maintain them when ruled by the Tsar of Russia and later, post-independence, by the President of the Republic of Finland, whose power was very strong until the early 2000s. This was the result of the culture created during the long

Swedish rule, and it reflected traditions where peasants and other subordinates as well as the aristocracy had different ways to be active in the kingdom's politics.

Unlike Sweden, Russia was an autocratic tsarist empire where subjects had no part in the decision-making process or in politics generally. They were merely 'souls' owned by the Tsar and the aristocracy. Finnish political traditions survived only because they were protected by the autonomy given by Tsar Alexander I and confirmed by his successors through the oath of allegiance given by the Finnish estates at Borgå in 1809 (Meinander, 2011). Thus, Finland became a 'nation among nations' according to Zachris Topelius, a leading Finnish intellectual during the following era of national awakening under the liberal Tsar Alexander II. Finland's Diet, inactive since Russian annexation, met in 1863, and regular sessions were established thereafter. Society and education in Finland began to develop according to liberal principles (Meinander, 2011). In 1858, the development of basic education began with Tsar Alexander II's proclamation that in future, primary schools could be founded with state support. Under the direction of Uno Cygnaeus, a new primary school system was planned, including the development and organization of teacher education in colleges. Nevertheless, many children grew up without going to school. It took decades to construct a comprehensive primary school network across Finland and to ensure that all schools had qualified teachers (Valtonen & Rautiainen, 2012).

The most important change during the period of 1809–1917 from the viewpoint of democracy in Finland took place in 1906 *via* parliamentary reform. Equal voting rights were given to all citizens aged 24 years and older. At the same time, the Finnish Parliament became unicameral, a radical development in Europe at the time (Meinander, 2011). Finland was the first country in Europe where women received equal suffrage to men. These changes, together with the rise of pan-Slavism in Russia (which threatened Finnish autonomy) and the spread of socialist thinking, accelerated the debate concerning the importance of civic school education.

After the civil war following independence from Russia in 1917, civic education was seen as a tool to prevent further internal strife and to develop national identity (Arola, 2003). Finland remained a democracy during the interwar years, despite an attempted coup in 1932 by the fascist Lapua movement. Nevertheless, school ethos remained right-wing and teacher-centered. In this context, democratic activity in school was very narrowly defined compared with the concept of democratic education being developed by Dewey at the same time.

Finnish society changed following, and as a result of, World War II. Of particular importance was that the hitherto-prohibited Communist Party became the center of power. Criticism of the school system grew and eventually led in the 1960s to radical school reform.

Compulsory basic education for all was extended to nine years. This was part of the building of the Finnish welfare state which aimed to create a more equal society for all citizens; education had an extremely strong position in this process. Education became not only a tool, but also a promise of a more democratic society embodied by the newly formed Social Democratic Party.

Education for democracy in England and Finland   11

School reform and the debate around the school system created tensions between the different stakeholders. One of these tensions resulted in a radical democratic experiment in the early 1970s. In the beginning of the 1970s, school councils became highly politicized in the 8-year grammar schools, a traumatic period for teachers. The experiment was quietly withdrawn towards the end of the 1970s and schools became islands where people were careful not to talk about politics, i.e., not to take a stand on contentious issues. With the introduction of the comprehensive school, assessment of learning moved more vigorously towards evaluation of how well individual pupils achieved the objectives set for each subject. Thus, by the start of the 1980s, schools had become socially neutral places (Kärenlampi, 1999; Rautiainen & Räihä, 2012). During the last fifteen years, there have been numerous different projects with the aim of democratizing schools, but so far little has happened. For example, pupils' unions do not have enough power in school decision-making. They have a social function, e.g., to arrange celebrations instead of contributing to decision-making processes in school. Playing 'the game' according to rules is a recognizable stereotype of being political in Finland (Luhtakallio, 2012:186).

The development of Finnish democracy has been a long-term development where the role of representativeness is significant. Spontaneous civic activism has been viewed negatively, and traumas emanating from the civil war in 1918 and the Communist era during the 1960s and 1970s are deep even today. The Finnish school is a typical example of this as active citizenship is construed as representing a democratic society. But is this enough? Is school actually creating passive subordinates, because teachers are limiting conceptions of democracy by defining what is the good and correct way to act democratically instead of giving pupils the opportunity to experiment with 'democracy in action' from their own viewpoints?

Why this book?

This book has been written because of the authors' concern for our children's future as involved and reflective citizens. One of the most important cornerstones of European cohesion is democracy, but according to Economist Intelligence Unit metrics, democracy has declined since 2008 in several EU Member States. Deep and prolonged economic crisis has strengthened anti-democracy movements, including the rise of extreme right- and left-wing parties, for example, the United Kingdom Independence Party and the Syriza anti-austerity party in Greece. The European Union emphasizes that schools should develop pupils' knowledge and understanding of active citizenship and democracy. One of the key competences for lifelong learning is stated to be social and civic competence:

> Civic competence, and particularly knowledge of social and political concepts and structures (democracy, justice, equality, citizenship and civil rights), equips individuals to engage in active and democratic participation.
> (Official Journal of the European Union L394:10)

12   *Andrea Raiker & Matti Rautiainen*

However, the EU's Member States have very different approaches to educating and developing children and young people to become active in democratic citizenship. What is more, they have sovereignty of affairs concerning educational policy. Democratic ideas appear in school systems in very different ways and forms, mostly because of their history, culture and politics. We argue that there is richness in diversity, but there is also a need to identify similarities as a basis for developing shared understanding and an agreed direction for educating Europe's young people in democratic citizenship. As a first step, this involves the analysis and evaluation of democratic practices in classrooms and education systems in different European countries. In this book, we begin the process by comparing policy and practice in relation to educating for democracy in England and Finland.

In order to gather data on the relationship between democratic and neo-liberalistic approaches to education in the two countries, recorded video seminars connecting the Universities of Bedfordshire (England) and Jyväskylä (Finland) were held, firstly in December 2012, when student teachers, schoolteachers and teacher educators presented their views on the theoretic aspects underpinning their work, and secondly in January 2014, when teacher educators debated conceptions of democracy. Thematic analysis according to the voice-centered rational method (Mauthener & Doucet, 1998) revealed that Finnish students have a more future-oriented and reflective approach towards their profession, while English students appear to focus only on the present and conceptions of professionalism are more taken for granted. Another finding indicated that, although England is the more neo-liberal of the two countries, wielding greater control over its education system, its teachers and their 'voice', Finland has greater success in international tests. The second seminar also stimulated debate on the relationship between neo-liberalism and the potential for developing democracy and informed citizenship through education. We decided to explore this relationship by inviting co-authors from each country to write chapters on educating for democracy through the lenses of key themes.

This introductory chapter has established the overarching socio-economic, historic and political factors that have resulted in attitudes to democracy influencing current education systems and practices found in England and Finland. Chapter 2 invites the reader to enter education 'through the school gate' through the author's reflections on her experiences of teaching in the two education systems. There is a purpose to this chapter's contrast in style with the conventional academic approach of the rest of the book. In the author's words, '. . . these reflections may help sensitise the reader to the subtle and profound features of the respective systems, as well as contributing to the overall notion that not only can we learn from each other but it might be wise and in the interests of democracy to do so'.

Chapter 3 explores the role of the teacher, a role pivotal for development of conceptions of democracy. The UK *Teachers' Standards* (2012) and the underlying social democratic ideology of Finland both imply teachers' knowledge and understanding of the concept. This chapter challenges such assumptions.

It explores national notions of democracy by investigating teacher education, ethics and pedagogies in relation to Freire's (2008) conceptions of teacher as competent technician and cultural worker. Consideration of the prescriptive processes to which English 'trainees' are subjected, the outcomes of which are reduced to simple statements that can be 'ticked off' and 'evidenced' through portfolios and structured observation, could be expected to produce competent technicians. In contrast, an initial assessment of Finland's more liberal and lengthy five-year master's program, which includes study of philosophy and the 'pedagogical sciences', could be seen to result in cultural workers. The debate presented in this chapter suggests greater complexity.

Democracy and classroom practices are considered in Chapter 4 through the focus of pre-service teachers' conceptions of excellence in teaching. The findings of a small-scale research project revealed insights not only into their classroom practices, but also into their characters and thoughts on how they should behave towards others and how others should act towards them, so the 'best good' can be achieved. The democratic frameworks underpinning their pedagogies, based on Dewey's conception of living the personal good life through social being, are revealed. The chapters' authors evaluate the extent to which these abilities might promote informed participatory democratic thinking and acting within teachers and pupils. Chapter 5 extends the argument by proposing that teacher education should give up 'banking' approaches and replace them with problem posing to enhance democratic education. This chapter describes, analyzes and evaluates an intervention course module *PedArt*, which was based on the democratic philosophies of Freire and hooks. According to the data of written essays from a participating group of class and subject teacher students, senses of community, equality and authenticity and faith in change were exposed as meaningful outcomes of the intervention. Along with student empowerment, the authors suggest teacher education programs should have more space for dialogue as a prerequisite for democratic education.

The theme of democracy and the curriculum is the focus of is explored in Chapter 6. In comparison with Finland, England has centralized the curriculum as a vehicle for economic efficiency and productivity. The division of 'core' and 'foundation' subjects in the *National Curriculum* has had the effect of pushing the arts and humanities to the periphery of both the primary and secondary curricula. However, the concept of stakeholders complicates the issue of curriculum control. The authors argue that England gives greater weight to students as stakeholders than Finland, while the reverse is the case with teachers. These differences form the context for the chapter's discussion of the complex and interesting ways the curriculum molds and reflects national perspectives on educating for democracy.

Chapter 7 examines an English and a Finnish progressive school to explore ideas of power within democratic education. Using data gathered from a small-scale research project, the nature of power is examined by considering who holds power within democratic schools and how power is distributed between pupils and staff. We undertook this exploration in response to assertions that

14   Andrea Raiker & Matti Rautiainen

progressive schools afforded too much freedom (and therefore power) to pupils. The findings reveal that while power is accessible to staff and pupils through a number of democratic devices in both schools, the ways in which it is distributed between pupils and staff is different. The power in the English school appears to be more equally and democratically distributed than in the Finnish case. We suggest these differences represent a complex picture which reflects the different socio-economic, historic and political positions occupied by England and Finland and their respective journeys towards educating for democracy.

Chapter 8 reveals the differences in accountability processes and explores the engagement of young people as active citizens. For example, although Finnish authorities gather statistical information about schooling, there is no standardized national testing before the matriculation test, taken by half the age group at the end of upper secondary school. In contrast, Standardized Assessment Tests in years two and six, together with the General Certificate in Secondary Education at age sixteen, are used as performance indicators for students and schools. Such quantitative data are used to produce targets for the intervening years, and is given greater weight than qualitative teacher assessment. The chapter demonstrates clearly how differences in accountability processes arise between a country that values the development of national identity and the teachers' role in this process and one that is driven by an escalating market-driven approach.

Inclusion is about identifying, reducing and removing barriers to learning and participation and can be viewed as a fundamental building block for participation in a democratic state. In Chapter 9, the authors focus on how inclusive education policy has developed in both Finland and in the United Kingdom. The impact of political ideology on the opportunities for learners with special educational needs to access education is discussed. The chapter covers the current worldwide focus on inclusive education systems as the most appropriate form of provision and comments on how both countries have responded to the *Salamanca Statement on Inclusive Education* (1994). The authors consider the factors that are important in fostering inclusive practice and in forming barriers, including those that can be linked to neo-liberal policy (e.g., non-supportive legislation). In conclusion, the authors discuss the promotion of inclusive policies, cultures and practices in both countries in relation to democracy and debate how inclusive education policy is likely to develop over the coming years.

The focus of Chapter 10 is educational research for democracy and the impact on it of a rapidly changing Europe in which neo-liberalism is increasingly prevalent. The authors present their own philosophical perspectives in relation to educational research as the context for discussions on equality, human rights and social justice. The chapter considers some synergies and differences in approach in Finland and England. The authors deconstruct and challenge existing practices and trends in educational research and offer educational researchers a democratic language for resisting what they perceive to be encroaching tides of neo-liberalism, conformism and accountability. Chapter 11 explores the role theory plays in the field of educational research and

Education for democracy in England and Finland 15

educational practice and how conceptions of educational theory can provide insights into the democratic processes at work in English and Finnish teacher education. By considering the manner in which theorizing education is constructed in England and Finland, the authors demonstrate a fundamental epistemological difference focused on conceptions of education as a discipline in its own right and as an amalgam of facets of contributing disciplines. The authors show how these conceptions reflect underlying political ideologies and their combined impact on teacher education and classroom practice. The keys findings from this and preceding chapters are concluded in the final chapter, Chapter 12, leading to an analysis and evaluation of the insights gained on the two questions posed in Chapter 1 and an assessment of the relevance and impact of these insights for practice leading to democratic education, educating for a democratic future and future research.

References

Aristotle. (1981) *The Politics* (transl. T. A. Sinclair). London: Penguin Books.

Arola, P. (2003) Tavoitteena kunnon kansalainen. Koulun kansalaiskasvatuksen päämäärät eduskunnan keskusteluissa 1917–1924. *Helsingin yliopiston kasvatustieteen laitoksen tutkimuksia 191*. Helsinki: Helsingin yliopisto.

Ball, S. (2003) 'The teacher's soul and the terrors of performability' in *Journal of Education Policy*, 18(2), pp. 215–228.

Boden, R. & Epstein, D. (2006) 'Managing the research imagination? Globalisation and research in higher education' in *Globalisation, Societies and Education*, 4(2), pp. 223–236.

Bourdieu, P. (1999) *Vastatulet. Ohjeita uusliberalismin vastaiseen taisteluun* (transl. T. Arppe). Helsinki: Otava.

Department for Education. (2012) *Teachers' Standards*. Available at: www.education.gov.uk [accessed 18 January 2016].

Dewey, J. (1939) 'Creative democracy: The task before us' in *John Dewey and the Promise of America, Progressive Education Booklet*, No. 14. Columbus, OH: American Education Press. Republished in John Dewey, The Later Works, 1925–1953, Vol. 14.

Dewey, J. (1966) *Democracy and Education*. New York: The Free Press.

European Union. (2013) *Citizens 2013*. Available at: http://europa.eu/citizens-2013/en/about/ [accessed 4 February 2016].

Foucault, M. (1984) 'Right of Death and Power Over Life' (pp. 258–272) in Rabinow, P. (Ed.) *The Foucault Reader*. London: Penguin.

Freire, P. (ed. Sonia Nieto) (2008) *Dear Paulo: Letters to Those Who Dare Teach*. Boulder, CO: Paradigm Publishers.

Harvey, D. (2005) *A Brief History of Neoliberalism*. Oxford: Oxford University Press.

Helliwell, J., Layard R. & Sachs. J. (Eds.) (2015) *World Happiness Report*. Available at: http://worldhappiness.report/wp-content/uploads/sites/2/2015/04/WHR15_Sep15.pdf [accessed 14 February 2016].

Kärenlampi, P. (1999) Taistelu kouludemokratiasta. Kouludemokratian aalto Suomessa. *Bibliotheca Historica 37*. Suomen kouluhistoriallinen seura.

Kerr, D., Sturman, L., Schulz, W. & Burge, B. (2010) *ICCS 2009 European Report: Civic Knowledge, Attitudes and Engagement Among Lower Secondary Students in 24 European Countries*. Amsterdam: IEA. Available at: http://www.iea.nl/fileadmin/user_upload/Publications/Electronic_versions/ICCS_2009_European_Report.pdf [accessed 4 February 2016].

16 *Andrea Raiker & Matti Rautiainen*

Locke, J. (1880) *Some Thoughts Concerning Education*. Cambridge: The University Press.

Luhtakallio, E. (2012) *Practicing Democracy: Local Activism and Politics in France and Finland*. Hampshire: Macmillan.

Mauthner, N. S. & Doucet, A. (1998) 'Reflections on a Voice Centred Relational Method of Data Analysis: Analysing Maternal and Domestic Voices' (pp. 119–144) in Ribbens, J. & Edwards, R. (Eds.) *Feminist Dilemmas in Qualitative Research: Private Lives and Public Texts*. London: Sage.

Meinander, H. (2011) *A History of Finland* (transl. T. Geddan). London: Hurst.

Moyn, S. (Ed.) (2006) *Democracy: Past and Future*. New York: Columbia University Press.

National Core Curriculum for Basic Education 2004 (2004) *Helsinki: Finnish National Board of Education*. Available at: http://www.oph.fi/english/sources_of_information/core_curricula_and_qualification_requirements/basic_education [accessed 17 June 2013].

Office for National Statistics (2014) *Annual Mid-Year Population Estimates*. Available at: http://ons.gov.uk/dcp171778_367167.pdf [accessed 4 February 2016].

Oravakangas, A. (2005) *Koulun tuloksellisuus? Filosofisia valotuksia koulun tuloksellisuuden problematiikkaan suomalaisessa yhteiskunnassa*. Jyväskylän yliopisto: Kokkola.

Peters, R. S. (1958) 'Authority' in *Proceedings of the Aristotelian Society*, 32, pp. 207–234.

Raiker, A. (2010) 'Creativity and Reflection: Some Theoretical Perspectives Arising from Practice' (pp. 121–138) in Nygaard, C., Holtham, C. & Courtney, N. (Eds.) *Teaching Creativity: Creativity in Teaching Improving Students' Learning Outcomes*. Faringdon: Libri Publishing.

Rautiainen, M. & Räihä, P. (2012) 'Education for democracy: A paper promise? The democratic deficit in Finnish educational culture' in *Journal of Social Science Education*, 11 (2), pp. 7–23.

Salamanca Statement. (1994) *The Salamanca Statement and Framework for Action on Special Needs Education: Access and Quality. Salamanca, Spain, June 7–10, 1994*. Salamanca, Spain: UNESCO and Ministry of Education and Science of Spain. Available at: http://www.unesco.org/education/pdf/SALAMA_E.PDF [accessed 10 November 2015].

Sinclair, R. K. (1988) *Democracy and Participation in Athens*. Cambridge: Cambridge University Press.

Spencer, H (1954) *Social Statistics*. New York: Schalkenbach.

Statistics Finland. (2015) *Population*. Available at: http://www.stat.fi [accessed 12 November 2015].

Thomson, P., Hall, C. & Jones, K. (2010) 'Maggie's day: A small scale analysis of English education policy' in *Journal of Education Policy*, 25(5), pp. 639–656.

United Nations. (2015) *Transforming Our World: The 2030 Agenda for Sustainable Development*. Available at: http://www.un.org/en/ga/search/view_doc.asp?symbol=A/RES/70/1&Lang=E [accessed 15 February 2016].

Valtonen, H. & Rautiainen, M. (2012) 'La educación finlandesa desde 1850 hasta el presente'. *ISTOR Revista de Historia Internacional*, 12(48), pp. 129–160.

2 Living between two education systems

Josephine Moate

I arrived in Finland as a newly qualified teacher in the summer of 1997. After teacher *training* in England, I was surprised to encounter teacher *education* in Finland. I arrived well-prepared for classroom management, syllabus development, lesson planning and engagement with pupils. My understanding, however, of what made my practice 'educational' was rather superficial. As a child, I thought that school should help pupils learn to live together. As a young graduate, I thought school should help pupils strive for more than life necessarily offered – whilst wondering why my education contained significant gaps, such as little understanding of the political system of the country. Just before completing my teacher training, a political canvasser phoned to ask whether I would vote for Tony Blair in the upcoming elections, whether I was convinced by his manifesto of 'education, education, education'. I was convinced and, thankfully, left to start my teaching career in a different educational context.

I initially saw few significant differences between the Finnish and English educational systems. Schools still seemed to be schools – generally rectangular, built around a playground with classrooms, a dining hall, a sports hall, staffroom and head teacher. For a long time, I did not recognise the hybrid space I was occupying. My classes and my educational thinking were physically located in Finland, warmed with a touch of intercultural curiosity, but interpreted through English 'teacherliness'. For example, textbooks seemed to be an anathema (e.g., Norris et al, 1996). I believed talk should be ubiquitous (Mercer & Littleton, 2007) and sought to create a stimulating environment with posters and displays of work (Alexander, 2001) offering a range of different activities pupils could choose from. Whilst these educational features are not the sole jurisdiction of English education, I assumed that this was the way education worked regardless of context.

As I began to encounter educationally significant figures – Vygotsky, Dewey, Bakhtin, Kemmis – and different theoretical conceptualisations, I began questioning my own practice and understanding. As I entered classrooms as a researcher and my own children entered the educational system, the differences became more pronounced, even though I had lived in Finland for over a decade. The liminal space between insideness and outsideness (McNess et al, 2015) became my lived reality. I began to consciously reflect on the differences

18   *Josephine Moate*

between Finnish and English education, rather than to dismiss them as mere idiosyncrasies. Indeed, I have come to regard these differences as key landmarks in the space I now occupy, landmarks that can help concretise the often abstracted space of educational research that can all too easily avoid '. . . the task of democracy . . . [to create] a freer and more humane experience in which all share and to which all contribute' (Dewey, 1940:230). This chapter outlines how my naïve first impressions changed as I engaged with education through the different roles of teacher, researcher and parent in two democratic societies.

First impressions

My initial impression of the Finnish school system was very positive. The primary school children appeared calm and well-behaved within relatively informal classrooms, calling teachers by their first name or 'ope' ['Teach']. The seven-year-old first graders seemed incredibly small, making me wonder how four-year-olds could be in school in England. It seemed to make sense that the seven-year-olds by and large were more ready to learn to read than the four-year-olds and that the whole class usually learnt to read within the first school semester (also noted by Alexander, 2003). This meant that the whole class could continue with similar tasks, leading to the surprising finding that the Finnish system has managed to keep all pupils above the international average (Sahlberg, 2011), albeit with a large discrepancy between different pupil groups (Reinikainen, 2012). I wondered to what extent these early experiences of education set up children for success or otherwise in their ensuing school career.

A second initial observation was the way in which the Finnish staff in schools wore comfy indoor shoes as did the children, yet the children could get all their outdoor clothing on every 45 minutes for a 15-minute break time. The children appeared to be quick and efficient at dressing and undressing and the classrooms more relaxed without outdoor shoes. It seemed strange that English, not Finnish, classrooms are carpeted, although English schoolchildren and teachers wore shoes all day. A third observation that came as a surprise during the early days was the way in which a teacher produced a wall display within a 15-minute break. She grabbed a box of dressmaker's pins and pinned the children's artwork to the wall. I wondered how she could trust the children with such easily available objects to stab one another, and then I was surprised that I would think children would stab each other. Why would they? Why would I expect them to? I thought of the hours I had spent helping teachers in England put up classroom displays with carefully chosen sugar paper backing and printed titles. I wondered why the Finnish display did not seem to be lacking and why English teachers worked so hard.

A final observation from the early days relates to the timetable. I was commissioned to teach different grades in a local school. With the early grades, I often found that I was asked to teach the same lesson in the same class on the same day, once at 8am and the second time at 12pm. This was possible because classes were regularly divided in half, with one group of children arriving and leaving earlier than the other half. This seemed like such a practical way to give a teacher the opportunity to work more closely with the pupils, getting to know them in a small group rather than with the whole class. On the other hand, this meant that different children started and finished school at different times on different days. How could parents keep up with when to take and collect their children, where was the ensuing chaos? Amazingly, parents do seem to manage with timetables that start and finish at different times on different days, although I know that it can require some adjustment when children start school and sometimes parents do get confused. Indeed, the use of time is an interesting contrast between the two systems. Whereas the standard number of lessons in English schools remains the same, throughout primary school in Finland, the number of hours incrementally increase from 20 x 45 minutes a week in the first and second grades to 24+ x 45 minutes in grades five and six. The number of hours per week in the later years of schooling can vary greatly. Moreover, Finnish teachers are only obligated to work the hours of the teaching timetable, whereas teaching obligations only amount to half of the salaried working hours for English teachers (OECD, 2011). Whilst I am sure teachers in both contexts often work more than these designated hours, the length of the working day differs in the contexts suggesting different conceptualisations of the teacher's role and duties.

After some initial adjustments – pupils without uniforms, first name acquaintances, shorter lessons, flexible timetables and no hierarchical positions for teachers except for the head – I settled into life as a teacher in Finland. Overall, my experiences as a teacher in Finland were mainly positive with little critical reflection. It was only when I began to enter Finnish classrooms in a different role that I began to recognise more significant differences between the two school systems.

A new perspective: from teacher to researcher

Over the last decade, I have observed classes, visited different schools in England and Finland, talked with many colleagues and teachers, read various academic texts and followed my children's education primarily in Finland but also in English schools. I no longer consider myself an 'insider' in the English system – many changes have taken place over the last nineteen years within the rampaging educational system of England. Nor do I consider myself a Finnish 'insider' – too many things still surprise me. Indeed, I find myself in a somewhat alien place in which similar landscapes can hide profound differences and raise unexpected questions.

During the school year 2009–2010, I recorded and observed two science courses, increasingly fascinated by the presence of the textbook. In 1996 Norris et al. observed that:

> ... whole [Finnish] classes following line by line what is written in the textbook, at a pace determined by the teacher. Rows and rows of children

20 *Josephine Moate*

all doing the same thing in the same way whether it be art, mathematics or geography. We have moved from school to school and seen almost identical lessons, you could have swapped the teachers over and the children would never have noticed the difference.

(Norris et al, 1996:29)

A decade later, little appears to have changed (Atjonen et al, 2008). I was particularly confused by the way in which the textbook appeared to rival, rather than resource, the teacher. The lessons were built around the chapters of the textbook, most of the tasks originating from the textbook, the learning conversations of the classroom often based on the textbook. How could teachers suffer this intrusion into their pedagogical space? How did pupils know how to expertly use the textbook, at least as assumed by teachers and textbook authors? How did textbooks come to occupy such a privileged position? I continue to seek answers to these questions but what began to intrigue me was the cultural hue of my reaction. Why was I offended by the presence of seemingly prescriptive textbooks when my national culture had one of the most prescriptive curriculum systems in the world policed by inspectors – an anathema in Finland, inspector-free since the early 1990s?

Over time, I have come to better understand the value of a text-based system. It does, nevertheless, seem strange that a system which invests so much in teacher education with class and subject teachers holding master's degrees and a non-prescriptive, beautifully open-ended curriculum would not foster greater variety between teaching methodologies. I rather suspect the answer may in part lie in the history of Finnish education and in the teacher education system. Attached to the University of Jyväskylä, for example, is a 'normal school', a practice school with nigh on 1,000 pupils aged 7–19 where 900 student teachers annually complete their teaching practices. With such a high turnover of student teachers, the textbook offers continuity between pre- and in-service teachers. It is perhaps the continuity provided by the textbook, however, that 'produces conforming and loyal teachers rather than critical teachers' (Rautiainen & Räihä, 2012:16), yet I would be hesitant to suggest that obliging teachers to produce their own materials creates a more democratic school system.

More recently I have been wondering whether the textbook explains the absence of a meta-text in the classroom; that is, a 'red line' that weaves together the different parts of the lesson, maintaining continuity in the learning conversations and activities of the classroom. Observing classes in England, teachers often stated the aim of most lessons, by and large reiterating this point at the end of the lesson. In Finland, lesson 'aims' can all too easily be defined by textbook chapters, homework given as textbook pages and test revision as textbook sections rather than the topic or the purpose behind the series of lessons. It is perhaps of little surprise that pupils can begin to equate learning a subject with covering the contents of a textbook (Aro, 2009). The full significance of these differences is not clear, but the absence of the meta-text demarcating the area for participation in Finnish schools may contribute to the passive participatory culture of Finnish schools, in which it can be seen as 'a virtue to dutifully achieve learning outcomes and not, for example, to talk about learning objectives and whether they were sensible' (Rautiainen & Räihä, 2012:10). Furthermore, textbooks can be used a tool for classroom management (Tainio, 2012) adding authoritative overtones to pedagogic action – an interesting contrast to teachers within English-speaking contexts that tend to use turn pedagogic talk into a tool for classroom management (Alexander, 2001).

Another noticeable difference between lessons in England and Finland is pace. I suspect a significant difference exists in the pace of life in the two countries as a whole, but it is particularly marked in school. English lessons seem to be fast and furious to keep pupils on track, on task and on their toes. Breaks between lessons are carefully designed to allow pupils to move from one classroom to the next but little else. As a girl in England I remember a morning break of 15 minutes, a lunch break of an hour and a second afternoon break. The morning break appears to still be in place, with the addition of a healthy snack, free or affordably priced, whereas the afternoon break seems to be shorter or non-existent. Finnish lessons are generally on task, but pupils are not kept 'on their toes'. Textbooks are expertly divided into sections following the school year, and even if there is concern that the textbook might not be completed by the end of the year, the Finnish curriculum provides the space for teachers to dwell on topics or areas of difficulty depending on the pupils. Absent pupils can catch up by following the textbook without parents being fined. I do not mean to suggest that absenteeism is encouraged in Finland, but a sense of urgency does not underpin the educational system. Finnish pupils start to read, write, learn multiplication tables and scientific formulae later than their English peers, but they catch up bringing the race of the hare and the tortoise to mind.

It is perhaps worth asking whether a gentler pace allows for deeper thought or engagement. Student teachers in Finland have a five-year period to engage with educational theory, to critically consider their options as teachers, as pedagogues. Whether these student teachers are fully prepared to take advantage of this opportunity, I cannot say, and I doubt that theoretical understanding alone necessarily creates a democratic or innovative educational system. Student teachers in England, however, if on a fast-paced, practice-oriented, evaluative, year-long course arguably have little time nor incentive to look at the bigger picture. Indeed, keeping teachers, parents and pupils bound to a furious pace can be rather cynically viewed as a convenient way to keep bigger educational questions from being asked, such as what is the purpose of education (Biesta, 2013:64)? Does this educational system 'form people so that they can live well in a world worth living in' (Kemmis, 2014:31)? The demanding pace of education in England seems to rather conveniently complement the removal of theory from teacher training in the 1990s (Alexander, 2008:19–20), limiting the theoretical tools as well as the temporal space for participating in democratic discussions around education.

A difference that has been pointed out in the literature is the role or presence of testing within the respective educational systems. Finland has no (obligatory) national tests until the matriculation exam at the age of 19. Entry into high school is determined by grades awarded throughout junior high school. It is not the case, however, that there are no tests in Finnish education. Tests are built into the school year on a regular basis, with test weeks featuring four to six times a year by seventh grade and on. Our two children in the local lower comprehensive school also have regular tests in each subject, bringing the printed copies home to be signed. In this way, Finnish pupils are carefully socialised into educational tests, encouraging them to review a recent topic concluded with a test. The key difference, perhaps, is the lack of published results, the absence of school assessment based on pupil achievement; in this way, tests become part of the day-to-day study experience, not a threat. As parents, we encourage our children to prepare for tests, but need not worry that they will be excessively stressed by the tests, unlike their peers in England. Finnish teachers are also trusted to be able to judge the quality of pupil work, with the national curriculum only detailing the basis for a grade 8 on the scale of 4–10 used to grade Finnish pupils (NBE, 2014).

Another absence that I have been trying to understand in the Finnish system is the absence of marking. Finnish teachers do on occasion mark pupils' activity books that accompany textbooks, but there are no piles of books in staffrooms patiently waiting for busy teachers to find time to sit down, to add marks and comments, acknowledging pupils' efforts and providing recommendations. In my observations, the marking of pupil work is not a key feature of the teachers' workload, perhaps because pupils are taught as quickly as possible to be responsible for and to mark their own homework. In practice, this means that pupils revisit the material, as the homework is marked within the public space of the classroom all together. In this way, the independent marking of pupil work remains part of the learning conversation in the classroom. Teachers ask and survey whether everyone has completed the homework and incomplete homework is marked into the electronic register system – Wilma. It does appear, however, that textbooks extend the 'learning space' of education beyond the classroom. As educational policy in England increasingly calls all participants to account – pupils to teachers, teachers to inspectors – one wonders at what stage pupils are encouraged to be independent or recognise their responsibilities as members of a democratic society.

The practical, pedagogically beneficial solution to the issue of marking does not mean that pupils always complete homework prior to lessons or that Finnish pupils necessarily learn how to actively participate (Rautiainen & Räihä, 2012). This point returns to a perhaps more fundamental difference between Finnish and English educational systems and the respective emphases on reading and writing. The full scope of this difference cannot be addressed here, but it is a point worth raising. The pedagogical guide in Finland at all levels of the Finnish educational system is the printed word, from the careful development of ABC readers in grade one, with textbooks for practically all curricular subjects throughout the school system, to book exams on theoretical literature in teacher education. Whilst quality texts are of great important in the development of reading skills, a text-based system does not necessarily require pupils to produce text. Answers to questions in textbooks rarely require more than a sentence or two. Socialisation into reading comprehension does not automatically lead to text production or critical engagement. I have often thought that combining the productive writing and speaking that is encouraged in the English system with the solid reading and independence of the Finnish system might well produce a powerful educational system. This might, however, be the aspiration of a parent caught between two educational systems.

The lived perspective of a parent

Our children attend the local school, as do most children in Finland, although this is slowly changing as school profiles differ. The specialised music classes, the Christian and the Steiner schools and the international classes of the town, for example, cross local boundaries. My first parents' evening in Finland, however, took me by surprise. Before long we were discussing the challenges of peeling boiled potatoes for new school children and the unsavoury alternative of slimy potatoes at the bottom of the vat for the final diners of the day. Perhaps that explains the mash and chips of English schools, I thought. I should quickly add, however, that school dinners are a point of pride in Finland. From the inception of the school system, free school dinners have been provided for all pupils, a principle that continues today with the legal proviso that the meals meet nutritional requirements. These free school dinners are, therefore, a statement reiterating the responsibility of schools to cater for the physical as well as intellectual needs of children whilst also avoiding socio-economic labels for 'haves' and 'have nots'.

In Finland, children generally walk to school or, from the third grade on, they can cycle once they have passed a proficiency test. The independent to-ing and fro-ing to school in Finland complements the more flexible timetable of the school day and encourages children to be independent, and perhaps alone, from an early age. For first and second graders, after-school clubs exist, offering a variety of activities and a daily snack for a reasonable fee. In our experience, this is a wonderful complement to the more formal school day. The children at the after-school club are well catered for, yet free to choose their activities and level of participation. Homework can be completed at the club, with help available if needed. Some third graders also attend, although the numbers are few. I confess I do wonder how many nine-year-olds manage at home, sometimes from 1pm onwards on a daily basis. When our daughter was a third grader she struggled to be home alone after school, not because she is unsafe, but just alone. With our now third-grade son the struggle is to keep him off screens from 1pm most afternoons. This can create an uncomfortable feeling for a parent torn between responsibly caring for one's child and responsibly completing duties as a full-time employee.

The contrast with England is vast. Our children first attended a country school in a small village surrounded by fields. The gate for the school was

24   *Josephine Moate*

unlocked ten minutes before the school day began, and the children were collected from the yard at the end of the school day once the teacher had seen the legally assigned guardian. The city school that the children attended the following year also had locked gates and only released children to the assigned guardian, but this school was not surrounded by fields. It was surrounded by a high brick wall and an electric gate. On one occasion, parents were invited in to watch puppet shows the year two children had produced. A group of parents and grandparents gathered at the gate. At the appointed time, the gate opened and we walked through the outer courtyard to sign our attendance into the school register. Returning to the yard, we waited at the inner gate, electronically opened from a distance. We marched towards the main door of the school and waited for the deputy head teacher to unlock the door. Standing aside, she greeted us each in turn. We entered the lobby and waited for the inner door to be unlocked. We walked through the hall to the classroom, sat, watched and left through the various doors and gates. Before this experience, I had found Foucault's comparison of school and prison difficult to comprehend when considering Finnish schools. I now felt that I had visited my six-year-old in prison.

Was our son safe, however, in that setting? What if a fire had broken out – how would the children leave the building? And surely, if someone really wanted to harm the school, these security measures would not stop them. The wall, gates, electronic systems, signings and monitoring created such a sense of dis-ease, but for what purpose? And yet, it seemed so normal for the general populace. It would be a grave disservice to English teachers, however, if this anecdote was not quickly followed by reference to the great investment that is made in imaginative freedom that is still fostered in English schools. In Finland, our children – and I am aware that this is very much based on personal experience – rarely speak about what they are learning, rarely show enthusiasm, even if school is going well. In England, our children were excited. Of course, for them it was stimulating to be in a different language environment, but when they came home they carried on with school-like activities. One Saturday, we woke to hear the children writing stories. Our six-year-old in Finnish pre-school was only required by the Finnish curriculum to learn the alphabet and to count to 10. As a year two pupil in England, he was required to write up experiments and to produce short stories. His then eight-year-old sister was writing down his story as he dictated it, he was then copying out what she wrote. When we returned to Finland, I asked how many stories our then second grade daughter had written in school: three, in a year and a half. Something was happening in the English classrooms to prompt imagination and the desire to share stories and developing understanding.

The English classrooms were also full of displays. Often, not only were the walls covered with displays, lines were strung across the ceilings and full of spelling words, illustrations of topic work, important reminders for the production of 'good' text. Indeed, the displays often seemed to be a curious combination of celebrating children's work and reminding them of rules, requirements and expectations, reflecting the cross-currents and contradictions of the wider

Living between two education systems 25

system – as noted elsewhere (e.g., Alexander, 2001). These contradictions, however, also seem to be reflected in the pedagogical activities of the classroom. Each morning on arrival at school, for example, our son selected a handwriting template and repeatedly practiced letter formation tracing over the letter template. The templates illustrated cursive writing rather than printed letters, almost as though the children were expected to immediately learn cursive writing to save time in an overcrowded curriculum.

In Finland, even the handwriting textbook is pedagogically oriented. The textbook was not merely a place for the practice of motor skills, but it encouraged the children to critically consider why the height of a letter should be clear and whether letter formation helped to convey understanding. A similar observation is made with regard to mathematics in Finland in a report by Ofsted inspectors (2010). It seems in some ways ironic that the system that invests heavily in teacher education would also 'rely' heavily on textbooks. Surely within any system, some teachers will be better than others, and perhaps textbooks compensate for any pedagogical lacks. On the other hand, it makes sense that a system invested in teacher education would also care enough to provide quality materials even if the relationship with the materials should be based on critical reflection rather than assumed usage. The need for critical reflection in both educational contexts is the focus of the final section.

Closing remarks

In 1940, Dewey stated, 'The present state of the world is more than a reminder that we have now to put forth every energy of our own to prove worthy of our [democratic] heritage' – (*ibid.*:278) a statement no less true today. For me, living between two educational systems has highlighted the way in which many different aspects of education are not because they have to be, but rather because they have *come* to be. This appears to be the case in the more open-ended Finnish educational system as well as in the driven educational system of England. It is, however, when 'we are not aware of what and why and how ... we cultivate a mindlessness that, in the end, reduces our own humanity ... even when it is not intended' (Bruner, 1996:79). It is this lack of awareness that can perhaps allow democratic values to be chipped away from educational systems, as pupils, teachers and other educational stakeholders conform to what is without considering what could be. If, however, democracy is a way of life based on a working faith in the possibilities of human nature (Dewey, 1940), it is perhaps this working faith that prepares and trusts teachers to do their work well, preparing and trusting pupils to participate well in an educational system that is prepared to face the challenge of living well in a world worth living in.

References

Alexander, R. (2001) *Culture and Pedagogy: International Comparisons in Primary Education.* Oxford: Blackwell Publishing.

26 Josephine Moate

Alexander, R. (2003) *The Education of Six Year Olds in England, Denmark and Finland: An International Comparative Study*. OFSTED: HMI 1160. Available at: http://www.educationengland. org.uk/documents/pdfs/2003-ofsted-six-year-olds-comparative.pdf [accessed 15 February 2016].

Alexander, R. (2008) *Essays on Pedagogy*. Oxon: Routledge.

Aro, M. (2009) *Speakers and Doers: Polyphony and Agency in Children's Beliefs About Language Learning*. Jyväskylä, Finland: University of Jyväskylä.

Atjonen, P., Halinen, I., Hämäläinen, S., Korkeakoski, E., Knubb-Manninen, G., Kupari, P., Mehtäläinen, J. Risku, A-M., Salonen, M. & Wikman, T. (2008) Tavoitteista vuorovaikutukseen. Perusopetuksen pedagogiikan arviointi. *Koulutuksen arviointineuvoston julkaisuja 30*.

Biesta, G. J. (2013) 'Prologue: On the Weakness of Education' in *The Beautiful Risk of Education*. Oxon: Routledge, pp. 1–10.

Bruner, J. S. (1996) *The Culture of Education*. Cambridge, MA: Harvard University Press.

Dewey, J. (1940) 'Creative Democracy: The Task Before Us' in Boydston, J. A. (Ed.) *The Later Works, 1925–1953, John Dewey, Vol. 14: 1939–1941 Essays, Reviews and Miscellany*, Carbondale: Southern Illinois University Press, pp. 224–230.

Kemmis, S. (2014) 'Education, Educational Research and the Good for Humankind' in Heikkinen, H. L. T. Lerkkanen, M-K. & Moate, J. (Eds.) *Enabling Education: Proceedings of the Annual Conference of Finnish Educational Research Association FERA 2013*. Jyväskylä, Finland, University of Jyväskylä: FERA. pp. 15–68.

McNess, E., Arthur, L. & Crossley, M. (2015) 'Ethnographic dazzle' and the construction of the 'Other': Revisiting dimensions of insider and outsider research for international and comparative education in *Compare: A Journal of Comparative and International Education*, 45(2), pp. 295–316.

Mercer, N. & Littleton, K. (2007) *Dialogue and the Development of Children's Thinking: A Sociocultural Approach*. London: Routledge.

Norris, N., Aspland, R., MacDonald, B., Schostak, J. & Zamorski, B. (1996) *An Independent Evaluation of Comprehensive Curriculum Reform in Finland*. Helsinki: National Board of Education.

OECD. (2011) *Education at a Glance*. Available at: http://www.oecd.org/education/skills-beyond-school/48631419.pdf [accessed 15 February 2016].

Ofsted. (2010) *Finnish Pupils' Success in Mathematics: Factors that Contribute to Finnish Pupils' Success in Mathematics*. Manchester: The Office for Standards in Education, Children's Services and Skills.

Perusopetuksen opetussuunnitelman perusteet. [Principles for planning the core curriculum]. (2014) Helsinki: National Board of Education. Available at: http://www.oph.fi/download/139848_pops_web.pdf [accessed 1 December 2015].

Rautiainen, M. & Räihä, P. (2012) 'Education for democracy: A paper promise? The democratic deficit in Finnish educational culture' in *JSSE-Journal of Social Science Education*, 11(2), pp. 8–23.

Reinikainen, P. (2012) 'Amazing PISA Results in Finnish Comprehensive Schools' in Niemi, H., Toom, A. & Kallioniemi, A. (Eds.) *The Miracle of Education: The Principles and Practices of Teaching and Learning in Finnish Schools*. Rotterdam: Sense Publishers, pp. 3–18.

Sahlberg, P. (2011) 'The fourth way of Finland' in *Journal of Educational Change*, 12(2), pp. 173–185.

Tainio, L. (2012) 'The Role of Textbooks in Finnish Mother Tongue and Literature Classrooms' in Lehti-Eklund, H., Slotte-Lüttge, A., Silén, B. & R. Heilä-Ylikallio (Eds.) *Skriftpraktiker hos barn och unga*. Rapport från Pedagogiska fakulteten. Vasa, Finland: Åbo Akademi, pp. 11–33.

3 The role of the teacher in educating for democracy

Andrea Raiker, Marja Mäensivu & Tiina Nikkola

Introduction

In England and Finland, the role of the teacher is regarded as pivotal for development of conceptions of democracy. The UK *Teachers' Standards* (DfE, 2012:10) explicitly states that teachers will demonstrate high standards of ethics ' . . . by not undermining fundamental British values, including democracy . . . ', implying that teachers know and understand the nature of democracy and will teach it directly in citizenship lessons or indirectly via the 'hidden curriculum'. Also in Finland, the value base concerning democracy, equality and active agency in civil society is embedded in the basic curriculum of the *National Core Curriculum* (Perusopetuksen opetussuunnitelman perusteet, 2014:12–13) and in the *Basic Education Act* (MoJ, 1998:1:22). Although it is not directly articulated, development of conceptions of these values is seen as the responsibility of teachers because they are the ones who can demonstrate these values every day in their classrooms.

This chapter will examine the role of the teacher in educating for democracy by comparing education policy documents and practice in England and Finland with the conception of the 'progressive teacher' proposed by Paulo Freire, the internationally renowned Brazilian philosopher and educator, whose experiences led him to a very political understanding of education as a force for democracy. He also contextualised education in historical, cultural and social as well as in political terms. As the purpose of this book is, in part, to research the relationship between democratic values and political ideologies in England and in Finland, we argue that comparisons with Freire's thinking will provide meaningful and informative insights.

Although the pivotal role of the teacher in educating for democracy is advocated by Freire, his writings, particularly the fourth letter in his *Teachers as cultural workers: Letters to those who dare teach* (2008), make it clear that he considers that only teachers with certain attributes are capable of educating for democracy. For example, on discussing elitist versus democratic approaches to teaching, he comments that he:

> . . . cannot see how one could reconcile adherence to an ideal of democracy and of overcoming prejudice with a proud or arrogant posture in which

28   *Andrea Raiker et al.*

one feels full of oneself. How can I listen to the other, how can I hold a dialogue, if I can only listen to myself . . .

(Freire, 2008:208)

In this extract, Freire is describing the conservative or traditional teacher described in detail in *The Pedagogy of the Oppressed* (2000). Shaull in his introduction to this translation reflects on the parallels between teaching in modern technologised societies and in teaching illiterates in Latin America. He concludes that in both scenarios, teaching can result in '. . . rapidly making objects of most of us and subtly programming us into conformity to the logic of its system' (Freire, 2000:33). Such a teacher could be termed a 'competent technician' who is awarded with the designation of competence by the dominant elite and acts on behalf of that elite as a narrator of a curriculum prescribed by that elite. 'Narration', writes Freire, considering the effect on pupils of the teacher as narrator:

. . . leads [them] to memorise mechanically the narrated content . . . it turns them into 'containers', into 'receptacles to be filled' by the teacher. The more completely she fills the receptacles, the better a teacher she is. The more meekly the receptacles permit themselves to be filled, the better students they are.

(Freire, 2000:71)

Freire contrasts this 'banking', authoritarian and undemocratic concept of teaching with that of 'progressive' teaching. The progressive teacher will not only be competent in the sense of 'scientific competence', but also in the spheres of affection and creativity. For Freire, the learning process itself is a creative force: it is other-seeking and dialogic. To be progressive, teachers must be aware of and empathise with the ways individual students learn based on their very personal experiences resulting in their unique 'reading of the world'. Students should:

. . . have full responsibility as an actor with knowledge and not as a recipient of the teacher's discourse. In a final analysis this is the major political act of teaching. Among other elements, this is the one which makes the progressive educator different from the reactionary educator.

(Freire & Macedo, 1993:47–48)

Encouraging students to speak, to give them voice, is fundamental to the democratic process. In order to give voice, Freire advocates questioning and engaging with the dialogic, with purposeful discussion, as necessary strategies to elicit students' prior knowledge and understanding. Although the teacher assuming the role of facilitator is regarded by many educators as being a democratisation of power in the seminar and classroom, Freire is dismissive of the notion. By diminishing emphasis on:

. . . the teacher's power by claiming to be a facilitator, one is being less than truthful to the extent that the teacher turned facilitator maintains the

The role of the teacher in educating for democracy   29

power institutionally created in the position. That is, while facilitators may veil their power, at any moment they can exercise power as they wish . . .

(Freire & Macedo, 1999:47.)

This chapter will now consider the extent to which the role of the teacher in England and Finland supports education for democracy through critical examination of policy and practice in teacher education focused particularly on Freire's categories of scientific competence, affection, facilitation, questioning and engaging with the dialogic, and generally on the creative and democratic process of learning.

The role of the teacher in England

According to Allen and Toplis (2013) in their contribution to a textbook on learning to teach in the secondary school, '. . . your primary role as expected by a prospective employer is to *teach the curriculum* [original emphasis], with the aspiration being every pupil in the class achieves the learning outcomes for each of your lessons . . . ' This is no different from countries as politically diverse as the United States of America (USA) and China. By 'curriculum' is meant the formal curriculum that is laid down by government as the *National Curriculum* (2014), comprising of overarching principles and specific subject content to be covered. The *National Curriculum*, when introduced in 1988, was substantial in size and highly prescriptive. Each subject had an appendix containing description of attainment levels, indicative of the required achievement of each child at the end of a specific teaching year. Reviews and subsequent redrafted and published documents, in 1999 (DfEE, 1999) and 2014 (DfE 2014), have reduced the *National Curriculum* in size and prescription. Attainment levels have been abolished. There is more scope for teachers to choose content and pedagogical approaches. This is similar to the USA, but not to China, where the central role of a teacher is to work with a prescribed curriculum in depth, with no or little opportunity to deviate from that curriculum (Yang, 2007).

In England, the quality of specific subject content, or subject content knowledge (Shulman, 1986), giving entry into Initial Teacher Education courses for secondary education has been identified by government as a cause for concern because children's achievement in international tests is declining. International comparisons in education are becoming increasingly important. Governments throughout the world are using them to identify nations that are high achieving. For the neo-liberalist British government, the interest lies in acquiring information '. . . on how we're doing compared with our international competitors' (DfE, 2010:3). The most recent OECD Programme of International Student Assessment (PISA) survey of 65 countries (OECD, 2014) shows that the performance of children in the UK is continuing to fall in comparison with other countries. Since the 2000 survey, the UK has slipped from seventh to 23rd in reading, although this shows improvement over the 2009 PISA position of 25th. In mathematics, the UK has fallen from eighth

30   *Andrea Raiker et al.*

to 26th and from fourth to 21st in science. The mean score of the UK was 496, with a ranking of 24th, the USA 481 at 36th and China Shanghai at 613 (first), China Hong Kong at 563 (third), China Taipei 560 (fourth) and China Macau 53 (sixth). The British government has extensively studied the education systems of top-performing countries such as China Shanghai, Canada, Singapore, Finland and South Korea and has concluded that a major cause is inadequate teacher subject knowledge. Therefore, only graduates having lower second degrees and above are now funded for teacher education (DfE, 2010). Despite Freire's assertion that 'narration' turns students ' . . . into 'containers', into 'receptacles to be filled' by the teacher', graduates aiming at becoming secondary teachers must have good subject and curriculum knowledge. The Chinese approach to tight control of teaching and teachers certainly ensures that. In England, teacher education secondary courses expand subject knowledge, but courses are generally only a year induration with a minimum of 24 weeks in school. This means that the expansion of subject knowledge must be pragmatic and didactic. Likewise, in school, the role of the teacher is to deliver the curriculum in a form that can be learnt. Constraints of time mean that essential knowledge has to be delivered didactically, or by narrative. However, like the USA, the UK's policy frameworks determining teacher education go beyond the narrative.

The role of the teacher in England is determined by the *Teachers' Standards* (DfE, 2012), which define the minimum level of specified competences to be achieved for the award of Qualified Teacher Status, a benchmark that can subsequently be used for future continuing development (CPD). The eight teaching standards and three statements defining personal and professional conduct are given in Table 3.1 below.

Table 3.1 The role of the teacher (adapted from the *Teachers' Standards* 2012)

PART 1	Teaching: a teacher must: Set high expectations which inspire, motivate and challenge pupils; Promote good progress and outcomes of pupils; Demonstrate good subject and curriculum knowledge; Plan and teach well-structured lessons; Adapt teaching to respond to the strengths and needs of all pupils; Make accurate and productive use of assessment; Manage behaviour effectively to ensure a good and safe learning environment; Fulfil wider professional responsibilities
PART 2	Personal and professional conduct: Teachers uphold public trust in the profession and maintain high standards of ethics and behaviour, within and outside school . . . Teachers must have proper and professional regard for the ethos, policies and practices of the school in which they teach, and maintain high standards in their own attendance and punctuality. Teachers must have an understanding of, and always act within, the statutory frameworks which set out their professional duties and responsibilities.

The role of the teacher in educating for democracy   31

Each standard and the first statement are broken down as a series of bullet points to be used as the bases for assessment and the CPD (DfE, 2012). It can be seen that the demonstration of good subject and curriculum knowledge, what Freire would describe as 'scientific knowledge', has no exalted position in the eight teaching standards. Even the *Initial Teacher Education Handbook* which is used by the Office for Standards in Education, Children's Services and Skills' (Ofsted) inspectors to assess the quality of initial teacher education providers goes beyond subject knowledge and its transmission, stating that inspections are '. . . to evaluate the quality of teaching and training, and their contribution to the learning of children/pupils/learners' (2015:15). Strong subject knowledge is regarded as embedded within, but not synonymous with, learning; emphasis is placed on the environments and interactive processes that should be established by the teacher to maximise the learning of subject knowledge according to socio-constructivist principles. This supports a learner-centred approach to education, resonating with the position taken in the USA but not in China, where education is viewed as teacher-directed and content-orientated. The English/USA approach echoes Freire's view of learning being a creative and dialogic process. Despite the underpinning need for accountability driving teaching and learning in the UK (see Chapter 8), the approach to teaching and teacher training in England goes beyond the 'banking', and therefore undemocratic concept of teaching, into the realms of 'affective' teaching.

The importance placed on environments and processes in the *Teachers' Standards* to promote learning reflect Freire's identification of 'affection' as being a necessary attribute of the progressive teacher and hence of teacher educators. By affection, Freire means a particular form of love:

> . . . I mean . . . the very process of teaching; to discover how beautiful it is to be involved in the process of teaching to the extent of the process of teaching is directed towards the process of education, which is rather different from training.
>
> (Freire & Macedo, 1995:20)

Freire considers 'training' to be a word with immoral overtones and semantic limitations. In England, teacher education is commonly termed 'teacher training and student teachers are called 'trainees'. 'Training' suggests external direction with elements of coercion so that a sequential pattern of events occurs to achieve a prescribed outcome. There are certainly aspects of the English system that support the use of the term 'training' rather than education: the rigorous Ofsted inspections of initial teacher education providers against the *Teachers' Standards* and a variety of other statutory frameworks; the right of Ofsted inspectors to place providers in special measures or even have their licenses to award Qualified Teacher Status (QTS: the academic award given when competences laid down *in The Teachers' Standards* have been achieved) rescinded.

However, the argument presented here is that the *Teachers' Standards*, because they require the adaption of ' . . . teaching to meet the strengths and needs of

32   *Andrea Raiker et al.*

all pupils' and the establishment of behavioural norms ' . . . to ensure a good and safe learning environment', do encourage Freire's conception of the word 'love' by incorporating elements of 'concern', used here in the Heideggerian sense. The *Teachers' Standards* encourage an approach to teaching where the learners are challenged, assimilate and take ownership for what they have observed and understood during a learning event; in other words, they are both concerned about and have a concern for their learning. Thus love, concern and empathy emanate from the processes and environments, which can be understood as 'events', and are established by the teacher to embrace the learner so that learning is maximised. In creating and managing teaching events, the teacher is acting as a facilitator. This is not relinquishing power, as Freire maintains, but sharing power from a position of pedagogic confidence and competence. Teacher educators and teachers show their concern, not only in the seminar and classrooms, but also in the pastoral care which is an essential aspect of their role and in the long hours they work to adapt their lesson plans and teaching to the strengths, areas for improvement and needs of their learners. An initial teacher education provider is never placed in special measures through being awarded the lowest grading, in the range 'outstanding', 'good', 'requires improvement' and 'inadequate', because of lack of love. There are strong and deep historical and cultural roots to affective learning in England. As Pepin (1999) points out, the learner-centred and individualistic education seen throughout primary, secondary and tertiary phases in England is philosophically based in humanism, a philosophy that gained ground during the English Renaissance and Enlightenment periods of the 16th and 17th centuries and was taken across the Atlantic by the settlers who were instrumental in founding the USA. According to Pepin (1999:126), humanism '. . . assumes that to acquire knowledge is not a logical, sequential and standardised process, as rationalists would claim, but learning is regarded as 'intuitive'. Standardised, methodical, systematic learning is not reconcilable with this view of education'. This latter approach to learning is indicative of the Chinese method, which is heavily dependent on rote-learning, repetition and the memorising of information. In contrast, in the USA and England, teachers are seen as managers of learning but sharing that responsibility with their pupils so that they will profit from individualisation of experiences; group work, cooperation and collaboration in learning are considered essential.

It appears that the aim of consecutive UK governments since and including that of Margaret Thatcher in the 1980s is to constrain and redirect a cultural stream that has existed for over 500 years. It could be argued that this could be a cause of the continuous publication of government initiatives and strategies over recent years, for example, the *National Literacy Strategy* (1998), *National Numeracy Strategy* (1999), *Excellence and Enjoyment* (2003), *Every Child Matters* (2004), *Vision Report of the Teaching and Learning in 2020 Review Group* (2006) and *The White Paper; the Importance of Teaching* (2010). However international comparisons on student achievement respected by governments, such as PISA, suggest that these initiatives are not having the desired effect as yet, perhaps because the extremes of individualistic, humanist thought and practice of the

The role of the teacher in educating for democracy   33

1960s have not yet been completely tempered. As will be outlined in Chapter 4, in this decade of liberation and facilitation, teachers could teach what they wanted to teach in a manner and to a timescale that suited them, albeit constrained in secondary education by the national Certificate of Secondary Education national examinations for children aged 15. Although the decade could be viewed as a time when the role of teacher embraced democratic freedom in terms of choice and personal responsibility, the period has been termed the era of 'uninformed professionalism' (Earl et al, 2003). In Chapter 4, it is argued that individualistic expression of freedom in the role of the teacher led to the de-professionalisation of teaching with government control replacing teacher autonomy. One could imagine Freire shaking his head sadly at this lost opportunity for teachers to act politically by demonstrating they could act responsibly through working ethically and thus professionally through their own authority. For Freire:

> . . . there is no freedom without authority, there is no authority without freedom. It is through the contradictory relationships between authority and freedom we can experience the value and the need for limits.
>
> (Freire & Macedo, 1995:210)

Despite growing government authority and control over teacher and school education, curtailing teachers' and teacher educators' freedom, there has been increasing emphasis on supporting questioning and engaging with the dialogic at all levels of education. Questioning to encourage learners to give voice to their thinking was identified as a key finding of the research carried out by the *Gillingham Partnership Formative Assessment Project 2000–2001* (2003) and the work undertaken by the Assessment Reform Group (2003). This research, commissioned by the government, was in response to the realisation that by the time a learner failed a summative assessment, regarded as assessment *of* learning, it was too late to take action. The purpose of assessment *for* learning is to raise achievement by identifying issues as early as possible and addressing them through appropriate interventions. It was recognised that learners, rather than produce shadows of themselves, a metaphor used by Freire, constructed their own views of the world based on reasons that have meaning for them. This constructionist view of learning means recognition has been given to pupils in schools and teacher trainees have an understanding of what they do and do not know. So they too must be brought into the assessment process. As a facet of educating for democracy, the educator and the learner both give feedback on the assessment with the educator taking the lead as the 'expert' on what is needed to meet the learning objective. It is the learner's responsibility to achieve the learning objective. Both assessment *for* and *of* learning are now contained in the *Teachers' Standards* under the heading of *Make accurate and productive use of assessment*. As demonstrated in a quotation given in the introduction to this chapter, the process of assessment for learning is in accord with Freire's views on the role of teaching as a political act in the promotion of democratic practices

34 *Andrea Raiker et al.*

The role of the teacher in Finland

Teachers' autonomy is a characteristic of Finland's educational system. Compared to the English system, teachers have strong autonomy to plan, teach and evaluate as they see appropriate. Finnish teachers' work is not officially monitored. For example, in the early 1990s, school inspectors stopped visiting teachers' classrooms; since then, there has not been any official surveillance by the Ministry of Education. Also, there are no official teachers' standards, either for teachers or student teachers. One of the reasons for the lack of assessment of the quality of teacher's competences might be that in Finland the teaching profession is a high-status occupation attracting top-grade applicants for teacher education. This contrasts with other Nordic countries like Norway and Sweden, where the role of the teacher is not as highly regarded as in Finland, and therefore, teachers' work is more controlled.

Another reason for the extensive autonomy enjoyed by Finnish teachers is the high standard of scientific education and practical competences instilled by their university education. In order to qualify as teachers, students are required to have master's degrees, in education for class teachers and in a specific subject for subject teachers. High-level qualifications and scientific competence are considered to be important factors in Finland's success in PISA (Kupiainen et al, 2009).

Teacher education is directed at establishing autonomy. All universities have the freedom to organise their teacher education as they see fit, because there is limited government control and few official standards. For example, to be qualified as subject teachers, students have to have 60 European Credit Transfer and Accumulation System (ECTS) points in pedagogical studies in addition to their specific subject studies but each University can decide the content. There are very few national standards determining teacher qualification, and those that exist mainly dictate the extent of the qualification, not its content. To become teachers, students have to pass university teacher education courses, but their competence is not assessed otherwise. After qualification, teachers' abilities to teach are not evaluated or controlled in any way; it is expected that newly graduated teachers will be ready to act autonomously. Because teaching is such a prized occupation, 'affection', love of the process of teaching, is neither a criterion for admittance to or emphasised in teacher education.

Of course, teachers' autonomy does not mean that teachers do not have any kind of guidance for their teaching. They have to follow the *National Core Curriculum* (Perusopetuksen opetussuunnitelman perusteet, 2014), which sets out the common principles guiding the value base of schools and also specific subject content for each grade. But this *National Core Curriculum* is not precise, leaving teachers freedom to make choices and execute their profession as they see appropriate. For instance, the value base of the curriculum is about learning, not about teaching, and there is only one small part where the curriculum explicitly states something about teachers: teachers are responsible for pupils' activity, learning and well-being and their task is to guide, to support as well

The role of the teacher in educating for democracy   35

as to observe and to recognise possible difficulties but also appreciate and treat all the pupils fairly (Perusopetuksen opetussuunnitelman perusteet, 2014:34). The teacher's role, then, is not precisely specified in the curriculum. However, if we perceive a teacher as someone who enables learning, there can be found, for example, the 'affection' stated in the curriculum *via* conceptions of learning. The curriculum states that encouraging guidance will reinforce the pupil's confidence to her/his potential (Perusopetuksen opetussuunnitelman perusteet, 2014:17).

Along with the *National Core Curriculum*, there are also locally designed curricula by which local education authorities can arrange teaching in the best way suited to local circumstances (see Perusopetuksen opetussuunnitelman perusteet, 2014:9–13). The local curriculum design not only engages teachers in developmental work, but also gives them power to reflect on the basis of their teaching, giving them wide pedagogic responsibility. Above all, teachers' autonomy is based on trust: compliance with national local curricula is not assessed because teachers are regarded as being highly professional and responsible.

Although there are not very strong official control systems over the teaching profession and teachers have an extensive autonomy, there are still some unofficial and maybe hidden elements that strongly direct and control teachers' work. For example, student study books are typically used in classrooms. Although a teacher has autonomy and thus the opportunity to teach the *National Core Curriculum* content in any way s/he wants, almost all teachers use these books. Because teachers' guideline books accompany the student study books, teachers follow the suggested 'pedagogy' in the guides, presented as tips on how to run each lesson, instead of exercising their autonomy. Such books can be useful to teachers; however, it is remarkable that there is no official scrutiny by the educational authorities to ensure that these market products follow the national and local curricula. As well as the convention of using study and guide books, school practices seem to be uniform everywhere. For example, it is common practice that the school day is divided in 45-minute lessons based on school subjects. Considering the emphasis placed on the autonomy of the teacher's role, it is surprising that teachers rely on these unofficial and unspoken control systems.

How do these 'autonomic' teachers promote democracy education in their everyday work? An interesting aspect of the Finnish system is that little is known of classroom practice, unlike in England, where information is disseminated through documents like Ofsted reports.

However, according to research, democracy education should be stronger in Finnish schools. Also, researchers have observed that knowledge about democracy and democratic practices do not transfer effectively into practical skills. (Suoninen et al, 2010.) Of course, Finnish schools provide knowledge about democracy in accordance with the *National Core Curriculum*. There are also opportunities for democratic practices because many schools have pupil associations to promote joint action and participation in matters relating to pupils, such as organising school events (MoJ, 1998:22). However, despite these activities,

36 *Andrea Raiker et al.*

pupils do not feel that they have opportunities to influence their own study conditions, and they do not consider politics as something that belongs to them (Suoninen et al, 2010). Young people's interest in politics and political issues is significantly below the European International Civic and Citizenship Education Study (ICCS) average (Kerr et al, 2010:108). They seem not to be interested in taking an active role in society, and do not think that they are educated for democratic citizenship during their school years (Demokratiakasvatusselvitys, 2011). The problem may be that although these practices, like school associations, are important they are just minor additions between normal schoolwork. They not have an influence and do not accumulate as practical skills. However, in the Freirean sense, democratic practices mean precisely normal, everyday schoolwork, not something extra.

Teachers should demonstrate democratic values and practices in their work as an essential element of promoting every pupil's 'reading of the world'. In Finland, the *National Core Curriculum*'s (2014:17) conception of learning emphasises the pupil as an active agent whose interests and experiences guide learning processes. This is laudable in theory, but in everyday teaching it is easier to emphasise subject content than these higher-order objectives. As mentioned before, teachers use study books to ensure that all the curriculum subject content is covered. This can lead to situations where the pupils' own active use of knowledge is minimal and hides pupils' own 'reading of the world'. Using study books can lead to, as Freire puts it, 'teacher as narrator': pupils memorise mechanically the study book content which presents teachers' narration. Although the internet is used a source of information in addition to study books, critical evaluation of online knowledge is difficult for many pupils (Kiili et al, 2008, 2016). This indicates pupils' poor ability to question, an ability which can be seen as essential for democratically influential citizens.

For educating for democracy, promotion of pupils' 'reading of the world' is not sufficient: teachers should also be giving pupils 'voice' in everyday school life. For Finnish teachers, this is one of the stumbling blocks. Firstly, engaging pupils with dialogue is not typical in Finnish classrooms. Despite the *National Core Curriculum* having moved in a more socially oriented and student-centered direction, some subjects, e.g., science, are taught in an authoritative and monologic manner (Lehesvuori, 2013). Instead of dialogue, pupils listen to teachers talk, read study books and fill up exercise books. Secondly, pupils' involvement in decision making is minimal and typically limited to organising school events. Decision-making is always in the hands of the teacher, who can dictate the opportunities for pupils to use their voice in the classroom. These both, lack of dialogue and pupils' opportunities to make decisions, originate from the teacher's role which has developed towards autocracy; although the Finnish teacher's role has nowadays developed more towards facilitator, authority is merely less obvious. The lack of possibilities for using voice and making decisions in everyday schoolwork has led to a situation where pupils do not learn about actions of democracy in Finnish school communities. The development of the teacher's role must be discussed to understand why.

The cultural and historical bases to the development of Finnish teacher professionalism since the 1850s are to be found in the belief that teaching is a national and divine calling. A further factor was introduced in the 1960s, with teachers engaged in developing the welfare state through comprehensive schooling. However, from the 1980s onwards, neo-liberal educational policy has brought new tensions to the teacher's role which are more difficult to perceive. The role has always involved being a loyal servant for the state, whatever the state's social and political aims and commitments. Even though the role of the teacher in social rebuilding has always been significant, it is interesting that this aspect has not been emphasised in Finnish educational discussion (Vuorikoski & Räisänen, 2010). Instead, the role of the teacher in Finland is based on social neutrality. Teachers do not act as democratically influential persons – which is essential in developing democracy education. The understanding of the role of the teacher among student teachers and schools is one of neutrality and political non-involvement (Syrjäläinen et al, 2005).

The culture of primary school teacher education, its content and form has remained mostly unaltered from that established in the teacher seminaries of the mid-19th century. This culture can be understood as being based more on the political will to establish Finnish identity than on education science. When the scientific bases of teacher education were criticised, it became necessary to raise it status by strengthening its academic standards (Rantala et al, 2013:64–65). Teacher education was transferred to universities in the late 1970s. During its whole academic existence, teacher education has developed strongly in the didactic-psychological direction, and the social aspect of education has had very little impact on the recruitment criteria of professors and lecturers for teacher education and on the content of the teaching curriculum. This has been criticised since the 1990s, and it has been said that it produces a narrow and unhistorical understanding about the role of teachers (Kivinen & Rinne, 1994; Simola et al, 1997). Lack of social aspect in teacher education might be a significant reason behind the political neutrality of the role of the teacher in Finland. The social connections of education and their influence on the role of teachers have been left almost invisible in Finnish teacher education and the school system. This has had an effect on how the possibilities for democratic action for teachers and pupils are being understood in schools. The working methods of teachers have responded to the idea of inquiry-based learning and the understanding of teachers as facilitators of learning. Nevertheless, the role of the teacher as a democratically influential person – which would be essential from a point of view of democracy education – is almost indifferent in both approaches.

Conclusions

It could be inferred from the emphasis in Finland on teachers' autonomy that teachers are seen as cultural workers more than competent technicians acting on behalf of the dominant elite. In comparison to English practitioners,

38 *Andrea Raiker et al.*

teachers in Finland have wide independence to act as they please. For example, the imprecision of the *National Core Curriculum* gives teachers space for autonomous action. Autonomic Finnish teachers have opportunity to use their creativity when organising everyday schoolwork. In England, there are more official systems which control their work, e.g., Ofsted and the *Teachers' Standards*. Therefore, teachers in England could be regarded as being competent technicians who are the executors of government ideology.

But the discussion in this chapter suggests greater complexity. The argument presented above suggests that *Teachers' Standards* are underpinned by English cultural norms: because of this document's importance in evaluating trainees, newly qualified teachers and experienced practitioners alike, the role of the teacher is essentially that of cultural worker. In Finland, teachers do not necessarily use their autonomic position to its full extent and are guided by unofficial systems like study books. Their autonomic position also gives teachers opportunities to give their pupils voice and support their reading of the world. However, although 'engaging with the dialogic' is considered to be an important part of the learning process, dialogue is not widely used in Finnish classrooms; if it is, it is an addition to normal schoolwork rather than a daily part of it. The teacher's autonomic position enables them to omit dialogue from curricula. From this point of view, Finnish teachers can be seen as being more like competent technicians. In contrast, in England, pupil voice is encouraged through group work grounded in socio-constructivist theory. Group work is seen as being an essential component of class lessons and seminars (see Chapter 4). In addition, learners are involved in assessment feedback and a pedagogic practice based on research and statutory frameworks such as the *Teachers' Standards* have the expectation that learners throughout the phases will be encouraged and supported to give voice. From the English perspective, it can be seen that the role of the teacher educator includes acting as a fulcrum to teaching and learning, modelling processes and environments that trainees will find in schools and embedding them in theory to create praxis.

Nevertheless, in Finland, teachers' scientific competence is trusted, whereas in England, the actions of successive governments demonstrate that it is not. PISA results since 2003 appear to confirm the UK government's view that teachers and teacher educators cannot be trusted with achieving high standards for their pupils. One result of this is that teacher education is slowly being taken out of universities and placed in training schools; these are schools that have been judged 'outstanding' by Ofsted. This means that the theoretical component of teacher education is decreasing. On the other hand, there are a growing number of schools, e.g., Free Schools and Academies, that are funded by government but are not controlled by local authorities. Such schools are able to employ teachers who have had no teacher education, theory or practice, the justification being that such individuals are subject specialist experts. Although nearly all schools are subject to Ofsted inspections, these occur less often and are not as lengthy. The UK government's view on, and rigorous evaluation of, what constitutes teachers' scientific competence is unclear.

The role of the teacher is composed in relation to wider social constructions. Finnish schools have succeeded in PISA evaluations and therefore seem to confirm that country's conception of the role of the teacher. Still, international comparisons of learning do not reflect the totality of the pupil learning experience. Every education system reflects the culture and history of the country concerned. As well as having highly competent teachers, Finland's success can be explained by the education system (uniform basic education for the whole age group) and the autonomy given to schools. Also, Finnish society is positivistic with regard to education, with only the core curricula designed for nationwide application. In Finnish schools, much attention is accorded to individual support for learning and well-being. Schools are developed in multiprofessional cooperation, and Finland has an efficient library system of very high quality (Kupiainen et al, 2009). The role of the teacher has been strongly supported by the structures of Finnish society, but despite this, individual and psychological aspects in teaching and in teacher education are being emphasised more than social and structural aspects. If the social significance of teachers is not being understood, then educating for democracy is inevitably shallow. In England, the culture of society since the Enlightenment movement of the 16th and 17th centuries has created an education system that is liberal and humanistic and hence democratic at its core. Since the 1970s, liberalism has been replaced in politics by neo-liberalism and the prescription of education in the years following has reflected the changing ideology. As has been argued above, the declining achievement of English students demonstrates that the English government's approach to teaching and the teacher's role at both school and university level requires further thought and action. For example, further research on the authoritarian and teacher-centred methods employed by various Pacific Rim regions might be instructive. This, together with deliberation on the contradictions revealed in this chapter on the relationship between authority and freedom, identified by Freire as fundamental for democracy, could increase understanding of the value of the teacher's role in educating for democracy as well as improving international test scores.

References

Allen, M. & Toplis, T. (2013) 'Student Teachers' Roles and Responsibilities' in Capel, S., Leask M. & Turner, T. (Eds.) *Learning to Teach in the Secondary School: A Companion to School Experience*. Abingdon: Routledge, pp. 28–44.

Demokratiakasvatusselvitys [*Report of Democracy Education*] (2011) Raportit ja selvitykset 2011:27. Helsinki: Opetushallitus. Available at: http://www.oph.fi/download/139654_Demokratiakasvatusselvitys.pdf [accessed 18 January 2016].

Department for Education. (2010) *The Importance of Teaching: The Schools White Paper 2010.* Norwich: The Stationary Office.

Department for Education. (2012) *Teachers' Standards*. Available at: www.education.gov.uk [accessed 18 January 2016].

Department for Education. (2013) *The National Curriculum in England: Framework Document.* Available at: www.education.gov.uk [accessed 18 January 2016].

40 Andrea Raiker et al.

Department for Education and Employment. (1998) *The National Literacy Strategy Framework for Teaching Mathematics from Reception to Year 6*. London: Her Majesty's Stationary Office.

Department for Education and Employment (1999) *The National Curriculum Key Stages 1 and 2*. London: Her Majesty's Stationary Office.

Department for Education and Employment. (1999) *The National Numeracy Strategy Framework for Teaching Mathematics from Reception to Year 6*. London: Her Majesty's Stationary Office.

Department for Education for Schools. (2003) *Excellence and Enjoyment: A Strategy for Primary Schools*. London: Department for Education for Schools Publications.

Department for Education for Schools. (2004) *Every Child Matters*. London: Department for Education for Schools Publications.

Department for Education for Schools. (2006) *2020 Vision Report of the Teaching and Learning in 2020 Review Group*. Nottingham: Department for Education for Schools Publications.

Earl. L., Watson, N., Levin, B., Leithwood, K., Fullan, M. & Torrance, N. (2003) *Final Report of the External Evaluation of England's National Numeracy and Literacy Strategies: Final Report. Watching and Learning 3*. DfES: Nottingham.

Freire, P. (2000) *Pedagogy of the Oppressed: 30th Anniversary Edition* (trans. Myra Berman Ramos). New York: Continuum.

Freire, P. (2008) (ed. Sonia Nieto) *Dear Paulo: Letters to Those Who Dare Teach*. Boulder, CO: Paradigm Publishers.

Freire, P. & Macedo, D. (1993) 'A Dialogue with Paulo Freire' in McLaren, P. & Leonard, P (Eds.) *Paulo Freire: A Critical Encounter*. London: Routledge, pp. 47–48.

Freire, P. & Macedo, D. (1995) 'A dialogue: Culture, language, and race' in *Harvard Educational Review*, 65(3), pp. 377–402.

Freire, P. & Macedo, D.P. (1999) 'Pedagogy, Culture, Language and Race: A Dialogue' in Leach, J. and Moon, B. (Eds.) *Learning and Pedagogy*. Buckingham: Open University Press, pp. 46–58.

Kerr, D., Sturman, L., Schulz, W. & Burge, B. (2010) *ICCS 2009 European Report: Civic Knowledge, Attitudes, and Engagement Among Lower-Secondary Students in 24 European Countries*. Amsterdam: International Association for the Evaluation of Educational Achievement.

Kiili, C., Laurinen, L. & Marttunen, M. (2008) 'Students evaluating Internet sources: From versatile evaluators to uncritical readers' in *Journal of Educational Computing Research*, 39(1), pp. 75–95.

Kiili, C., Leu, D. J., Marttunen, M., Hautala, J. & Leppänen, P. H. T. (2016) *Sixth Graders' Critical Evaluation Skills of Online Sources*. Manuscript in preparation.

Kivinen, O. & Rinne, R. (1994) 'The thirst for learning, or protecting one's niche?' in *British Journal of Sociology of Education*, 15(4), pp. 515–528.

Kupiainen, S., Hautamäki, J. & Karjalainen, T. (2009) The Finnish Education System and PISA. *Ministry of Education Publications 2009:46*. Helsinki: Opetusministeriö. Available at: http://www.minedu.fi/export/sites/default/OPM/Julkaisut/2009/liitteet/opm46.pdf?lang=en [accessed 15 January 2016].

Lehesvuori, S. (2013) Towards Dialogic Teaching in Science: Challenging Classroom Realities Through Teacher Education. *Jyväskylä Studies in Education, Psychology and Social Research 465*. Jyväskylä, Finland: University of Jyväskylä. Available at: *https://jyx.jyu.fi/dspace/handle/123456789/41268* [accessed 18 January 2016].

Ministry of Justice. (1998) *Basic Education Act*: 21.8.1998/628. Available at: http://www.finlex.fi/en/laki/kaannokset/1998/en19980628 [accessed 18 January 2016].

Office for Standards in Education, Children's Services and Skills. (2015) *Initial Teacher Education Inspection Handbook*. Available at: www.gov.uk/government/organisations/ofsted [accessed 17 February 2016].

The role of the teacher in educating for democracy 41

Organisation for Economic Co-operation and Development. (2014) *PISA 2012 Results in Focus: What 15-year-Olds Know and What They Can Do and What They Know.* Available at: www.oecd.org [accessed 18 January 2016].

Pepin, B. (1999) 'The Influence of National Cultural Traditions on Pedagogy: Classroom Practices in England, France and Germany' in Leach, J. & Moon, B. (Eds.) *Learning and Pedagogy.* Buckingham: Open University Press, pp. 124–135.

Perusopetuksen opetussuunnitelman perusteet [*National Core Curriculum*] (2014) Määräykset ja ohjeet 96. Helsinki: Opetushallitus. Available at: http://www.oph.fi/saadokset_ja_ohjeet/ opetussuunnitelmien_ja_tutkintojen_perusteet/perusopetus [accessed 18 January 2016].

Rantala, J., Salminen, J., Säntti, J., Kemppinen, L., Nikkola, T., Rautiainen, M. & Virta, A. (2013) 'Luokanopettajakoulutuksen akatemisoitumiskehitys 1970-luvulta 2010-luvulle' [The academic development of teacher education from 1970's to 2010's] in Rantala, J. & Rautiainen, M. (Eds.) *Salonkikelpoiseksi maisterikoulutukseksi.* Luokanopettaja- ja opinto-ohjaajakoulutusten akatemisoitumiskehitys 1970-luvulta 2010-luvulle. *Suomen kasvatus-tieteellisen seuran tutkimuksia 64.* Jyväskylä: Suomen kasvatustieteellinen seura, pp. 61–81.

Shulman, L. S. (1986) 'Those who understand: knowledge growth in teaching' in *Educational Researcher,* 15, pp. 4–14.

Simola, H., Kivinen, O. & Rinne, R. (1997) 'Didactic closure: Professionalization and peda-gogic knowledge in Finnish teacher education' in *Teaching and Teacher Education,* 13(8), pp. 877–891.

Suoninen, A., Kupari, P. & Törmäkangas, K. (2010) *Nuorten yhteiskunnalliset tiedot, osallis-tuminen ja asenteet. Kansainvälisen ICCS 2009-tutkimuksen päätulokset.* [*Social knowledge of the youth, their participation and attitudes. The main results of international ICCS 2009 research.*] Jyväskylä: Jyväskylän yliopisto, Koulutuksen tutkimuslaitos.

Syrjäläinen, E., Värri, V-M., Piattoeva, N. & Eronen, A. (2006) 'Se on sellaista kasvattavaa, yleissivistävää toimintaa – opettajaksi opiskelevien käsityksiä kansalaisvaikuttamisen merkityksestä' [How student teachers understand the meaning of active citizenship] in Rantala, J. & Salminen, J. (Eds.) Kansalaisvaikuttamisen edistäminen koulussa ja opetta-jankoulutuksessa. *Historiallis-yhteiskuntatiedollisen kasvatuksen tutkimus- ja kehittämiskeskuk-sen tutkimuksia 5.* Helsinki: Historiallis-yhteiskuntatiedollisen kasvatuksen tutkimus- ja kehittämiskeskus, pp. 39–68.

Vuorikoski, M. & Räisänen, M. (2010) 'Opettajan identiteetti ja identiteettipolitiikat hal-lintakulttuurien murroksissa' [The identity of teachers and identity politics in turning points of governmental rationalities] in *Kasvatus & Aika,* 4(4), pp. 63–81. Available at: http://www.kasvatus-ja-aika.fi/site/?page_id=350 [accessed 7 February 2016].

Yang, F. (2007) 'Education in China' in *Educational Philosophy and Theory,* 34(2), pp. 135–144.

4 Democracy, classroom practices and pre-service teachers' conceptions of excellence

Andrea Raiker & Matti Rautiainen

Introduction

All countries in the European Union (EU) are representative democracies. By democracies, we mean the abilities of peoples to choose and change their governments (Hollifield & Jillson, 2013). In Chapter 1 of this book, we argue that it is the responsibility of governments to establish environments where citizens' abilities to engage effectively with democracy and its processes could be developed. A corollary of this argument is that governments and the education systems they support must create teachers and students who can voice critically appraised judgements to guide their citizenship. We ask: how do education systems develop the abilities of citizens in the EU so that they are prepared to fulfil their democratic role in choosing and changing their governments for the good of themselves and others, within and beyond their national borders? How are these abilities acquired and developed? Choosing and changing a government involves responsibilities of the highest order. So it is paramount that each individual engaging in representative democratic processes knows what s/he is voting for and why, so that the individual can recognise and support through her/his vote the representative of the political party whose policies most closely align with her/his views.

An important aspect of democracy and its processes and outcomes has already become apparent. At the heart of democracy is the relationship between the individual and society, as demonstrated both as the voter registering her/his choice and the individual candidate representing a political party. Dewey recognised this symbiotic relationship. For Dewey, belief in democracy involves free and critical thinking, expression and debate in the:

> . . . formation of public opinion, which in the long run is self-corrective, except faith in the capacity of the intelligence of the common man to respond with commonsense to the free play of facts and ideas which are secured by effective guarantees of free inquiry, free assembly and free communication?
>
> (1939:3)

In other words, democracy is not merely political: it is social and moral, social in the sense that individuals are members of societies, and moral in that societies are governed by shared, understood and agreed ways of behaving. These may well reflect the desires and expectations of individuals, but principally in the sense that they reflect the judgements of the majority. These shared and understood ways of behaving or rules are clearly of greater importance than exercising one's right to vote. They determine the boundaries of everyday life; elections happen only once every four of five years. Nevertheless, the formal and informal laws governing the individuals comprising the social will reflect those devised and mandated by government and, as a consequence, Dewey maintained that democracy is a personalisation of individuality, and is exhibited by certain ways of behaving, certain traits of character, certain ways of living a good life as a social being. As Jackson (2014:15) summarises, 'Dewey's theory is indeed founded on its notion of a democratic individual way of life, for it is this exhibition of democratic behaviour by individuals that is meant to be our primary standard for evaluating the presence of democracy'.

If this is the case, then education systems should include within their curricula learning spaces for the development of character and behaviours, and of knowledge and understanding to support the development of social, democratic beings; in other words, as fully participating citizens who demonstrate their abilities to choose and change their political representatives by the characters and behaviours they exhibit. As Hopkins and Tarnanen indicate in Chapter 6 of this volume, such a curriculum will be democratic in '. . . that [it] embodies, from a pedagogical point-of-view, the social interaction and collective enterprise necessary for active citizenship in a democratic society'. To deliver such a democratic curriculum will require the involvement of teachers who are themselves democratically and politically knowledgeable and active. So the curricula offered in higher education, especially teacher education, should include content and pedagogical approaches that will continue the development of informed and participatory citizenship established in the compulsory school phases.

Pupil and teacher education, then, is of prime importance in developing citizens who have the knowledge and understanding to make critical judgements on how they and their political representatives should act on the issues confronting communities locally, nationally and globally. Almost every child in the EU passes through approximately 10 years of schooling. Every child has parents that have also experienced a similar time in formal education. Hence, the questions we asked at the beginning of this chapter: how do education systems develop the abilities of citizens in the EU so that they are prepared to fulfil their democratic role in choosing and changing their governments for the good of themselves and others, within and beyond their national borders? How are these abilities acquired and developed?

To initiate debate focussed on these questions, we consider student teachers' perceptions and classroom practices in England and Finland. We focus on Aristotle's notion of the 'best good', being '. . . a habit disposed towards action by deliberate choice . . . defined by reason as a prudent man would define it' (Aristotle 1990:4). We propose that the term 'excellence' is equivalent to the notion of 'the best good' and that obtaining the views of pre-service teachers

44   *Andrea Raiker and Matti Rautiainen*

on conceptions of excellence in teaching will reveal insights not only into their classroom practices but also into their characters and their thoughts on how they should behave towards others and others act towards them, so that the 'best good' can be achieved. This, in turn, will reveal the abilities, in terms of character and behaviour, that pre-service teachers believe to be important. In so doing, student teachers will disclose the democratic frameworks underpinning their pedagogies, based as they are on is a personal way of living a good life as a social being, as Dewey argues. We will then be able to make judgements on the extent to which these abilities might promote informed participatory democratic thinking and acting within teachers and pupils.

Teacher education has a key role to play in education. It reflects the solutions made in the past, but it should also look to the future. This is the reason why we focus on teacher education in this chapter. Our research into conceptions of teaching excellence, or the 'best good' in their respective education establishments, has been taking place since 2010 and is ongoing (see, e.g., Raiker & Rautiainen, 2012). We use empirical data, including quotations as examples, collected from Finland (subject student teachers) at the end of their pedagogical studies and reflections on excellent teaching collected from English Postgraduate Certificate of Education (PGCE) students at the end of their course. In Finland, conceptions of teaching excellence are based on teacher's own reflections. This is the reason, why a reflective and inquiry-based approach is emphasised in Finnish teacher education. The quotations given in the discussion below represent the authentic voice of students' reflective processes. This data is gathered from 18 subject teacher students in 2011 at the University of Jyväskylä. In these essays, students had to describe and argue their pedagogical thinking and reflect their theoretical and practical understanding concerning teacher's profession. In contrast, in England, conceptions of excellence are more closely defined in documents concerning standards of teaching and professional conduct and are controlled by Ofsted. These differences impact on classroom practices. Because of broad pedagogical freedoms enjoyed by teachers in Finland, their classroom practices are not only individual but also personal; England's more hierarchical and controlled system attempts to normalise practice. Therefore, conceptions of excellence from 18 English PGCE teachers were collected outside course activities through a mind-mapping exercise.

Student teachers' conceptions of excellence and classroom practices

Max Horkheimer has described man's position in his famous work *Eclipse of Reason* in the following way:

> It seems that even as technical knowledge expands the horizon of man's thought and activity, his autonomy as an individual, his ability to resist the growing apparatus of mass manipulation, his power of imagination, his independent judgement appear to reduce.
>
> (Horkheimer, 1947:v–vi)

It appears that the education system in England exhibits the reductivism described by Horkheimer. On the other hand, the Finnish system, acclaimed in the introduction to the UK government's White Paper *The Importance of Teaching* (2010:16) as being a factor influencing the significant changes in teacher and pupil education appearing in the subsequent Education Act (2011), seems to oppose it. Whereas in England, the philosophy and theory of education has all but been abolished from the initial teacher education curriculum (see Chapter 10), in Finland, the formation of personal pedagogies based on critical evaluation of ontologies and epistemologies is fundamental to the award of teacher status. The situation in the two countries appears to reflect Paolo Freire's (in Leach & Moon, 1999:53) division of teachers into competent technicians who can modify previously given instructions so that they become part of one's own classroom activity and his ideal of critical pedagogy with the 'teacher as cultural worker' (see Chapter 3).

Such an interpretation would be misleading, however. In fact, student teachers' conceptions of excellence in teaching are remarkably similar in both countries. Both emphasise child-centred learning, the promotion of thinking and personal conceptions of teacherhood. Both groups are also enthusiastic, even passionate, about their chosen profession, and both in different ways appear to be prescribed by external factors, tradition in Finland and government in England (Raiker & Rautiainen, 2012.) Finnish teachers have substantial autonomy based on shared understanding with their political partners of education's role in developing individual and social wellbeing, and in Finland's emergence as an international player. Unlike in England, the Finnish Ministry of Education sees no need to for change. In other words, the country's confidence in the current abilities and status of teachers is stable. This can be seen also in teacher education, where student teachers are supported and encouraged in developing their pedagogical thinking from their personal perspectives:

> According to me, enthusiasm is the most important part of pedagogy. Motivated learners learn, because they are eager to learn. The teacher's role is to inspire learners. I thought this way already before I started my pedagogical studies, but now I know how to motivate learners!

This quotation is taken from a Finnish subject student teacher's report entitled *My pedagogical thinking and its theoretic and philosophic background*; this report is the final task in their pedagogical studies (60 European Credit Transfer and Accumulation System (ECTS) points). It reflects the synthesis of all the teacher education that student has received, internalised and then articulated. New teachers have high consciousness of their pedagogical freedom in their classroom with their classes. They know the system is not controlling them.

However, new teachers' pedagogic freedoms do have constraints in the form of the traditions of the Finnish school culture. Student teachers with new ideas to improve classroom practice recognise the pressure of tradition. They are aware that, as teachers, they will be expected to introduce innovative

46   *Andrea Raiker and Matti Rautiainen*

ways of learning and teaching into schools, but at the same time, they will be expected to uphold traditional pedagogic practices. This contradiction makes them uncertain of their choices during their studies. Rautiainen (2008) compared students' conceptions of community in relation to the idea of democracy and political ideologies such as anarchism, liberalism and conservatism. The majority of the students are conservatives even if they show great willingness to increase interaction between teachers and pupils. Only a small minority is willing to change basic school practices. Nevertheless, some student teachers have thoughts that have are similar to those of John Dewey (1966). The quotations below are from the data collected from subject student teachers concerning the changes needed in school according to student teachers.

> Besides, how can an educator demand of his students the ability to cooperate or to get along with other people if he himself as an adult human being is incapable of functioning as an active member of his own community or in cooperation with other teachers or with the home?
>
> In a school community, pupils should be given the opportunity of directly influencing school activity. A simple example would, for example, be defining the objectives for courses. Pupils should have the possibility of influencing all kind of activity. Admittedly, participation does presuppose sufficient knowledge about how schoolworks, but this could be gradually taught even during lessons. Pupils should have equal chances of influencing the school community and everybody should have the opportunity and right to affect matters. The issues and the decisions should have a real meaning and appropriate goals. The community must approve the goals democratically, but be open to new suggestions and ideas. Pupils could be given different roles and tasks in the community. Through joint action and planning pupils commit themselves to developing the community.

In everyday life, the task of developing a new culture of democracy will face the problem of lack of time. If a student teacher feels there is not enough time for completing the basics in a school subject, how can time be found for making explicit living democratically? In this context, education for democracy is a secondary aim compared to achieving objectives in each subject. This is also a deeply rooted tradition of school: the pupil's unquestioned position as learner and the teacher's as supervisor. In other words, the pupil's role is subordinate to that of the teacher. This is interesting, because there does not seem to be a strong connection between learning practices and education for democracy in student teachers pedagogical thinking. The primary nature of learning methods compared to educating for democracy has created classroom practices without a strong ethos of democracy.

A typical Finnish classroom is still laid out with rows of tables and seats. The teacher's table is in the front of the classroom. This arrangement is not conducive for educating for democracy, as one pupil is looking at the neck of another pupil, and the only face the learner can see is that of the teacher. The difference compared with classroom design in England is striking. In England, many classrooms are arranged for group work but with the wherewithal for each child to look to the front, where the teacher and the interactive whiteboard are generally situated. Teachers' desks are often pushed to the side; some teachers do not have desks at all. Lessons are designed to include not only whole class delivery of subject matter to meet specific learning outcomes, but also group work focused on differentiated tasks so all pupils can access the learning presented. Group work is learner-centred and can be either cooperative or collaborative, depending on the task. In Finnish classrooms, lesson plans and furniture arrangements are designed for teaching from the front, in other words, teacher-centered in nature. Finnish classroom-design solutions are logical from a traditional perspective. Teaching from the front to pupils sitting in rows emphasises the teacher's central role in and control of the learning process. However, it appears that the English approach, where control moves from teacher to pupil and back again, with the teacher holding the overarching role of facilitator, has greater resonance with Dewey's conceptions of the democratising power of education or of 'faith in the capacity of human beings for intelligent judgment and action' (Dewey, 1939:3).

Character and behaviour

Interestingly, the changes in direction of democratic teacher professionalism, characterised by character and behaviour, have the same root in England and Finland, the period of experimental education known as 'progressive education' practised in the 1960s. Progressive education involved a move towards child-centred education, informality with an emphasis on personalisation and learning by discovery. In both Finland and the UK, selective schools were replaced with comprehensive schools (though public schools and some grammar schools in the UK avoided replacement). However, whereas in Finland, collaboration at all levels and by all stakeholders ensured the development of a cohesive approach to teacher education with shared understanding of required standards and their method of application, there was no similar uniform approach in the UK. Partly, this was due to the relative size of the two countries. In 1960, the population of Finland was 4.43 million (Statistics of Finland, 2007), whilst that of the UK was 52.4 million (ONS, 2014) and growing rapidly due to the post-war 'baby-boom'. Also, whilst Finland had been able to adopt comprehensive education throughout the nation, diversity was maintained in the UK. The reasons lie in the attitudes to mass education held by the Conservative government of 1951–1964. The Conservatives were committed to the public and grammar schools where they themselves had been educated. Despite the efforts of Harold Wilson's Labour Government (1964–70) to increase opportunity within British society, by abolishing the 11 plus examination on which selection to grammar schools depended and spending more on education than defence, by 1970, only 30 per cent of secondary-aged children were attending secondary comprehensive schools. However, the increase of access to secondary education

48   *Andrea Raiker and Matti Rautiainen*

given by the 1944 Education Act had resulted in a more knowledgeable and politically aware populace that recognised the unfairness of the selective system and believed that education should be more child-centred, particularly in primary schools. The system of streaming in primary teaching, and thus whole class teaching, was gradually discarded.

Newly qualified teachers found their professionalism and status advanced by teaching becoming a graduate profession through the introduction of the Bachelor of Education degree following recommendations of the 1963 Robbins report. Local Education Authorities (LEAs) encouraged innovation in the classroom. This, together with a decline in the inspectoral role of Her Majesty's Inspectors and LEA inspectors of schools increased teachers' autonomy and they were stimulated to be creative and innovative in their practice. This was a golden time for democratic teacher professionalism, but, as Galton, Simon and Croll (1980) point out, the direction of teacher autonomy and professionalism in future years '. . . can be found in this period and the apparent subsequent reaction from ideas and practices then regarded as positive' (Galton et al, 1980:39). This was an age of permissiveness: teachers could teach what they wanted to teach in a manner and to a timescale that suited them. This period has been termed the era of 'uninformed professionalism' (Earl et al, 2003), and it had significant consequences for teacher and child education.

In the 1980s, an international focus on achievement in language and mathematics raised concerns about teaching and learning methods; emphasis was placed on determining the causes of underachievement. In response, the role of government in education changed and became explicitly interventionist. The Conservative Government introduced a series of initiatives that attempted to democratise education whilst pressurising schools to demonstrate school improvement and increasing achievement in return for increased funding. Parental choice in schools increased, and many aspects of school management were taken from the LEAs and given to schools. *The National Curriculum* was introduced in the late 1980s (revised 1999 and 2014); it was a legal statement of what schools were required to teach. Pupil achievement was measured by *Standard Assessment Tests* at the end of each Key Stage at ages seven, 11, 14 and 16, success in the latter being awarded by General Certificates in Secondary Education. School performance was inspected in depth during a round of inspections by Ofsted beginning in 1996. The shift from teacher autonomy to government prescription was completed in 2012 when the General Teaching Council of England was abolished and its *Code of Practice for Registered Teachers in England* were replaced by the *Teachers' Standards* (TS, 2012). Devised and published by the Secretary of State for Education, the TS prescribe principles or criteria to be followed by student teachers and nearly all practising teachers, regardless of their career stage.

Character and behaviour feature strongly in the TS. In the *Personal and Professional Conduct* part of the TS (2012:10), character and behaviour are linked to the term 'ethics' and are defined as including and maintaining dignity and mutual respect between teachers and pupils, ' . . . at all times observing proper boundaries appropriate to a teacher's professional position', and safeguarding pupils' well-being ' . . . in accordance with statutory provisions'. This strongly suggests that the parameters of teacher character and behaviour are determined by the government. What is more, the parameters are defined in deficit terms, suggesting that they are not naturally part of a teachers' culturally generated self, that is, the totality and embodiment of her/his thoughts and experiences organised into perceptions of correctness of practices; in other words, teachers do not intrinsically have the character to behave in the 'best good'. However, our research into student teachers' conceptions of excellent teaching has revealed a healthy scepticism as well as an appreciation of the framework provided by the *Teachers' Standards*. The following is representative of the views of the English students who contributed to our research:

> What is excellence in education? Well, when I found out I was going to be speaking about tis today, the first thing I did was to ask the teachers in my school what they thought excellence in education was and I got a lot of different answers. The main answer I was given was that excellence in education was achieving an outstanding at Ofsted. Ofsted are like a governing body that assess teaching in the UK. But I spoke to my mentor about this and she gave me the opinion that getting an outstanding at Ofsted was not a sign of excellence, it could be luck. So this made me question what my definition of excellence is, and I think it's such a hard question to answer because it is based on your personal views. The UK government have come up with eight Teachers' Standards that Student C stated to talk about. It was to create a uniform goal of teaching across the UK. These standards came into implementation in September of this year and they are the standards by which we as PGCE students and teachers in general are judged . . . Although these standards are given to be the minimum level of practice, I personally think that of you are implementing all of the standards then you are on your way to achieving excellence.

There are no such government-directed and prescribed principles for acting in the 'best good' in Finland. Finnish teachers have broad pedagogic autonomy in their work compared to English colleagues. This has arisen from philosophic and historic perspectives based on social meta-practices evolving from European, in particular, German, traditions of education and socio-political development in the Nordic countries. According to Heikkinen et al. (2011:2):

> . . . in Finland and the Nordic countries, the European tradition of 'Bildung' has been adopted and developed along with the Scandinavian welfare state, based on strong values of democracy, equity and solidarity . . . The development in Finland can be understood within this social, political, cultural and material-economic context.

50   *Andrea Raiker and Matti Rautiainen*

'Bildung', following the Hegelian tradition, is defined by Heikkinen et al. as being not only an intense pursuit of personal intellectual and practical development, but also of development of one's society. This involves the consistent and continual questioning of the existing state of affairs, challenging both government and society to realise its own highest thoughts and designs.

The result of this in terms of teacher education was that changes in society in 1990s strengthened what Finnish educators call 'teacherhood'. Teachers' duties became more demanding than in earlier decades through the adoption of pedagogical approaches that placed greater focus on the ethical dimensions in teacher education. Established traditions made way for a constructivist orientation which presupposed constant assessment and renewal of one's pedagogical practices and approaches. The National Core Curriculum lost its prescription and became guidelines for school-based curricula. Also, the national school inspection system and inspection of school textbooks were abolished. At the same time, there was extensive discussion of basic concepts associated with learning and the status of the school. The idea of collaboration in its various forms spread in Finland at the same time as the shift to school-based curricula resulting from the curricular. The resultant rise of responsibility and autonomy required broader reflections on professional character and behaviours and teachers' responsibility for the ethical dimensions of their practices.

The same requirements for autonomy and professional responsibility in terms of character and behaviour were applied to teacher educators. National legislation provided the framework for academic and pedagogic programmes of study by defining the qualifications required for teacher status, but this framework is open to interpretation. This allows university faculties of education to have strong autonomy in deciding the aims and curricula content of teacher education. Traditionally in Finland, teacher education has been didactically and psychologically oriented; the role of the social sciences has been always been minimal (Rantala & Rautiainen, 2013). Therefore, the ethos of teacher education has emphasised student teachers' personal growth through reflection and reflexivity focused on personality, choices and the resulting outcomes (for further reading on the historical roots of the Finnish approach to teacher education, see Haavio, 1948; Niemi & Jakku-Sihvonen, 2006; Niemi et al, 2012.) Areas of study, for example, ethics and values, educational philosophy and theory, and legislation, provide the bases for pedagogic studies, professional development and growth, but the final conception of 'teacherhood' lies with the individual, both pre- and in-service. In other words, teacher education in Finland can be likened to a 'supermarket', where student teachers can select the arguments to support his/her conception of teacherhood (character and behaviour) to become and be a teacher. The cornerstone for teacher professional development is clearly liberal in nature.

> The goal of the Teacher education programme is to support students' professional development to become autonomous and ethically responsible experts who are able to critically analyse and reform the culture of school

Democracy 51

and education as well as their own activities. The goal is to create a strong academic identity and the basis thus formed for teachers to contribute to scientific and professional development in their own field. The work of a teacher requires both mastery of practical procedures and the ability to justify the choice of a particular way of working. At the core of a teacher's work lies the understanding and supporting of a pupil's and a group's development. The dialogue between theory and practice takes place particularly during teaching practice periods, which offer a holistic view of a teacher's work.

(Curriculum plans, 2014–2017, Department of
Teacher Education, University of Jyväskylä:1–2)

This situation is possible only where the community has confidence and trust in the teaching profession. In Finland, teachers have the community's confidence and trust. Their strong ethical basis for the work they do in school is recognised, resulting in teaching being a highly regarded and high-status profession, in the same orbit as medicine or law. Because of the emphasis on autonomy, ethical responsibility and expertise, it could be expected that school and classroom practices should be wide-ranging, because the interpretation inherent in the constitution of teacher status mentioned above makes possible pedagogic experimentation and creativity. It is therefore surprising that the differences between schools and classroom practices are small. In other words, despite the potential for diversity of practices, there is strong agreement on the purpose of education, its content and how it should be taught amongst teachers and other stakeholders, such as parents and the wider school community. This is interesting because teachers have pedagogic freedom of choice without external hindrances or constraints and their teacher education programmes include intellectual engagement with philosophy, ethics, educational theory and legislation. Finnish teachers might therefore be inclined, even expected, to be strong promoters of democracy in their classrooms, but they seem to be more like 'princes of their domains'. This contradiction can be explained by the strong role of traditional teaching and learning in Finland which is embedded in the schooling culture. Newly graduating teachers have come from this tradition schooling culture and they will be socialised back into it when they take up their first teaching post, whatever innovative pedagogic ideas on school and classroom development they have engaged with at university (Ruohotie-Lyhty, 2011).

Conclusions

It would appear that, although conceptions of excellent teaching should include explicitly education for democracy, it is not among the primary objectives of schoolwork in either country. In both countries, the teacher's task is to attain the learning outcomes of his/her subject as prescribed in England's *National Curriculum* or as guided by the equivalent in Finland. However, despite being presented as admonishment to teachers not to undermine them, democracy

52 *Andrea Raiker and Matti Rautiainen*

and its related virtues of the rule of law, individual liberty, mutual respect and tolerance are present in England's *Teachers' Standards* and in the everyday processes of classroom practice. In Finland, teachers' activities reflect the values of Nordic society like equality, caring and welfare for all. Visiting a Finnish school is a confusing experience for foreigners because they can see the two faces of Finnish education at the same time. In Finnish schools, learners attain high standards, as evidenced by the Programme of International Student Assessment (PISA), and the interaction between teacher and pupils and the various groups in school is informal. However, visitors are also aware of the passive learner waiting and following his/her teacher's instructions, a pupil who does not have a role in the decision-making process. It is clear that the teacher is in the position of 'expert' who rules the classroom and its state of democracy. The diversity of students in English classrooms means that the pedagogic strategies used within them have to be directed primarily at inclusion and equal opportunities in terms of accessing the curriculum. In spite of the class system still present in Westminster and the policies emanating from government, in schools and classrooms, educating for democracy exists in practice.

England and Finland are not alone with their teaching cultures and the challenges they are facing in their schools and classrooms. Teachers are using more and more active teaching practices as well as pupil-centred methods all around Europe (see, e.g., OECD, 2014). In addition, the European Union is emphasising citizenship education's significance in education. The vision is clear: more participatory, active and democratic citizens (Citizenship education in Europe, 2012). However, as we have demonstrated, the change is complex because education is carrying the weight of history, not only in practices, but also intellectually. In spite of differences, intellectuality including values of democracy and critical thinking is also connecting us though the same aim, but a different framework.

References

Aristotle. (1999) *Nicomachean Ethics* (trans. Ross, W. D.). Available at: http://socserv2.socsci. mcmaster.ca/econ/ugcm/3ll3/aristotle/Ethics.pdf [accessed 2 March 2016].

Citizenship education in Europe. (2012) *EURYDICE.* Available at: http://eacea.ec.europa.eu/ education/eurydice/documents/thematic_reports/139EN.pdf [accessed 26 February 2016].

Curriculum Plans 2014–2017. (2014) University of Jyväskylä, Department of Teacher Education. Available at: https://www.jyu.fi/edu/laitokset/okl/opiskelu/luokanopettajakou lutus/luokanopettajakoulutus/Curriculum2014_English.pdf [accessed 15 January 2015].

Department for Education. (2010) *The Importance of Teaching: The Schools White Paper 2010.* Norwich: The Stationary Office.

Department for Education. (2012) *Teachers' Standards.* Available at: www.education.gov.uk [accessed 18 January 2016].

Dewey, J. (1939) 'Creative Democracy: The Task Before Us' in *John Dewey and the Promise of America, Progressive Education Booklet,* No. 14. Columbus, OH: American Education Press. Republished in John Dewey, The Later Works, 1925–1953, Vol. 14.

Dewey, J. (1966) *Democracy and Education.* New York: The Free Press.

Democracy 53

Earl. L., Watson, N., Levin, B., Leithwood, K., Fullan, M. & Torrance, N. (2003) *Final Report of the External Evaluation of England's National Numeracy and Literacy Strategies. Final Report. Watching and Learning 3.* DfES: Nottingham.

Freire, P. & Macedo, D. P. (1999) 'Pedagogy, Culture, Language and Race: A Dialogue' in: Leach, J. & Moon, B. (Eds.) *Learning and Pedagogy.* Buckingham: Open University Press, pp. 46–58.

Galton, M., Simon, B. & Croll, P. (1980) *Inside the Primary Classroom.* London: Routledge and Kegan Paul.

Haavio, M. H. (1948) *Opettajapersoonallisuus.* Gummerus: Jyväskylä.

Heikkinen, H., Tynjälä. P. & Kiviniemi, U. (2011) 'Interactive Pedagogy in Practicum. Meeting the Second-Order Paradox in Teacher Education' in Mattsson, M., Ellertson, T.V. & D. Rorrison (Eds.) *A Practicum Turn in Teacher Education.* Rotterdam: Sense, pp. 91–112.

Hollifield, J. F. & Jillson, C. (2013) *Pathways to Democracy: The Political Economy of Democratic Transitions.* Abingdon: Routledge.

Horkheimer, M. (1947) *Eclipse of Reason.* New York: Oxford University Press.

Jackson, J. (2014) The democratic individual: Dewey's back to plato movement. *The Pluralist*, 9(1), pp. 14–38.

Niemi, H. & Jakku-Sihvonen, R. (2006) (Eds.) *Research-Based Teacher Education in Finland – Reflections by Finnish Teacher Educators.* Turku: Finnish Educational Research Association.

Niemi, H., Kallioniemi, A. & Toom, A. (2012) (Eds.) *The Miracle of Education: The Principles and Practices of Teaching and Learning in Finnish Schools.* Rotterdam: Sense.

OECD. (2014) *Talis 2013 Results: An International Perspective on Teaching and Learning.* Talis: OECD Publishing. Available at: http://www.keepeek.com/Digital-Asset-Management/oecd/education/talis-2013-results_9789264196261-en#page3 [accessed 2 February 2016].

Office for National Statistics (2014) *Annual Mid-year Population Estimates, 2013.* Available at: http://www.ons.gov.uk/ons/dcp171778_367167.pdf [Accessed on 1 July 2016]

Raiker, A. & Rautiainen, M. (2012) *A Comparison of Student Teacher Conceptions of Excellence in Teaching at Two Universities in England and Finland.* British Educational Research Association (BERA), Manchester: UK, 4–6 September 2012. Manchester: BERA, paper 0166. Available at: http://www.leeds.ac.uk/educol/documents/213353.pdf [accessed 10 December 2015].

Rantala, J. & Rautiainen. M. (2013) (Eds.). Salonkikelpoiseksi maisterikoulutukseksi: Luokanopettaja- ja opinto-ohjaajakoulutusten akatemisoitumiskehitys 1970-luvulta 2010-luvulle. *Suomen kasvatustieteellisen seuran tutkimuksia 64.* Helsinki: Suomen kasvatustieteellinen seura.

Rautiainen, M. (2008) Keiden koulu? Aineenopettajaksi opiskelevien käsityksiä koulukulttuurin yhteisöllisyydestä. *Jyväskylä studies in education, psychology and social research 350.* Jyväskylä: Jyväskylän yliopisto.

Ruohotie-Lyhty, M. (2011) Opettajuuden alkutaival: vastavalmistuneen vieraan kielen opettajan toimijuus ja ammatillinen kehittyminen. *Jyväskylä studies in education, psychology and social research 410.* Jyväskylä: Jyväskylän yliopistoStatistics of Finland (2007) Väestönkehitys itsenäisessä Suomessa - kasvun vuosikymmenistä kohti harmaantuvaa Suomea. Available at: http://www.stat.fi/tup/suomi90/joulukuu.html (Accessed: 1 July 2016).

5 Searching for the roots of democracy

Collaborative intervention in teacher education

Emma Kostiainen, Ulla Klemola & Uvanney Maylor

Introduction

Education is challenged by the demands of educating future citizens who are capable of responding to multiple societal demands. Analysis of global societal trends reveals consequences for Europe with outcomes such as rising inequality, more vulnerable groups and uneven opportunities for individual empowerment (Hoorens et al, 2013). Results of an *International Civic and Citizenship Education Study* (ICCS) indicate how countries are devoted to enhance young peoples' civic and citizenship education, which prepare them to meet the demands facing societies in the 21st century (Schultz et al, 2010). When defining 21st-century skills for professionals in the labour market, the capacities of sharing, teamwork and innovation are crucial (Binkley et al, 2012).

Most of the 38 ICCS countries emphasise participation and engagement in civic and civil society as well as communicating through discussion and debate. By contrast, fewer countries emphasise opportunities for student involvement in decision-making and reflecting on change processes in school. Comparisons between England and Finland suggest that the English school system better supports positive attitudes toward being active, participating citizens (Schultz et al, 2010), whilst Finnish youngsters' civic knowledge and performance, e.g., in mathematics, science and reading is at a higher level (OECD, 2014).

Teacher education is responsible for educating teachers capable of making changes and encouraging student/adult respect and democracy in society. Although democratic practices are developed, teacher education is burdened with hierarchical traditions such as unequal teacher-learner relationships and emphasis on school subjects instead of building a collaborative culture. This chapter analyses changes made in one Finnish teacher education programme at the University of Jyväskylä through one case study. In the Department of Teacher Education, emphasis has been placed on developing teaching courses focused on interpersonal competence (Klemola, 2009; Klemola et al, 2013; Rasku-Puttonen et al, 2011). The research-based evidence from these courses shows that such studies generate 21st-century skills, including collaboration and problem-solving as well as motivating learning. Due to these findings, we wanted to emphasise developing 'impressive' education (as described by students – see method) based on democratic philosophies (Freire, 1996; hooks, 1994). An intervention course

Searching for the roots of democracy 55

module *PedArt* was implemented where changes were consciously made at constructional and ideological levels.

In theorising democracy and dialogue, this chapter describes the *PedArt* intervention, considers the implications for teacher education, whilst also reflecting on the findings in light of the student teacher populations in Finland and England.

Dialogue as a basis for democracy and change

The space of dialogue and the emphasis on interaction must be present to enhance democracy and democratic practices in education. 'Democracy calls for citizens to think for themselves about the lives they want to lead and so democratic education must bring about citizens who can do this' (Blacker, 2007:146–147). According to Dewey, democratic education requires individuals to be personally involved in the decisions they make and to experience 'individual growth' (Blacker, 2007:42). In order to achieve this in the context of multiethnic societies such as the UK, the United States and, to a lesser extent, Finland, two things need to be understood. First that 'democratic education has largely committed itself to the enterprise of expanding its ideas and assumptions about culture from . . . a relatively narrow middle-class Anglo ideal to a more encompassing 'multicultural' approach that 'celebrates' or at least acknowledges diversity' (Blacker, 2007:43, emphasis in original). There are questions regarding the precise nature of this multicultural commitment in these countries. Second, critical thinking is required by the individual if s/he is to 'examine for *oneself* the assumptions about the world that one has been accepting' (Blacker, 2007:141). To do this, Descartes maintained, individuals should:

> . . . reject all their beliefs together in one go, as if they were uncertain and false. They can then go over each belief in turn and re-adopt only those which they recognise as true and indubitable.
>
> (Cottingham et al, 1985:481)

Blacker observes that many will question whether it is possible to reject all their beliefs and replace them only with correct beliefs. Moreover, how does one know which are the correct beliefs to have? This could be the role of the teacher and teacher educator. However, it is recognised that understanding whether students or indeed teachers are ready to have their taken-for-granted-beliefs challenged can be daunting for both teachers and teacher educators.

Notwithstanding, Freire suggests that education should be concerned to make students:

> more fully human i.e. 'conscious beings', subjects and creators of knowledge. A subject is someone who has the capacity to adapt oneself to reality *plus* the critical capacity to make choices and transform that reality.
>
> (Freire, 2008:4)

56   *Emma Kostiainen et al.*

Freire views teachers and other professionals as determined by a culture of (middle class) domination and ultimately being miseducated, and it is this miseducation which is addressed through dialogue and transformative pedagogy. However, true teacher–student dialogue cannot exist if teachers/teacher educators do not understand their own backgrounds, the world they live in and the backgrounds of those they teach and if they continue to regard students as 'ignorant' (Freire, 2008:71) and close their minds to the knowledge that students bring to the classroom. Similarly, hooks (1994:202) argues that '. . . without the capacity to think critically about ourselves and our lives, none of us would be able to move forward, to change, to grow' (hooks, 1994:202). In other words '. . . dialogue creates a critical attitude . . . ' and '. . . only dialogue truly communicates . . . ' (Freire, 2010:40). Being aware of and considering these challenging issues related to democratic education is difficult, but not impossible. The aim of the *PedArt* intervention was to find the voices of students as well as teachers, which in turn could enable critical thinking concerning the predominant structures and flaws in school with regard to democratic education and citizenship.

In the classroom, if dialogue is to communicate, there has to be understanding of the issues being raised and this comes through teacher–student and student–student discussion/negotiation of shared meanings. Further, to develop critical consciousness amongst students, it is important that educators understand the role of education and that of the teacher. According to Freire (2010, p.111):

> If education is dialogical, it is clear that the role of the teacher is important, whatever the situation. As s/he dialogues with the [students], s/he must draw their attention to points that are unclear or naïve, always looking at them problematically. Why? How? Is it so?

Put simply, educators are required to move from the banking approach where students are filled with knowledge to problem-posing, whereby '. . . education affirms men and women as beings in the process of *becoming*' (*ibid.*:65), capable of building democratic futures through critical questioning/dialogue. The expectation is that engaging in dialogue about real '. . . concrete situations' (*ibid.*) should lead to the transformation of both student and educator and their ability to transform the world.

Freire's philosophy encourages teachers to be self-reflective and at the same time seek to transform their practice. To do this, and to create possibilities for dialogue and educational change, hooks (1994:207) contends that teachers should '. . . teach in a manner that respects and cares for the souls of [their] students if [they] are to provide the necessary conditions where learning can most deeply and intimately begin' (hooks, 1994:13). hooks (1994:84) also called for teachers to '. . . bring to the classroom pedagogical strategies that affirm [student] presence [and] their right to speak, in multiple ways on diverse topics'. These notions were cherished in the *PedArt* intervention discussed below and provided opportunities for teacher educators and student teachers to engage in dialogue, enhance voice and teacher–student transformation through a new pedagogical strategy.

Method

Case description: PedArt-project in one Finnish teacher education programme

A research-based intervention course entitled *PedArt* was implemented at the University of Jyväskylä. In the spirit of critical pedagogy, the underlining ideas of *PedArt* were to change the school and conventional teaching and learning practices and to combine pedagogy and art.

Experiences and views of teacher educators and students undergoing the intervention course module were examined. The participants were a group of class teachers and subject student teachers (majoring in biology, Finnish language, foreign languages, health education, philosophy and psychology) together with sixth graders and two teacher educators. Every subject student teacher and a second-year class student teacher had an opportunity to join *PedArt*; 13 out of 350 used this opportunity. The course took seven months and attracted seven credits. The aim of the project was to generate possibilities for dialogues between students and between students and teacher educators. Replacing the banking by the problem-solving approach (Freire, 2008) meant that, from the beginning, the project's principles relied on pedagogical strategies of non-hierarchy between teacher educators and students, giving possibilities '. . . for all to grow' (Freire, 2008). Changes were made in the following epistemological ways:

- teaching orientation to research orientation;
- customary teaching and learning methods to more creative methods and art;
- static to dynamic;
- structured to open;
- fragmentary to holistic;
- formal to informal;
- knowing to being;
- working alone to working together;
- monologue to dialogue.

PedArt was implemented by emphasising an open basis-approach, the role of arts, co-teaching and linking theory and practice. The *open basis-approach* means that the 'teacher-students' and 'students-teachers' plan and construct the project together. The teachers offered only curriculum-defined loose frameworks, e.g., credits, university course aims and the context, school class. The *role of arts* was apparent in the learning assignments and teaching methods in various ways throughout the project. The *PedArt* project started with an art-adventure which ended up in a home garden. Two teacher educators intensively worked together modelling the idea of *co-teaching*, implemented by combining separate teacher education programmes of class and subject teachers, and collaboration between students as well as students and teachers. *Emphasising the link between theory and practice* was enhanced by studying theory in real environments and facing real problems.

58   *Emma Kostiainen et al.*

Research questions, data and data analysis

This study sought to answer the following questions:

What do student teachers find impressive during interventions emphasising democratic philosophies?
What issues do they raise in their writings?

The data consisted of students' (n=13) written essays in the form of letters (n=26) in the middle and at the end of the intervention. The form of letter was chosen because of its informal nature. In the letter, the students were asked to write about their thoughts and feelings about the *PedArt* project and what was meaningful to them.

Qualitative content analysis was used to reveal the significance of the student teachers' experiences. The data was analysed step by step, consisting of three interactive sub-processes (see Table 5.1): creating initial codes, searching and revealing themes, defining and naming themes (Braun & Clark, 2006; Miles & Huberman, 1994). In the first phase, the data were analysed according to those qualitatively different expressions that students described as being impressive, either during or as a result of the intervention. The first analysis phase revealed nine sub-code categories. The second phase consisted of the cross-analysis between the nine sub-categories and resulted in six themes which were experienced as impressive. Further, in the third analysis phase, three meta-themes on democratic philosophies were identified, namely: (1) the sense of community, (2) equality and authenticity and (3) faith in change.

The student's own voice is significant when presenting the results. Therefore, citations from their letters have a notable place in the text. For the purposes of this chapter, the data presented have been translated from Finnish into English.

Table 5.1 The phases of the data analysis

Phase 1 Creating initial codes	Phase 2 Searching and revealing themes	Phase 3 Defining and naming themes
Expressions of support given by the group	Meaning of the group and collaboration	The sense of community
Challenging task combines the group	Empowerment	Equality and authenticity
Openness creates collaboration	Allowing diversity	Faith in change
Well-being	Appreciation, trust and gratitude	
Mutual respect	Informality	
Expressions of emotions	Desire and courage to do things differently	
Facing various difficulties and disappointments		
Unconventional learning spaces		
Dreams and vision concerning future school		

Results

Sense of community

According to the analysis, the sense of community comprised a central theme identifying the impressiveness of the intervention based on democratic philosophies. The characterising dimensions in this theme were: meaning of the group, collaboration and empowerment.

Meaning of the group and collaboration

The group was exceptionally important for the students. The group was required because a lengthy, challenging project was not a mission that could be accomplished alone. The project, including the resistance of some sixth graders, required joint effort, brainstorming, support and social interaction competence among the students. The group was experienced both as being supportive and as being the source of inspiration.

> Concerning this [difficulties with the class] next spring is still like a television screen showing only a static blur – unclear. But nothing is impossible for our group!
>
> (S9)

> This group we have feels oddly intimate, a little bit like a family. It's empowering to be involved with people who have similar dreams for the future as you do! It's empowering to be involved with people who are so creative and enthusiastic!
>
> (S7)

The orientation to one another was characteristic of students' expressions. Getting interested in one another was supported by various teaching and learning methods. Using art as an integral role in assignments provided routes in mutual understanding. In a lengthy project, it was possible for the participants to become acquainted with each other, which was seen as a precondition for mutual trust. Also, teachers' situational sensitivity to the group and regular support proved to be important.

> It was interesting to notice how many different ways there can be for interpreting the word 'art'. Even though we are all different and we think differently about different subjects, we are all still similar in some ways. I'm not sure, maybe it's the art that makes us tolerant and interested in the viewpoints and opinions of other people as well.
>
> (S11)

> I feel it's great that I can trust every member, because we are committed. I can be honest and open when saying things to them and I am accepted.
>
> (S8)

60 *Emma Kostiainen et al.*

At times the stress levels began to rise but this group has offered so much peer support. Your [teachers'] advice has been really supportive as well.

(S3)

Empowerment

The intervention can be interpreted as empowering students in various ways, giving them breathing space and increased well-being. Further, the project was experienced as offering perspectives to see other studies and one's everyday matters and self in a new way. Understanding their own role as being special in changing the school was considered especially empowering.

> On the other hand, *PedArt* has given us the means to also rest and relax, because our meetings have genuinely been like a comfy couch for rest in the middle of packed schedules and overall anxiety. I began finding the sides of myself that have been dormant under the surface. I especially found a way to being a better and more tolerant person. Less envious.
>
> (S9)

> I thought that maybe the structures of the elementary school system are too stifling after all and my motivation to study to be a teacher was down in the dumps. The project has instilled me with belief, hope, and new ideas as well as dreams.
>
> (S12)

> Our group contains everyone who wanted to be on this course. A small portion of a humongous crowd that makes this even more important. Are we really the only ones who want to change the school world?
>
> (S9)

While recognising the importance of being a teacher, some students nevertheless found it a strain to question their career choice, once accepted into a teacher education programme. The intervention also enabled those uncertain and lacking knowledge about teaching to explore these issues.

> One of my teachers has said that there are teachers who should not concern themselves with anything remotely close to teaching. I know myself well enough to state, that I will very carefully measure whether or not being a teacher is my thing. Right now, that particular gate is not showing a green light. *PedArt* gives me the opportunity to think of issues such as this.
>
> (S10)

Equality and authenticity

Equality and authenticity appeared to be other important dimensions necessary to enhance democratic values (democracy, the rule of law, individual liberty, fairness/equality, respect and tolerance) in education. The features characterising these dimensions were allowing diversity and various emotions as well as experiences of appreciation, trust and gratitude.

Allowing diversity and various emotions

The analysis raised the issue that even in a group of thirteen white female students, the experience of being different and valued as such was important. They felt they were individually allowed to experience and express authentic emotions in their full variety, from disappointments to joy and success. The students appreciated the possibility of being '. . . more fully human . . .' (Freire, 2008:4) in a permissive and safe atmosphere.

> *PedArt* is not just a course. It allows us to be just how we are. Every personality is given sufficient space. I don't have to fear anything, not even giving constructive criticism to somebody. Thank you for giving our personalities space. It's wonderful that we don't have to be afraid of ourselves.
>
> (S9)

Appreciation, trust and gratitude

The students appreciated that the ideas based on democratic values and 'to move beyond boundaries, to transgress' (hooks, 1994:207) did not '. . . remain only as lovely thoughts but became concrete and apparent in the operational culture of the intervention' (S5). Further, students had a great sense of being valued and experience of being important and trusted.

> This project has made me feel that we students are important. That I'm important.
>
> (S7)

> I'm impressed by the fact that in the beginning, we had a completely open opportunity to do something really new and different. We were able to work on tolerance through art. I am forever grateful for the trust that we were shown in letting us plan this thing through.
>
> (S8)

The role of the teacher seemed to be very important. In their letters, the students were candid when describing the meaning of the teachers involved in the intervention. The teachers in turn were concerned that they did not appear to be 'above' the students and owning the 'right' answer. In general, the students expressed gratitude towards the project and the teachers.

> I think there is an exceptionally good team spirit, trust and emotional bond within this group of students that we have. But what is even more unusual is how close a relationship we have had with you too. You have dared to let us get close to you. You have been more to us than what teachers usually are for students – you have been present and open for us as human beings. I think there is no greater gift that you could be giving.
>
> (S7)

62   *Emma Kostiainen et al.*

> During this course, I learned to thank people.
>
> (S2)

Faith in change

The features in the data attached to faith in change were informality in learning spaces and the desire and courage to do things differently. Analysis indicated that faith in change supported the idea of democratic values in education.

Informality in learning spaces

Students described the more informal and unexpected situations and surroundings as important. These situations tended to give a certain nuance throughout the intervention.

> The highlights of this autumn have been the first meeting in Ulla's wonderful garden, the princess games and the meeting at the Gardner's house.
>
> (S3)

> I think it [team spirit] was affected by the unifying bicycle trek we did early on. Right away, it clearly knit us together into a group. Simply dressing up in red was so surprising and nice. I never thought that something like that would happen in a UNIVERSITY! But being invited into a teacher's home and the wonderful sense of hospitality that the teacher gave us . . . it totally took us off guard.
>
> (S8)

Desire and courage to do things differently

The students attending the intervention were motivated to change the school towards being more democratic and holistic, even with '. . . trying something quite radical that would really give children something to think about' (S13). Some of them had been frustrated in the current 'banking' school system and desired change.

> I loved the thought of an opportunity to go and teach in a new and different manner. During my student years, I wondered where my creativity had gone. When school came into my life, I was suddenly given a set of rules and orders that were telling me where to be, how to behave and what had to appear on paper as the tip of my pencil was moving on it.
>
> (S8)

Desire for change remained, even strengthened, within the project. In students' letters, there were strong words of faith, taking steps towards Freire's (2008) idea of dialogue.

> In a simple rhyme, you could say that *PedArt* gives you strength, faith and courage to strive towards a more humane, innovative school. And that counts for a lot. Thanks to *PedArt*, I believe that a school can operate

communally, by giving space and a voice to everyone. I believe that a teacher should be an idealist.

(S5)

The best way to wake people up to think, question and notice things is to spring into action for your own visions and believe in them. It is the only way to improvement.

(S13)

Discussion

In the spirit of bell hooks and Paulo Freire, we discuss the findings using dialogue to consider the role of art, teachers and possible interventions to enhance democracy. We also compare the results with Finnish and English student populations.

What is the role of art and the teacher in enhancing democracy?

Uvanney: Emma and Ulla, when you started this intervention, what did you have in mind the role of art and finding one's voice would be?

Emma and Ulla: One idea was that teacher education would be more holistic, not only a question of brains and thinking but would affect the whole human being through their heart and emotions (that you face or cannot face) and help students to find the strength and interests that they have concerning art. Even though the teaching of art and skills subjects rests in a solid basis in Finnish basic education, there is an ongoing debate concerning the need for increasing them (Ministry of Education and Culture, 2010). Our students, other than art student teacher, saw the need and wanted to strengthen the role of art in school. Art raises more questions than traditional teaching methods, and the questions are very important, as they raise critical thinking and encourage seeing things differently, more freely. Uvanney, what is the role of art in English schools and its relationship towards education for democracy?

Uvanney: Art is part of art and design within the national curriculum in England. Emphasis is placed on creativity, students thinking critically and developing a 'more rigorous understanding of art and design' (DfE, 2013a). There is no specific role for art in promoting democracy in the National Curriculum that falls within the remit of citizenship education (DfE, 2013b). However, art has been used in the UK to engage young people, particularly those described as disengaged from school and to explore issues of culture, citizenship and democracy (Finney et al, 2005; Meade & Shaw, 2011). It is also increasingly being used to explore migrant communities (and subsequent generations) experiences of integration and multiculturalism in Europe and the USA (DiMaggio & Fernandez-Kelly, 2010; Martiniello,

2014; 2015). The medium of art could be used to help teachers develop students 'democratic imagination' and foster an understanding of democracy as 'an active social, political and cultural process through which change occurs in different contexts and spaces by means of subversion, opposition and resistance as much as by participation and consent' (Meade & Shaw, 2011:65). Such understanding is particularly important for teachers and teacher educators in multiethnic societies, where a lack of knowledge about minority ethnic communities (including their beliefs and values) has contributed to minority ethnic cultures, particularly in Europe, being blamed for them being perceived as not sharing a state's democratic values (Cameron, 2011; Lesin´ska, 2014).

For these reasons, I think your project of using art as a vehicle to create dialogue is very helpful in working across different class/ethnic/gender/faith groups because it allows those opportunities for dialogue and new understandings to emerge. Importantly, you found art also provides a means for student teachers specialising in subjects other than art to develop democratic understandings and apply these in their teaching. But you said it is not art alone that gives the voice, so what else gives voice then?

Emma and Ulla: In this intervention, we put effort into us and the students getting to know each other personally, to enhance mutual respect. When we got to know each other it was easier to express and share all kinds of emotions. We think that one of the main points is that if you care and dare to open your innermost feelings, and the others in the group accept you, we may notice that my voice is equal to yours. This increased the trust between us all.

Uvanney: What do you think the role of the teacher is?

Emma and Ulla: Listening and aiming for dialogue are teachers' key skills for equality. Our bond with the students after a couple of years is still very strong; for example, one sent us an email concerning her current work for human rights. We think one reason for this was that we put effort into listening to our students and we were quite sensitive towards their needs and their emotions. Still, when we read their letters, it is a little bit embarrassing when they say such beautiful words about us. How can we report such results without praising ourselves?

The teacher being a member of the group was important. Actually, it might have been a cultural shock to our students that instead of saying, 'you have to do this and that', we said, 'we will create the project together'! So for some of our students it was hard to bear this uncertainty. But then when reflecting on hooks's and Freire's ideas, we became uncertain: are we as middle-class university teachers able to ask the right questions to enhance democracy?

Searching for the roots of democracy 65

How did the intervention reach for the roots of democracy?

Uvanney: You talked about being able to question yourselves and what you were doing. This suggests you [sought to] understand your own background as part of the process and used that to help you teach, which is what Freire and hooks say teachers should do. Did the students have the same class background as yourselves?

Emma and Ulla: If we look at the big picture, they were all white, young, Finnish ladies. Yet in their letters, many of them wrote about how this is a group of various different types of persons and still they felt they were accepted as their own unique person. Actually, the background didn't appear to be an issue in the project. What was an issue were students' feelings of inequality. For example, students felt that sharing the work in the project was uneven.

Uvanney: This inequality would suggest that even if you and the group you are teaching share the same background, it doesn't necessarily mean you will be able to communicate and have that shared dialogue. You have to find ways of creating that dialogue and shared understanding, which is what you did. It seems to me that you are also saying as part of that process that time is essential, to understand your students, for your students to understand you where you are coming from and what you are expecting as part of the learning process. In addition, another key point that comes out of your work, is that teachers need to see students as individuals.

Emma and Ulla: Exactly! According to the data this project managed to do it. The students felt they were accepted as individuals and they saw their own specialties, strengths, weaknesses and skills. Uvanney, would it be possible to organise similar projects like PedArt in English teacher education? Can the results with Finnish and English student populations be compared?

Uvanney: The school populations in Finland and England are clearly different. Yet there are some similarities with the teaching population in that the majority of teachers are predominantly white (DfE, 2015a). In some schools, classrooms are ethnically diverse, whereas within others, it's predominantly white. So having a predominance of white majority students in some English classrooms would not be dissimilar to those in Finland, where there are few minority ethnic students. While England is more ethnically diverse (ONS, 2012) than Finland, nevertheless I think the same issues as found in your PedArt project would apply, in that teachers would need to have an understanding of the backgrounds of their students and be sensitive to and respectful of those experiences when exploring

66   *Emma Kostiainen et al.*

democratic issues. So for example, in England you will have white British students but their everyday experiences are very different (e.g., because of geographical location, class, gender, disability), so they are coming to the classroom from different perspectives. Because their experiences are different their understandings are different, and they bring those differences to the learning process. The same would apply to minority ethnic students. Applying this to the teacher education context where the majority of student teachers are from white backgrounds (DfE, 2015b) means teacher educators cannot make assumptions about what knowledge students have (hooks, 1994) or the type of experiences or perspectives they might bring into teacher training. Do you want to discuss those interesting issues that you said the students did not mention in their letters?

Emma and Ulla: Yes, it was interesting that after this project they didn't raise those issues we normally get with university course feedback, like, 'I already knew this and didn't want to study it again'. With the PedArt project, they said, 'at last this is what we want'.

Uvanney: Any idea why they didn't do that?

Emma and Ulla: Because everything we did was so real, we used proper questions and we had real problems with the children for the students to solve. When there was a conflict with the pupils, we discussed it and practiced social and emotional skills which could be helpful in such situations. So theory and practice went hand in hand.

Uvanney: So that would be similar to Freire's problem-posing which he says is important in the creation of dialogue.

Emma and Ulla: The other part of this project was that we as teachers strengthened our own voice. It allowed us to dare to believe in these democratic values and continue our work towards dialogue and listening to students' voices and their ideas. And maybe that is the reason why every now and then tears come to our eyes when we talk about this project because it is something that we deeply believe in.

Implications

In the *PedArt* project, changes towards democratic education were made in various ways.

The project partly confirmed the students' desire to do things differently and change their teaching. Although a Finnish project, it has relevance for democratic education globally, as it supports seeing '. . . education as the practice of freedom . . . ', school as '. . . a location of possibility . . . ' and helped students '. . . to move beyond boundaries, to transgress ...' (hooks, 1994:207). The intervention empowered these student teachers to share, discuss and debate issues previously not explored. Possibly, through the positive experiences they highlighted, they will implement elements of democratic philosophies and practices in their future schools. Acts for childrens' empowerment would enhance democracy in school more widely, which is not obvious in Finnish schools (Rautiainen & Räihä, 2012).

Even though the experiences of the democratic intervention were highly positive, the question of equality remains under continuous negotiation. Work for equality and democracy demands commitment and sensibility of students and teachers. We believe that if teacher educators create a space for dialogue in teacher education, then teachers will be able to promote democracy and democratic values in their practice. It is important to recognise, however, that the shift towards democratic education is demanding. If the physical space (e.g., formal seminar room) and intellectual space (e.g., collegial pressure to be moderate) forces teachers to proceed using customary practices, they cannot strike against what is conventional. Instead, it becomes tempting to remain in one's 'comfort zone'. If the surroundings regulate teachers' work rather than foster an intellectual future-oriented dialogic community, democratic education will not be achieved. In democratic education, individuals are personally involved in the decisions they make (Blacker, 2007:42). Therefore, democratic pojects are worth doing and supporting in teacher education.

References

Binkley, M., Erstad, O., Herman, J., Raizen, S., Ripley, M., Miller-Ricci, M. & Rumble, M. (2012) 'Defining Twenty-First Century Skills' in Griffin, P., Care, E. & McGaw, B. (Eds.) *Assessment and Teaching of 21st Century Skills*. Dordrecht: Springer, pp. 17–66.

Blacker, D. (2007) *Democratic Education Stretched Thin*. Albany New York: SUNY Press.

Braun, V. & Clarke, V. (2006) 'Using thematic analysis in psychology' in *Qualitative Research in Psychology*, 3(2), pp. 77–101.

Cameron, D. (2011) *PM's Speech at Munich Security Conference, Speech delivered at Munich Security Conference, Munich, 5 February 2011*. Available at: http://www.number10.gov.uk/news/pms-speech-at-munich-security-conference/ [accessed 2 February 2016].

Cottingham, J., Stoothoff, R. & Murdoch, D. (Eds.). (1985) *The Philosophical Writings of Descartes*. Cambridge: Cambridge University Press.

DfE (Department for Education). (2013a) *National Curriculum in England: Art and Design Programmes of Study for Key Stage 3*. London: DfE.

DfE (Department for Education). (2013b) *National Curriculum in England: Citizenship Programmes of Study, Key Stages 3 and 4*, London: DfE.

DfE (Department for Education). (2015a) *The Teacher Workforce*. London: DfE.

DfE (Department for Education). (2015b) *Initial Teacher Training Census for the Academic Year 2015 to 2016*, SFR 46/2015, 19 November, England. London: DfE.

DiMaggio, P. & Fernandez-Kelly, P. (Eds.). (2010) *Art in the Lives of Immigrant Communities in the United States*. New Brunswick: Rutgers University Press.

Finney, R., Morrison, M., Nicholl, B. & Rudduck, J. (2005) *Rebuilding Engagement through the Arts: Responding to Disaffected Students*. Cambridge: Pearson Publishing.

68 *Emma Kostiainen et al.*

Freire, P. (1996) *Pedagogy of the Oppressed.* 3rd edn. London: Penguin Books.

Freire, P. (2008; 2010) *Education for Critical Consciousness.* London: Continuum.

hooks, bell. (1994) *Teaching to Transgress: Education as the Practice of Freedom.* New York: Routledge.

Hoorens, S., Ghez, J., Guerin, B., Schweppenstedde, D., Hellgren, T., Horvath, V., Graf, M., Janta, B., Drabble, S. & Kobzar, S. (2013) *Europe's Societal Challenges. An Analysis of Global Societal Trends to 2030 and Their Impact on the EU.* Rand Europe [Online]. Available at: http://www.rand.org/content/dam/rand/pubs/research_reports/RR400/RR479/RAND_RR479.pdf [accessed 15 November 2015].

Lesińska, M. (2014) 'The European backlash against immigration and multiculturalism' in *Journal of Sociology,* 50(1), pp. 37–50.

Klemola, U. (2009) Opettajaksi opiskelevien vuorovaikutustaitojen kehittäminen. [Developing student teachers' social interaction skills in physical teacher education]. *Studies in Sport, Physical Education and Health 139.* Jyväskylä, Finland: University of Jyväskylä.

Klemola, U., Heikinaro-Johansson, P. & O'Sullivan, M. (2013) 'Physical education student teachers' perceptions of applying knowledge and skills about emotional understanding in PETE in a one-year teaching practicum' in *Physical Education and Sport Pedagogy,* 18(1), pp. 1–14.

Martiniello, M. (Ed.) (2014) *Multiculturalism and the Arts in European Cities.* London: Routledge.

Martiniello, M. (2015) 'Immigrants, ethnicized minorities and the arts: A relatively neglected research area' in *Ethnic and Racial Studies,* 38(8), pp. 1229–1235.

Meade, R. and Shaw, M. (2011) 'Community development and the arts: Sustaining the democratic imagination in lean and mean times' in *Journal of Arts and Communities,* 2(1), pp. 65–80.

Miles, M. B. & Huberman, M. (1994) *Qualitative Data Analysis.* Thousand Oaks, CA: Sage.

Ministry of Education and Culture. (2010) *Arts Education and Cultural Education in Finland. Policy analysis reports of the Ministry of Education and Culture* [Online]. Available at: http://www.minedu.fi/export/sites/default/OPM/Julkaisut/2010/liitteet/okmpol022010.pdf?lang=fi [accessed 11 February 2016].

OECD. (2014) *PISA 2012 Results in Focus: What 15-Year Old-Olds Know and What They Can Do with What They Know.* OECD [Online]. Available at: http://www.oecd.org/pisa/keyfindings/pisa-2012-results-overview.pdf [accessed 4 February 2016].

ONS (Office for National Statistics). (2012) *Population Census 2011.* London: ONS.

Rasku-Puttonen, H., Klemola, U. & Kostiainen, E. (2011) 'Supporting Student Teachers' Social Interaction Competence in Teacher Education', in Kontoniemi, M. & Salo, O.-P. (Eds.) *Educating Teachers in the PISA Paradise. Perspectives on Teacher Education at a Finnish University.* Jyväskylä, Finland, University of Jyväskylä: Jyväskylä Teacher Training School, Publications 12, pp. 89–102.

Rautiainen, M. & Räihä, P. (2012) 'Education for democracy: A paper promise? The democratic deficit in Finnish educational culture' in *Journal of Social Science Education,* 11(2), pp. 7–23.

Schultz, W., Ainley, J., Fraillon, J., Kerr, D. & Losito, B. (2010) *ICCS 2009 International Report: Civic Knowledge, Attitudes, and Engagement Among Lower-Secondary School Students in 38 Countries.* International Association for the Evaluation of Educational Achievement (IEA) [Online]. Available at: http://www.iea.nl/fileadmin/user_upload/Publications/Electronic_versions/ICCS_2009_International_Report.pdf [accessed 28 January 2016].

6 Democracy and the curriculum

English and Finnish perspectives

Neil Hopkins & Mirja Tarnanen

Introduction

The issue of democracy and the curriculum in the English and Finnish educational contexts is a vexed one. Is democracy even an appropriate concept when discussing the curriculum, and, if it is appropriate, what do we mean by democracy? Ultimately, what is studied as part of a curriculum revolves around debate over knowledge and control. What constitutes appropriate or sufficient knowledge that is necessary for students to study, and who determines what this knowledge is? Such questions go to the very heart of democracy and the curriculum. As authors of this chapter, we have defined democracy as the processes that are in place to allow the various stakeholders a voice in how the curriculum is constructed, maintained and modified. We appreciate that this is a loose definition of democracy, when compared to debates within political philosophy or theory, but it will serve our purpose within the parameters of this chapter.

This chapter will discuss the levels of government control of the curriculum in England and Finland from a largely historical and theoretical perspective. As stated by many commentators and academics within education and outside, many countries in Western Europe and North America have adopted an increasingly centralised approach to their educational systems, often accompanied by reference to 'standards', 'economic efficiency' and the need for 'social inclusion'. Again, many commentators have aligned these arguments with neo-liberalism, in the sense that the state is viewed as working closely with the demands of the 'free' market as a 'provider' of students who are 'work-ready' for industry and business.

Our collaboration has revealed some interesting perspectives on government control, stakeholders and the curriculum. On the surface, England seemingly conforms to many of the neo-liberal assumptions regarding government control of a prescriptive 'national curriculum', high-stakes testing to maintain and improve 'standards' and a belief that education is inextricably entwined with employability. Finland, on the other hand, has a long-established culture of negotiation and consultation with stakeholders on the curriculum that allows individual schools and local authorities considerable freedom on what is taught and when.

Methodology

The methodology adopted in this chapter has been primarily theoretical. Both authors have researched and analysed a range of legislation, government policy, professional and academic literature to provide insight into the issue of educating for democracy within given curricula. The selection of references was chosen in order to give a wide perspective of the issues discussed from a variety of different viewpoints.

English perspectives

The curriculum in England: a brief historical outline

In England, as with many other countries in Europe, there has been a decisive shift towards control of the school curriculum by central government authorities over the past 30 years. The key event in this development was the implementation of the *National Curriculum* in 1988. For the first time, the school curriculum for state schools in England was divided into 'core' and 'foundation' subjects and the division of students into four key stages. From 1944 until 1988, Local Education Authorities (LEAs) had considerable influence on the creation and content of the curriculum for the schools under their jurisdiction. This was to change in 1988 – the subjects studied within the curriculum became, to a large extent, statutory. Considerable powers were given to the Secretary of State for Education, and the LEAs' role became that of supervisors of a centrally established curriculum rather than devisors of a range of local curricula.

The centralising tendency in England has been enhanced and extended in several ways since the adoption of the *National Curriculum*. Standard Assessment Tests (SATs) were created at the end of each Key Stage to measure children's progress according to nationally set levels for the 'core' subjects. In 1998 and 1999, the Labour government, fearing a decline in standards in English and mathematics, introduced the *National Literacy and National Numeracy Strategies*. These *Strategies* focused not only on the content of what was to be taught but also on the way the subjects of English and mathematics were to be taught. Based on research, the government demanded specific types of pedagogy, incorporating elements of whole class and group work, in what became known as a 'literacy' or 'numeracy' hour for schools in primary phase of Key Stages 1 and 2. Since 2010, further changes have been discussed and implemented. A form of 'deregulation' and 'decentralisation' of the school curriculum has come into force. State primary and secondary schools have been encouraged to become 'academy' schools, where funding is provided directly to the school. Academy schools are not required to follow the *National Curriculum*. Alongside this, the government has also promoted the creation of 'free' schools – like academy schools, free schools are not required to follow the *National Curriculum*.

The current position of the *National Curriculum* in England is, therefore, a complicated one. It is still a statutory requirement for those state schools under

LEA control. As was stated above, academies and free schools are not required to follow the *National Curriculum*, which could, it is argued, give them a certain latitude with regards to what is taught. However, the *National Curriculum* still exerts a significant influence, even on academies and free schools as Office for Standards in Education, Children's Services and Skills (Ofsted) inspects schools based on government priorities that are usually reflected in the *National Curriculum*.

Centralising the curriculum: causes and effects

The centralising tendencies of the English state education system have been criticised by a number of authors (Alexander, 2010; Wyse, 2008). This concern operates on at least two levels. Firstly, centralisation of the curriculum inevitably puts power in the hands of government ministers and civil servants in the Department for Education. This creates a tension between a perceived need to maintain 'consistency' and 'standards' at a national level and a potential decrease in the voice and influence of educational professionals within individual schools. It is important not to over-romanticise the period before the *National Curriculum* as a period of unfettered local democracy. However, the issue of curriculum control is a live one in England. The appeal to 'standards' in education goes back to the Black Papers of the 1970s. Successive goverments have taken the concept of 'standards' to devise a series of targets and benchmarks against which schools, teachers and students are measured and judged (Lingard in Wyse et al, 2013). The debate has often focused on how 'standards' can be devised in education and who has control over the drawing up of such standards. Many commentators in education have been concerned that the focus on standards and centralisation of curriculum control have led to a situation where schools feel they are unable to take risks due to the demands of SAT results, Ofsted inspections and other government targets.

The second major concern regarding the centralisation of the school curriculum is the perceived 'neo-liberal' educational agenda followed by various governments since the late 1970s. James Callaghan's 'Great Debate' speech of 1976 set the focus of the school curriculum very much on the need for economic efficiency, productivity and progress. The creation of 'core' subjects in the *National Curriculum*, SATs for these subjects and the *National Literacy and Numeracy Strategies* have had the effect of overemphasising literacy and numeracy to the detriment of other subjects and disciplines in the curriculum. Competency in English and mathematics have been seen as essential in England's attempt to maintain and improve its educational standing *vis-à-vis* other competitor nations (see DfE, 2010b). Successive government reports have stated the vital links between competency in English and mathematics and the needs of industry and business in a competitive international climate (HM Treasury, 2006). The curriculum in primary and secondary schools (as well as sixth form and FE colleges) has reflected this focus.

The division of 'core' and 'foundation' subjects in the *National Curriculum* had the effect of potentially pushing the arts and humanities to the periphery

72   Neil Hopkins and Mirja Tarnanen

of both the primary and secondary curricula. There are several implications for democracy with this trend. The marginalising of arts and humanities subjects narrows the opportunities for teachers and students to explore issues and themes that are central to being an active and informed citizen in the twentieth and twenty-first centuries (this trend was alleviated, to a small extent, by the introduction of Citizenship into the *National Curriculum* at Key Stages 3 and 4 in 2002). Alongside this is the message such a curriculum projects to students, parents and other stakeholders that state education is fundamentally a preparation for employment. The notion of education as an experiment in and preparation for democratic citizenship is difficult to maintain when the focus in the state curriculum is so heavily on what is perceived as instrumental to economic growth and productivity. It will be interesting to see if academies and 'free' schools will veer from this course towards other curriculum priorities and models.

Democratising the curriculum: the concept of stakeholders

There have been various proposals to address the perceived overcentralisation of the school curriculum in England. The concept of local stakeholders is, perhaps, one of the most promising ideas to develop as a means of opening out discussion on the issue of content and control of the curriculum. A stakeholder is an individual or group that has an important vested interest in a given organisation or institution (see Hutton, 1996). In terms of education, stakeholders would include: government (local and central), teachers, students, businesses, voluntary organisations, community representatives.

One interesting example of research into stakeholders influencing curriculum policy and delivery is the work of Luís Armando Gandin and Michael Apple (2002) in Porto Alegre, Brazil. In the 1990s, the city government implemented a policy of *Orçamento Participativo* (OP, or Participatory Budgeting). As part of OP, a series of 'Citizen' schools were established in the city. One of the ways participation is demonstrated within the Citizen School is through the local negotiation of curriculum aims and objectives. The curriculum is seen, at a fundamental level, as a construct of the local community, something the local population plays an active role in discussing and creating. According to Gandin and Apple, '[t]he starting point for the construction of curricular knowledge is the culture(s) of the communities themselves' (Gandin & Apple, 2002: 367; Hopkins, 2014).

Whilst it must be acknowledged that any experiment in school governance is culturally specific and does not readily translate from one context to another, the Porto Alegre project shows how attempts to democratise the school curriculum might work 'on the ground'. In terms of the English context, Michael Reiss and John White have proposed the idea of a 'Commission' that would oversee curriculum aims every five years and would be independent of the government of the time. Reiss and White also suggest that the *National Curriculum* should be non-statutory, but schools would be expected to justify any

Democracy and the curriculum   73

deviation from the broad-based aims outlined by the Commission (Reiss & White, 2013:70–74). It is important to state here that any proposal to allow greater freedom for schools in the curriculum should be balanced by schools consulting with stakeholders to ensure changes or experiments have a degree of democratic accountability (Hopkins, 2014).

The role for local stakeholders might be enhanced by proposals set forth in the *Cambridge Primary Review* (Alexander, 2010). The *Review* advocates a curriculum where 30 percent of the teaching time is devoted to a 'the community curriculum' that is locally proposed and non-statutory. Accordingly:

> Each local authority would convene a community curriculum partnership (CCP) to consider what might be included in the local component of each domain [of learning]. The CCPs would include primary, secondary and early years teachers, domain experts and community representatives, and would have domain-specific sub-committees . . . Children would be involved in the consultations, probaly through school councils.
>
> (Alexander, 2010:273–274)

This, in essence, is not radically different from Reiss and White's Curriculum Commission envisaged on a local basis. It goes a considerable way towards acknowledging the need to include a variety of perspectives and voices in the planning of school and college curricula. Where it differs from Reiss and White is in the statutory/non-statutory distinction.

Finnish perspectives

The curriculum in Finland: a brief historical outline

In Finland, the basis of the current basic education was established in the 1960s, and implementation of the comprehensive school system throughout Finland was completed in the 1970s. This comprehensive school reform focused on everything from curriculum and textbooks to salaries and administration. Also, teacher training underwent substantial revision as it was raised to university level (Jakku-Sihvonen & Niemi, 2006). The comprehensive school reform was part of a larger change in the Finnish society as the entire country turned from an agrarian society to a Scandinavian welfare state. Education played an essential role in this change, not least due to the ideas behind the *Comprehensive School Curriculum*: pluralism, pragmatism and equity (Välijärvi, 2012). The idea was that every child was provided with a good education regardless of family income, social status or place of residence, and these principles and values have remained mostly unchanged since the 1960s (Aho et al, 2006).

The comprehensive school reform was, from the start, a top-to-bottom reform and implemented centralised management and steering of both primary and secondary education in Finland. In practice, this meant that the first national curriculum published in 1970 was strongly centralised. Schools were

74   *Neil Hopkins and Mirja Tarnanen*

visited and audited by the authorised inspectors, and textbooks were examined and approved by the national authorities. The transformation phase was considered successful, both administratively and politically, so this centralised management of education continued for the next two decades. The next phase of change was created by a push to decentralise that took place in the late 1980s and 1990s. The *Basic Education Act* in 1983 and the *Curriculum Reform* in 1985 launched the first steps towards decentralisation and teacher autonomy as they set higher goals for all students instead of streaming. This turned the focus onto the individual needs of students and provided more decision-making power for municipalities (Vitikka et al, 2012). Also, education experts and professionals were involved in the reform more actively, although many basic matters concerning education (such as the core subjects taught to all pupils and the distribution of teaching hours between various subjects) were and are still decided by the government and parliament (see also Aho et al, 2006).

The 1990s can be considered the start of an era of trust-based culture in Finland, which meant that the system (in the form of the Ministry of Education and the National Board of Education) believed that teachers, together with principals, parents and their communities, knew how to provide the best possible education for their children and youth (Aho et al, 2006). Consequently, the curriculum reform of 1994 provided an even larger degree of autonomy for local authorities, as they were now free to make decisions of their own in terms of state funding and organising schools as part of the education process. The educational reform legislation of 1998 continued the decentralisation process and enhanced the local decision-making power and emphasised goals for learning, pupil rights and duties. Thus, as a natural continuation of this, the curriculum reforms of 2004 emphasised moving away from a centrally prescribed national curricula toward the development of school-based curricula with active learning pedagogies, resulting in changing roles and responsibilities for teachers (Webb et al, 2004). The curriculum of 2004 was introduced as a normative document for each locally devised curriculum and provided criteria for student assessment at the end of lower secondary school (this being introduced for the first time). At the time of writing this chapter, the latest curriculum reform is the *Core Curriculum for Basic Education*, introduced at the end of 2014 and coming into effect in 2016. Local curricula based on the national ones are under construction by schools and school districts throughout Finland.

The curriculum and enabling different voices in schools

According to the *Basic Education Act* (628/1998), state education is governed by a unified National Core Curriculum in accordance with the *act*. The government determines the general national objectives of education referred to in the *Basic Education Act* and the allocation of lesson hours to the teaching of different subjects and subject groups. The National Core Curriculum is provided by the National Board of Education (NBE), a national agency in the education sector and responsible for implementation of the education policy under the Ministry of Education and Culture. The NBE determines the objectives and core contents of different subjects and cross-curricular themes, guidance counselling and the basic principles of home-school cooperation and pupil welfare under the purview of the local education authority. In practice, the *National Core Curricula* is compiled in working groups as a collaboration process lead by the NBE. Teacher educators, university researchers, schoolteachers and educational authorities specialising in the learning and teaching of specific school subjects are represented in the working groups. Municipalities, as autonomous authorities, are obliged to provide a curriculum within the framework decided in the core curriculum, and these curricula are guidance documents at the local level.

In principle, the National Core Curriculum in Finland is formed, at least partly, through a democratic process where teachers, parents and other citizens are welcome to participate in discussions in seminars and online settings to give their comments on the draft version of the curriculum. After discussion and comment rounds, the *National Core Curriculum* becomes a binding document. Those who have analysed the Finnish process of national curriculum reform from Habermas's discourse theory of justice point of view consider the process relatively democratic, though they question its validity at both the local and the national levels when focusing on moral and ethical acceptability in terms of setting up factual norms through a truly democratic process (Heikkinen et al, 2014). In other words, at the national level, individuals seem to have the autonomy of deliberating in public spheres, as they are provided differents forms of participation, and they are even encourage to do so, whereas at local level, the curriculum appears to be devised mainly by the authorities (Heikkinen et al, 2014).

On a global scale, Finnish teachers seem to be highly educated, holding master's degrees and enjoying high levels of autonomy in a culture of trust regarding their performance. As a body, they can decide their teaching methods, textbooks and other materials without interference. Also, in comparison to the Anglo-Saxon tradition of accountability in education, Finland has not followed the testing-oriented assessment culture that makes schools and teachers accountable for learning results, but assessment is, as it has been traditionally, the task of each teacher and school in Finland. In the Finnish education system there is only one standardised high-stakes test, the matriculation examination at the end of upper secondary school. Thus, the teachers are free to create their own assessments based on common learning goals, and when yearly given school reports are provided, the schools can decide if the grades (on the scale from four to ten) or literal assessments are used on the report (see also NBE (Finland), 2014).

Accordingly, the pedagogy in the schools seems to differ considerably from the pedagogy applied in systems characterised by explicit tracking and streaming (Välijärvi, 2012). As a result of valuing equality and pluralism, classrooms are grouped heterogeneously, meaning that all students, including students with learning difficulties and the ablest students, work together in the most cases. According to studies conducted in the 1970s and 1980s, heterogeneous

76 *Neil Hopkins and Mirja Tarnanen*

grouping appears to be of the greatest benefit to less able students. The performance of the ablest students, in contrast, seems to remain virtually the same irrespective of how the groups are formed (Välijärvi, 2007:40–41).

Opportunities for a multi-voiced society within schools

In general, as described above, the Finnish education system provides excellent potential for listening to student voices in relation to many aspects of the school system, from curriculum to teaching practices and assessment of learning (Lansdow, 2001). However, enhancing democracy in the schools and fostering student voice do not seem to be evident throughout the various curriculum reforms in recent Finnish education history. According to Harinen and Halme (2012), who have analysed Finnish children's well-being based on the outcomes of the international comparison study, Finnish elementary schools have problems especially with regard to the right to participate – children's voices are seldom heard in terms of the content of education, pedagogical practices, schedules, length of schooldays and issues related to the equipment at school. Harinen and Halme (2012) also point out that when approaching children's rights as a question of self-fulfillment, this side of well-being, as well as the ability of Finnish students to express themselves and be heard within the official school environment, seems to have been overlooked due to the emphasis on internationally recognised results in knowledge and skills when discussing Finnish children.

In this sense, Flutter's (2007) idea of pupil voice is a term which embraces strategies that offer pupils opportunities for active involvement in decision-making within their schools – something which is not currently actualised in Finnish schools. FitzSimmons et al. (2013) introduce three key tenets: reflection, the active implementation of the verb to speak and the powerful verb to act in the framework of action-oriented critical pedagogy. According to FitzSimmons et al. (2013), when looking at the meaning of these tenets for the Finnish curriculum, learning should become a 'shock and awe' experience as students learn to embrace the notions of 'formal' and 'authentic' freedom with the understanding that authenticity comes from within. Thus, learning should not be attached to closed physical settings and teacher-led and textbook-based pedagogies, which has been traditionally the case in many schools in Finland (Luukka et al, 2008; Pohjola, 2011).

There seems to be a belief among authorities, educators and experts that children's wishes and visions have been taken into account in shaping the ongoing reform of the *National Core Curriculum*. For example, the Head of Curriculum Development, Halinen (2015), points out: 'Developing schools as learning communities, and emphasizing the joy of learning and a collaborative atmosphere, as well as promoting student autonomy in studying and in school life – these are some of our key aims in the reform' (Halinen, 2015;Harinen & Halme, 2012)). This might be the case at the policy document level, in terms of intended curriculum. In the sense of the enacted curriculum, school communities and teachers play a key role as they produce, reproduce, manifest and contest through their attitudes and behaviour what they think about their students and how they listen and respond to students' ideas and how they understand good teaching (see Porter, 2006). Teachers are also influenced by policies as they are a multi-layered, multispatial and locally informed process where people produce and reproduce policies in interaction with each other and with the policy processes (Halonen et al, 2015).

Conclusions

This chapter has explored the issue of how and whether democracy has any role to play regarding the construction and maintainence of curricula. As noted in the introduction, we have taken a relatively loose and expansive notion of democracy as the participation of important stakeholders in the process of deciding what should be taught and studied as part of a given curriculum. The levels of negotiation and consultation between stakeholders might be seen as a possible sign of how 'democratic' the curriculum within an education system or jurisdiction might be. In England, the idea of stakeholders in the formulation of policy and delivery of the school curriculum is a potentially constructive way of facilitating a range of perspectives on this issue. The movement towards a negotiated stance amongst the various stakeholders regarding the curriculum could be seen as a means of democratising a vital area of education. Although the current government's policy emphasis is on deregulation and decentralisation of powers to individual schools, it remains to be seen whether this will result in an increase in local participation and accountability in regards to the curriculum or become yet another means of control by government minsters and civil servants. Currently, the centralised nature of the curriculum still generates concerns amongst many educationalists regarding the level of government control and the focus towards a neo-liberal model where education is strongly linked to economic productivity and efficiency.

The Anglo-Saxon accountability movement has not reached Finland yet, although there is public discussion in the media and amongst education experts if there should be a standardised testing system at the end of basic education to ensure reliability of assessment and control the differences between schools. Generally speaking, public opinion seems to be mostly against testing-orientation so far. According to Rinne et al. (2002), the Finnish populace has always had a proud mentality and stood its ground, even though the prevailing political and economic elite at various periods in history would, if left to their own devices, have quickly changed course in the direction indicated by world trade or the political expediencies of the age. However, Finnish society is going through profound demographical, cultural and structural transitions regarding the globalisation and internationalisation of its economy and trade.

Finland is considered to be culturally and linguistically homogenous, but this is changing as the country becomes more diverse. Alongside this diversity is a society more complex and unpredictable, which makes it challenging for schools to prepare their students for future citizenship. Thus, children and young people's participation cannot be understood in isolation from social, cultural and political context in which it occurs. The current curriculum reform has not shown, yet, if it provides equal and appropriate opportunities for all students to manifest their individual agency and participate in decision-making in their school communities. Such participation can, hopefully, have a positive impact on the attainment levels of the students themselves and on the well-being of all members of the community.

Nevertheless, a notable area of difference concerns teacher autonomy and professionalism in the two countries. England's attempts at making teaching into a master's profession in the 1990s and early 2000s has now been quietly shelved, while the emphasis in Finland is still on teacher education as a master's discipline. Since 1994, Finland's process of decentralisation has continued, with teacher autonomy and school-based curricula becoming central themes in a series of reforms. These reforms are part of a process of giving more power to local municipalities in Finland, and it will be interesting to see whether schools involve other local stakeholders when devising the curriculum. One potential danger of decentralisation and deregulation is the power that could be vested in teachers and head teachers in relation to the school curriculum at the expense of other interested parties in the locality. There is possibly more likelihood of this in Finland than England due to the culture of teacher autonomy and the regard that the profession is held in there. Whether the 'free' school movement in England offers the prospect of genuine stakeholder involvement in school-specific curricula is something that will be watched over carefully especially with the announcement of an increase in 'free' schools from 2015. Interestingly, however, England's system appears to be more open than Finland, at present, on the inclusion of student voice in the governance of schools. Whether this openness goes as far as discussion of the curriculum will depend on the phase, context and culture of the individual school, but this observation challenges, in certain instances at least, the idea that England has an exclusively 'top-down' approach to education. Finland's adoption of 'active-learning pedagogies' since 2004 also opens the way, potentially, to more student involvement into what is studied and how as part of their learning.

It could be argued that in England, the focus on English, mathematics and science as a drive towards greater economic productivity and growth leaves little room for exploring issues, themes and subjects that are conducive to active citizenship. The marginalisation of arts and humanities subjects is a worrying trend in many educational jurisdictions because these disciplines facilitate the creativity and sense of debate necessary for active citizenship in the twenty-first century. This trend is not exclusive to England or other countries normally associated with neo-liberalism in education. The situation in Denmark, for instance, has also shown signs of leaning heavily towards measurability and employability in education over the past couple of years. The Danish government has implemented a series of policies to increase the proportion of curriculum time

Democracy and the curriculum 79

devoted to literacy and numeracy alongside an expansion of school hours. This, alongside other issues, led to an industrial dispute between the government and teacher unions and a six-week 'lockout' when the schools were closed. This might be seen as evidence of what Pasi Sahlberg (2012) has referred to as the Global Educational Reform Movement or GERM, a tendency within various educational jurisdictions to look for instrumental 'improvements' in educational 'performance' at the potential expense of the wider concerns of any given curriculum or programme of study. It is within these wider concerns where democracy in education is most likely to flourish and any movement towards an instrumental approach to the curriculum will have negative consequences for our topic of discussion.

References

Aho, E., Pitkänen, K. & Sahlberg, P. (2006) *Policy Development and Reform Principles of Basic and Secondary Education in Finland since 1968.* Education Working Paper Series Number 2. World Bank.

Alexander, R. (2010) (Ed.) *Children, Their World, Their Education.* London: Routledge.

Basic Education Act (Finland) 21.8. 628/1998. Available at: http://www.finlex.fi/fi/laki/kaan nokset/1998/en19980628.pdf [accessed 4 October 2015].

Department for Education (England). (2010a) *Academies Act.* London: DfE.

Department for Education (England). (2010b) *The Importance of Teaching.* London: DfE.

FitzSimmons, R., Uusiautti, S. & Suoranta, J. (2013) 'An action-oriented critical pedagogical theory' in *Journal of Studies in Education,* 3(2), pp. 21–35.

Flutter, J. (2007) 'Teacher development and pupil voice' in *The Curriculum Journal,* 18(3), pp. 343–354.

Gandin, L. A. & Apple, M. (2002) 'Challenging neo-liberalism, building democracy: Creating the Citizens School in Porto Alegre, Brazil' in *Journal of Educational Policy,* 17(2), pp. 259–279.

Halinen, I. (2015) *What Is Going on in Finland? – Curriculum Reform 2016.* Available at: http://www.oph.fi/english/current_issues/101/0/what_is_going_on_in_finland_curriculum_reform_2016 [accessed 13 October 2015].

Halonen, M., Nikula, T., Saarinen, T. & Tarnanen, M. (2015) 'Listen, There'll be a Pause After Each Question': A Swedish Lesson as a Nexus for Multi-Sited Language Education Policies' in Halonen, M., Ihalainen, P. & Saarinen, T. (Eds.) *Language Policies in Finland and Sweden: Interdisciplinary and Multi-sited Comparisons.* Bristol, UK: Multilingual Matters, pp. 220–246.

Harinen, P. & Halme, J. (2012) *Hyvä, paha koulu: Kouluhyvinvointia hakemassa.* Helsinki: Unigrafia.

Heikkinen, H. L. T., Kiilakoski, T., & Huttunen, R. (2014) Curriculum design as collective will-formation in the light of Jürgen Habermas' discourse theory of justice.in *The Finnish Journal of Education,* 45(1), 20–33.

HM Treasury (England). (2006) *Leitch Review of Skills.* London: HMSO.

Hopkins, N. (2014) 'The democratic curriculum: Concept and practice' in *Journal of Philosophy of Education,* 48(3), pp. 416–427.

Hutton, W. (1996) *The State We're In,* London: Vintage.

Lansdown, G. (2001) *Promoting Children's Participation in Democratic Decision-Making.* Florence: UNICEF Innocenti Research Centre.

80 Neil Hopkins and Mirja Tarnanen

Luukka, M-R., Pöyhönen, S., Huhta, A., Taalas, P., Tarnanen M. & Keränen, A. (2008) *Maailma muuttuu – mitä tekee koulu? Äidinkielen ja vieraiden kielten tekstikäytänteet koulussa ja vapaa-ajalla.* Jyväskylä: Soveltavan kielentutkimuksen keskus.

Jakku-Sihvonen, R. & Niemi, H. (2006) 'Introduction to the Finnish Education System and Teachers' Work' in Jakku-Sihvonen, R. & Niemi, H. (Eds.) *Research-Based Teacher Education in Finland – Reflections by Finnish Teacher Educators.* Turku: Finnish Educational Research Association, pp. 7–16.

National Board of Education (Finland). (2014) *Perusopetuksen opetussuunnitelman perusteet 2014.* Available at: http://www.oph.fi/download/163777_perusopetuksen_opetussuun nitelman_perusteet_2014.pdf [accessed 30 September 2015].

Pohjola, K. (2011) (Ed.) *Uusi koulu: Oppiminen mediakulttuurin aikakaudella.* Jyväskylän yliopisto: Koulutuksen tutkimuslaitos.

Porter, A. C. (2006) 'Curriculum Assessment' in Green, J. L., Camilli, G. & Elmore, P. B. (Eds.) *Complementary Methods for Research in Education.* 3rd edn. Washington, DC: American Educational Research Association, pp. 141–159.

Reiss, M. J. & White, J. (2013) *An Aims-based Curriculum: The Significance of Human Flourishing for Schools.* Available at: http://eprints.ioe.ac.uk/16408/1/Reiss_White_2013_Aims_based_Curriculum.pdf [accessed 28 February 2016].

Rinne, R., Kivirauma, J. & Simola, H. (2002) 'Shoots of revisionist education policy or just slow readjustment? The Finnish case of educational reconstruction' in *Journal of Educational Policy,* 17(6), pp. 643–658.

Sahlberg, P. (2012) *GERM that Kills Schools* (TEDxEAST talk). Available at: https://www.youtube.com/watch?v=TdgS—9Zg_0 [accessed 19 January 2016].

Välijärvi, J. (2012) *The History and Present of the Finnish Education System.* Available at: http://cice.shnu.edu.cn/LinkClick.aspx?fileticket=U5rzr6FYThQ= [accessed 15 September 2015].

Välijärvi, J., Kupari, P., Linnakylä, P., Reinikainen, P., Sulkunen, S., Törnroos, J. & Arffman, I. (2007) *The Finnish Success in PISA – and Some Reasons Behind it 2.* Jyväskylä, Finland, University of Jyväskylä: Institute for Educational Research.

Webb, R., Vulliamy, G., Hämäläinen, S., Sarja, A., Kimonen, E. & Nevalainen, R. (2004) 'A comparative analysis of primary teacher professionalism in England and Finland' in *Comparative Education, 40*(1), pp. 83–107.

Wyse, D. (2008) 'Primary education: who's in control?' in *Education Review,* 21(1), pp. 76–82.

Wyse, D., Baumfield, V. M., Egan, D., Gallagher, C., Hayward, L., Hulme, M., Leitch, R., Livingston, K., Menter, I. & Lingard, B. (2013) *Creating the Curriculum.* Abingdon: Routledge.

7 Power, democracy and progressive schools

Sakari Saukkonen, Pentti Moilanen,
David Mathew & Eve Rapley

Introduction

At the time of writing, it is half a century since Donald Winnicott contributed to a conference on 'The Future for Progressive Education' in 1965. The title of his submission was *Do progressive schools give too much freedom to the child?* It is interesting to note that in the fifty years since Winnicott posed the question, not only have we failed to arrive at a consensus, but the matter has rarely left academe's lips. As a contribution to the ongoing (and potentially irresolvable) discussion, this chapter is also an attempt to see if we can agree if Winnicott's question remains pertinent, while regarding the part that power of responsibility and choice plays in educator/learner relationships.

Writing in notes, Winnicott conjectured that progressive schools exhibited the following characteristics: 'Operating from a creative if not actually *rebellious* element in someone's nature. This means that general acceptance has the effect of undermining motivation. Awkwardness in individuals may cause waste in terms of energy, but the advantage is to be measured in terms of originality, experimentation, tolerance of failure, leadership' (Winnicott, 1990:214). Although this summing-up is brief, it is compact and thought-provoking, ushering in as it does such a host of questions that one cannot help but notice certain *non-sequiturs*. For example, why should the fact that a school is spurred on by a creative element in someone's nature be a pre-requisite for the suppression of motivation? Why should 'awkwardness' necessarily lead to the dissipation of (presumably student) energy?

As debatable and intellectually provocative as such points are, however, most educators would probably agree on Winnicott's final assertion: that 'originality, experimentation, tolerance of failure, leadership' are positive and advantageous qualities. Winnicott was of the opinion that such traits were healthy by-products of a good progressive education, but what do we mean by *progressive*?

Progressive education and democratic schools

There is no exact definition of progressive education, but there are some characteristics that summarise the nature of it: self-determined learning and a learning

82   *Sakari Saukkonen et al.*

community based on equality and mutual respect. Pedagogical progressivism means teaching young people:

> . . . the skills they need in order to learn any subject, instead of focusing on transmitting a particular subject . . . promoting discovery and self-directed learning by the student . . . work[ing] on projects that express student purposes and that integrate the disciplines around socially relevant themes . . . promoting values of community, cooperation, tolerance, justice and democratic equality.
>
> (Labaree, 2005:277)

Korkmaz and Erden (2014) define the characteristics of democratic schools. The first and most important characteristics are their strong principles and philosophy. Democratic schools have been established to provide an alternative to mainstream education. The number of democratic schools worldwide is not known exactly, although according to the listing by the Alternative Education Resource Organization (n.d), there are about 270 schools and centres in 34 countries that describe themselves as democratic. The second characteristic of democratic schools is their participative decision-making mechanisms. In the most radical form, democracy is manifested in democratic schools in the direct participation of everybody in school administration with equal votes (*ibid.*). According to the European Democratic Education Community (n.d):

> Democratic schools have school meetings in which all members of the community have an equal vote, regardless of age or status. Students and teachers can sit together as equals to discuss and vote on school rules, curricula, projects, the hiring of staff and even budgetary matters.

The pedagogies of the democratic school are usually based on flexibility, learner suitability, active participation and individualisation according to learner needs. The democratic schools movement – a radical species of progressive education – stresses the characteristic of democratic equality. This means that every member of the school community has equal power. Is this idea a romantic illusion, or is it a definitive characteristic of good education?

Power within education

Power can be considered as a system of control and a tool that teachers can use over their students, over their colleagues and over the students' parents. Teachers are also affected by the power of these same groups of people; furthermore, they are affected by the power wielded by educational authorities and by traditions and ideologies. In a larger picture, power can be defined as a set of relations among actors.

Power can also be considered along more nuanced lines, with its weight and utility being positioned along a power spectrum, with 'hard power' at one pole, and "soft power" at the other. The concepts of hard power and soft power

Power, democracy and progressive schools   83

describe two different ways of using power. These concepts are mainly used in the research of world politics, but they might also be helpfully applied to progressive schools in order to understand the ways in which power is used. Hard power is based on commands, coercion, inducements and threats, whereas soft power is based rather on persuasion and argument and ability to entice and attract. Successful use of soft power shapes actors preferences and makes them to want what the power-user wants them to want (Jones, 2009; Nye & Wang, 2009).

Power can be further understood as a network of relations and as a structuring force (Hannus & Simola, 2010). Opposite to the layman's idea of power as a purely repressive force, we can adapt Foucault's idea of generative power (Foucault, 1981). Actors have different resources to build upon and they are differently positioned. This leads to a Bourdieusian view of the importance of practices and social positions. As Hannus and Simola (2010) conclude, the idea of generative power is a combination of Foucault and Bourdieu.

Methodology

From this perspective, a case study of the lower secondary Alppila School in Helsinki, Finland, becomes interesting. Alppila School has aimed to be a democratic school over the years, but how successful has this been? In a democratic school, power relations among teachers and students are different from mainstream schools; power has to be re-distributed and negotiated. This should be visible in daily practices, routines and discourses. In order to evaluate the success of Alppila School, during the winter of 2014/15, semi-structured in-depth interviews were carried out with four staff members: the headmaster, vice headmaster, a subject teacher in social sciences and history and a guidance counsellor. The headmaster and vice headmaster were interviewed twice, on each occasion of our two visits to the school. In addition, we followed five different lessons during the two visits. Interviews were recorded and later transcribed by a research assistant. During the lessons, we wrote notes.

From this material, the most typical narratives which shaped the basic groundings in terms of conceptions and practices of pedagogical power in school were located. The analysis was based on techniques of close reading and narrative research (Bold, 2012). In this case study, we relied on the interviews, but our observations and experiences during the two visits influenced our interpretations and conclusions of them. During the two days we spent in Alppila School, we gathered a sense of what it is like to live, learn, learn and teach there. Our research foci were the teachers and the ways they executed, articulated and used their pedagogical power over their pupils and how this pedagogical power was distributed among teachers. The distribution of pedagogical power tells us what kind of community Alppila School is in terms of democracy. In describing this, we have to evaluate in parallel the power used by the school authorities, headmaster, teachers and students. We use the findings made to discuss 'progressiveness' in relation to concepts of democracy with a progressive school in England, Summerhill in Leiston, Suffolk.

84 *Sakari Saukkonen et al.*

Alppila School

The Alppila neighbourhood has historically been inhabited by working-class people, although this feature is diminishing. During the last decades, people with higher incomes have moved to Alppila as real estate prices have risen. The school principal described pupils as '. . . more colourful than in some other schools so near the centre'.

The Alppila School was established in 1959 as a state-run experimental school. Its mission was to develop new pedagogy and prepare a new pedagogical vision for Finnish schools. The school was municipalised in 1972 when the comprehensive school started in Helsinki as one of the latest cities in Finland. After this, there have been many pedagogical developmental projects in the school supported by the educational authorities of the Finnish state and also the city of Helsinki. In relation to other Finnish schools, Alppila School may be called progressive, but one has to remember that Finnish schools are quite traditional.

The school is basically a lower secondary school for teenagers 13–16 years old. It has seventh, eighth ninth grades. In Alppila School, structures of schooling are diverse. There are no age-based classes or basic groups. In an administrative sense there are, but because pupils are given freedom in choosing their studies, those basic groups very seldom form the basis for studying. The Alppila School curriculum is phenomenon-based. This means that school subjects have mostly vanished from course headlines. At the beginning of every course, the teacher invites the pupils to join in a meeting focused on deciding how the course should be implemented. Pupils also are asked to discuss what the exact content and aims of the course should be and, more importantly, what would be the best ways to learn the content. Should we use textbooks, internet databases, individual or group work, and what is the role of the teacher?

The Helsinki School Authority administers all municipal schools in Helsinki, including the comprehensive and upper secondary schools of the city. Equality between the schools seems to be important. Officially, all schools are equally good, and the School Authority encourages schools to share their expertise. Schools are encouraged to initiate pedagogical development. Sharing the result of this development is considered to be one way of supporting the equality of schools. This suggests that the official line that all schools are equally good is questionable.

The headmaster describes the relationship between her school and the School Authority quite warmly. She receives support from the School Authority whenever she needs it, but never in an authoritive, controlling or prescriptive manner. When we asked the headmaster and vice headmaster if the School Authority has ever prohibited some of the school initiatives, the answer was abrupt: never. In her mind, the School Authority is eager to listen to what she has to say and there seems to be mutual respect.

> How the Helsinki school authority is present in everyday school life, well, there has been a tremendous change over the decades. The authority is

more and more present on school level in a way there is a channel for sharing information and ideas. There is a sense of openness and both sides listen to each other.

The education providers, usually the local education authorities and the schools themselves, draw up their own curricula within the framework of the National Core Curriculum. Accordingly, the city of Helsinki has prepared its own curriculum based on the National Core Curriculum. In Alppila School, much effort was put into writing the latest school curriculum. As part of this, a working group of teachers took advantage of the general nature of the National Core Curriculum to select and write the curriculum in a language that was understandable for the students, their parents and also for the teachers. They used their expertise and the autonomy enjoyed by Finnish teachers to create a curriculum that would serve the best interests of both students and school.

Teacher autonomy in Finland finds expression in the understanding shared throughout the community that every teacher in Alppila School may teach in the way he or she wants to because teachers are *the* experts in education. This kind of pedagogical freedom is very dear to Finnish teachers. The role of the headmaster is simply to encourage and support teachers, not to direct and control them. The relationship between coercion and conceptions of self-worth is understood. If teachers were forced to adopt certain pedagogy, the older teachers particularly would feel that their work was not valued. So pedagogical freedom is connected to well-being and the feeling of being valued, and therefore, it should not be questioned.

An Alppila School Board includes representatives of parents, teachers and students, and it formally ratifies decisions made by the school community concerning major topics (budget, curriculum etc.). As these decisions include the results of collaboration between students and teachers, the approach of the Board can be said to be progressive. However, at Alppila, as at other Finnish schools, the headmaster has power and can use it is as s/he thinks fit. In other words, the democratic process can be overruled. The potential of widening power relations is mediated, though, through the headmaster sharing his leadership role with the vice headmaster and executive group (headmaster, vice headmaster and three teachers). Overall, our discussions with the Alppila School headmaster and vice head demonstrated democratic process through the emergence of three predominant themes: openness, discussions and teachers' pedagogical freedom. This comes through strongly in the headmaster's assessment of teacher autonomy and collaboration at Alppila, in which she concluded:

> Of course there has been self-willed teachers in the past doing things solo, but it has changed a lot. You don't see anybody locking the classroom door and doing things on your own, it just does not happen anymore.

This is significant because in Finnish schools, there is a long tradition of teachers working in isolation from other teachers, a practice that can be seen as a positive feature, as it indicates expertise and autonomy (Afdal, 2014; Simola, 2005). In Alppila School, there is a strong culture of negotiating and sharing amongst teachers. The vice head said that the headmaster frequently wants teachers to discuss topics and to take part in the subsequent decision-making. We asked if there is opposition among teachers towards those decisions and if they have to compromise between rival conceptions or principles. No opposition and only a few compromises, was the answer. One reason for this is that most teachers have been working at the school for some years and they know each other. In past years, there have been cliques among the teachers, but not anymore. Openness and discussions go hand in hand in Alppila School. So the pedagogical freedom noted above is a shared as well as being an individual freedom. However, openness and discussion cannot be seen as a determinant of progressiveness at Alppila; according to recent work by Sahlberg (2011), there has been a change from isolation to collaboration in many other Finnish schools.

So collaboration between School Board, headmaster and senior teachers, teachers and students is indicative of the potential of power-sharing relations. This is made possible *via* various groups: the School Board, as outlined above, subject groups and smaller teacher teams. These groups are for discussion but also for preparing everyday activities and developmental actions in school life. Having power in Alppila School as a teacher is related to her or his willingness to take part in various groups. Evidence suggests that the curriculum group in particular seems to have had a major impact on the learning culture at Alppila School. One of the subject teachers (NN) stressed that teachers are able to influence their work through choosing subject content and appropriate pedagogies. We discussed above the democratic approach taken by teachers at Alppila to write the curriculum in user-friendly language. However, encouraging *students* to take part in the democratic opportunities available to them appears to be an issue.

In line with the school's democratic ideals, the students have power in school in educational matters, but not all of them want to use that power. There are only about 20–30 active students out of the 400 who take part in various student associations. We were informed by the staff that the tutoring group, environmental agent group and student council are the main channels for participation. Also the immersion in Swedish language course students are exceptionally active. There are also two student members on the School Board. Considering the school's democratic ethos and the efforts made by teachers for power sharing, the proportion of students taking part in these formal activities provided by school is small.

The same reluctance to engage was seen in students' response to student-centred pedagogies. We were told that at the beginning of every course, the teacher invites the pupils to join in a meeting focused on deciding how the course should be implemented. NN told us that the students are not very active in proposing new ways for learning, and that many students are satisfied with teacher-centred teaching methods. This notion was confirmed in an interview with the school guidance counsellor, who found it strange that students do not

Power, democracy and progressive schools 87

use their opportunities to influence their learning. The headmaster also warned us in the first interview that we will not see progressive pedagogy but quite traditional teaching methods in the school. We followed seven different classes over two school days, and our observations confirmed the headmaster's view. To be honest, we were a little disappointed.

NN is still dreaming of students being more active but is not frustrated with student passivity. He does admit that there is a certain conflict of ideals and reality in this respect. Nevertheless, NN described the teacher/student relationship as direct and non-formal. Teachers have to be sensitive and flexible with the students. When asked how teachers experience the active students, he said that these students were a helping hand for teachers. The next week after the first interview, there were both Statute Labour Day and 'open doors day' events at the school. In both of these, students seemed to have quite a central role in planning activities with teachers.

Having illustrated Alppila School and the ways in which democracy is valued, how democratic decision are made and the stakeholders involved, we move now to introduce an English progressive school as a means of comparison.

A progressive school in England

A.S. Neill and his Summerhill School are considered by many as being the bedrock upon which progressive, democratic schools are founded. Creative and original, Summerhill proudly pronounces itself as being 'the oldest child democracy in the world' (Summerhill School, n.d). Its progressive outlook has not always been well viewed by others within the English education system. Indeed, the school successfully fought off the UK Government Office for Standards in Education, Children's Services and Skills (Ofsted), who sought to close Summerhill in the 1990s, claiming an inadmissible philosophy with abysmal practices (Stronach, 2012).

Founded in 1921, Summerhill was created as a 'non-repressive environment' where students would be able to become '. . . self-motivated and self-directed students who would never lose the early joy of learning' (Andersen et al, 2002:2). As a proponent of democratic education, Neill and others of his ilk argued that students who are endowed with '. . . freedom and choice will ultimately become better democratic citizens because they have learned how to negotiate with others, to name obstacles, and to know themselves' (Morrison, 2008:54).

Summerhill School is a fee-paying, non-religious, independent school, primarily made up of students who board at the school, with many coming from all over the world. With a school community of around a hundred people, 75 of which are children aged five to 17 (Summerhill School, n.d), the school has served as a model democratic schools internationally (Stronach & Piper, 2008). There are timetabled activities and most students do sit the General Certificate in Secondary Education examinations towards the end of their time at Summerhill, although there is no compulsion to attend lessons. Students are also

88 *Sakari Saukkonen et al.*

able to enjoy '. . . free access to art, woodwork and computers. There are also open areas where pupils not in classes can hang out, amuse themselves, socialise, play games, be creative' (*ibid.*).

Staff and students are stakeholders in the ongoing democratic life of the school, with teachers being expected to '. . . value classroom activities and play equally' (*ibid.*), whilst older students (Ombudsmen) can take the role of mediators to provide support between meetings, as well as resolving conflicts (*ibid.*). Unlike mainstream schools in England, Summerhill does not send school reports to parents or comply with the Ofsted regulation of 'tracking children's progress through the school' (Clifton, 2014:38).

The 2014 Summerhill General Policy Statement (Community Life) outlines fundamental tenets upon which the school operates, stating:

- Summerhill students live as equal members in a democratic community.
- Any member of the community, pupil or staff, has the right to charge another or bring up a business in the General Meeting or call a Special Meeting about anything they wish to. Thus, both pupils and staff are answerable to the whole community. Nobody in the school is exempt from this, and no subject is beyond the community's discussion.

The democratic principles upon which the school is founded are firmly rooted in the school rules (laws), of which there are around 200, and the notion of 'The Meeting'. The laws guide the everyday life of the school, from rules about smoking and who can use particular toilet facilities to a means of managing bullies and establishing the policy regarding the use of profane language beyond the school grounds. These laws are constituted and decided upon by staff and students on a one person-one vote basis (Stronach & Piper, 2008) within the confines of 'The Meeting'. Within this collective arena, problems of the community can be organised and managed (Clifton, 2014).

Comparing Alppila with Summerhill

In broad terms, Alppila and Summerhill share many progressive features. Alppila has clearly both ideologically and practically 'borrowed' from Summerhill by virtue of its own use of a school council, by not having age-related classes and by using student-staff negotiation with regard to what and how to study a particular subject. At first glance, it might be assumed that Alppila is as progressive and democratic as Summerhill. But upon closer scrutiny of both schools, we are compelled to question the extent to which Alppila has achieved its aspiration to be a progressive, democratic school whereby students and staff share power *via* a negotiated and equally distributed model. We also need to return to the opening question posed by Donald Winnicott, namely: 'Do progressive schools give too much freedom to the child?' Given what has been observed by us in Alppila School, coupled with our discussions regarding democratic education and Summerhill, are we now able to offer a definitive response to this question,

Power, democracy and progressive schools 89

a question which has hitherto failed to achieve consensus amongst educators for nearly 50 years?

Discussion

We proffer a response to Winnicott's question, and this that such schools do not afford too much freedom to the children who attend them. This conclusion is based upon both the empirical primary evidence gathered within Alppila School, and from the extant literature regarding Summerhill School.

We argue that the positive impact of the democratic schools movement, particularly the legacy of A.S. Neill and Summerhill School is one that is felt today, not only in progressive, democratic schools, but in mainstream schools around the world. The United Nations Committee of Rights of the Child is unequivocal in its position regarding the influence of Summerhill upon children and the ways in which its progressive and democratic principles have directly shaped the Rights of the Child convention. When acting as Secretary of the Committee on the Rights of the Child, Paulo David confirmed the role played by Summerhill by commenting, 'The convention of the Rights of the Child makes particular reference to children's rights to participate in decisions affecting them and Summerhill, through its very approach to education, embodies this right in a way that surpasses expectation' (Bailey, 2013:157).

The reach of Summerhill extends further *via* the model of school councils, which are integral to mainstream schools within the UK, yet which can trace their roots back to Summerhill with its Meetings and Ombudsmen model. The premise of school councils with pupils electing fellow peers to represent the views of all pupils and to improve their school are directly influenced by the democratic and egalitarian principles espoused by Summerhill.

Other external validation and approval of Summerhill and its quest for instilling and fostering democracy comes from Ofsted. Despite well-publicised historic dissonance between this UK government audit inspectorate and the liberal philosophies of Summerhill, the 2011 *Ofsted Report* judged the school as being good overall but outstanding in regard to its quality of provision for spiritual, moral, social and cultural development and for the behaviour of its pupils. According to Ofsted (2011), strengths of the school include:

> ... the mature and co-operative interactions between pupils and staff that lead to closely-tailored activities matching the needs, abilities and interests of every individual pupil. As a result, all pupils have opportunities to acquire and develop a love of learning and interest in the world.
>
> (2011:5)

The *Report* continues by describing how pupils develop clarity on:

> ... how to live their lives and there is a tangible atmosphere of tolerance and harmony ... The democratic approach to how the school runs ensures

90   *Sakari Saukkonen et al.*

that pupils develop a high level of respect for the privacy of others. Pupils are prepared for their future lives and responsibilities extremely well.

(ibid.:6)

We take the view that if the democratic and progressive schools offered 'too much freedom', why would influential bodies such as the United Nations and Ofsted as well as mainstream schools globally adopt its key principles and philosophical ideals? Clearly, such wholesale embracing of democratic principles can only sensibly be seen as being an endorsement for freedom, and a rejection of notions of 'too much freedom'.

Having refuted 'too much freedom' as being the issue, we contend this chapter and our small-scale investigation at Alppila School has revealed the disparity in the way in which democratic decision-making and power is distributed between the English and Finnish examples. In Alppila and Summerhill schools, one can notice examples of both 'hard' and 'soft' power, but the emphasis seems to be on 'soft' power, power that is based on persuasion and argument rather than one based on coercion or threats. Given the philosophical outlook of each school, this is perhaps unsurprising. What we are faced with is to wonder who has the power. Is it equally distributed, or does one or more stakeholder have more of it than another?

The 2011 *Ofsted Report* on Summerhill singles out the School Council for praise, describing it as being a forum where '. . . pupils and staff meet to share and discuss information and make decisions as a community of equals . . . pupils are extremely skilled in assuming roles such as Chair, Secretary and Ombudsmen' (*ibid.*:5). We contend this appears to point towards a more egalitarian and balanced relationship between students and staff than might be said to be seen at Alppila School.

In terms of active engagement participation in their learning, the 2011 *Ofsted Report* comments that pupils are engaged and '. . . absorbed in what they are doing and make good progress, both in lessons and in the other activities they choose to do' (*ibid.*:5). This does not appear to be the case with Alppila School. As described by those of us who observed classes at Alppila School and by Alppila staff themselves, issues of passivity were seen and reported. Comments from teachers hoping students would become more active and from those of us who observed classes who reported being 'disappointed' by the classroom interaction are in sharp relief to the portrayal of Summerhill.

There is no strong democratic tradition in Finnish schools. Even though Finnish schools may be said to based on humanistic and holistic pedagogy, traditionally, the students do not have much to say to what, how and when to learn. At Alppila, the power and responsibility concomitant with democracy have been offered by staff, yet have not been readily accepted by the Alppila students when compared to their English peers at Summerhill.

The Alppila case shows that students are not all willing to take the power into their hands. Naturally, we are left to consider why this might be. Alppila may be considered as a newcomer in the progressive, democratic schools tradition, but it does stress values like respect, equality, justice, collaboration and solidarity (Korkmaz & Erden, 2014). In attempting to live up to these values, Alppila does use phenomenon-based studies where teachers and students have an active role in the planning of these projects. We believe that phenomenon-based project studies are an important step in giving to students more power in Finnish schools, but this step is not enough if the students do not get opportunities to exert more power to influence about how and what they study in their in subject studies. This juxtaposition of a democratic learning culture with the phenomenon-based studies with a more traditional, authoritarian learning culture associated with subject studies creates an uncomfortable contradiction. We suggest that this lack of a uniform approach to infusing democratic, consultative approaches is likely to contribute to the passive approaches seen and reported. We also suggest that reasons for the unwillingness of many students to fully participate and to plunge themselves into a liberating, democratic culture lie beyond the confines of Alppila. The reticence observed by us and described by staff is symptomatic of historical, cultural and socio-political factors which shape Finland and the traditions in which Finnish society operates.

Concluding thoughts

There can be no doubt that Alppila does subscribe to educating for democracy, but it has not been fully realised as yet. In Alppila School, those who we interviewed mentioned several times the 'Alppila spirit'. This spirit unifies the members of the school community and creates a strong culture of conversations and tolerance for difference. What we have identified is that, unlike Summerhill, Alppila is on a different trajectory towards becoming a progressive democratic school. It is starting from a different time, from a different place and from within a society where ideas surrounding education are more conservative and bound up in more traditional, authoritarian model of education. Unlike Summerhill, where power is willingly shared by and between staff and students, the power at Alppila does seem to be more in the hands of the staff. Only when this is more democratically distributed and exercised can Alppila be considered to be a truly democratic, progressive school.

References

Afdal, H. W. (2014) 'Does teacher education matter? An analysis of relations to knowledge among Norwegian and Finnish novice teachers' in *Scandinavian Journal of Educational Research*, 58(3), pp. 281–299.

Alternative Education Resource Organization (n.d). Available at: www.educationrevolution. org/store/findaschool/democraticschools/ [accessed 8 March 2016].

Andresen, L., Boud, D. & Cohen, R. (2002) 'Experience-Based Learning: Contemporary Issues' in Foley, G. (Ed.) *Understanding Adult Education and Training*. 2nd edn. Sydney: Allen & Unwin, pp. 225–239.

Bailey, R. (2013) *A. S. Neill*. London: Bloomsbury Library of Educational Thought, Bloomsbury Academic.

Bold, C. (2012) *Using Narrative in Research*. Chennai: SAGE.

Clifton, G. (2014) 'In Conversation with . . . Zoë Readhead, Principal of Summerhill School, Leiston, Suffolk' in *Journal of Pedagogic Development*, 4(2), pp. 33–41. Available at: www.beds. ac.uk/jpd/volume-4-issue-2/conversation-zoe-readhead [accessed 8 March 2016].

European Democratic Education Community (n.d). Available at: www.eudec.org [accessed 8 March 2016].

Foucault, M. (1981) *The History of Sexuality, Vol. 1: An Introduction*. Harmondsworth: Penguin.

Hannus, S. & Simola, H. (2010) 'The effects of power mechanisms in education: Bringing Foucault and Bourdieu together' in *Power and Education*, 2(1), pp. 1–17.

Jones, P. (2009) 'Hard and soft policies in music education: Building the capacity of teachers to understand, study, and influence them' in *Arts Education Policy Review*, 110(4), pp. 27–32.

Korkmaz, H. & Erden, M. (2014) 'A delphi study: The characteristics of democratic schools' in *The Journal of Educational Research*, 107(5), pp. 365–373.

Labaree, D. (2005) 'Progressivism, schools and schools of education: An American romance' in *Paedagogica Historica*, 41(1&2), pp. 275–288.

Morrison, K. (2008) 'Democratic Classrooms: Promises and Challenges of Student Voice and Choice. Part One' in *Educational Horizons*, 87(1), pp. 50–60. Reprinted in Noll, J. W. (2012) *Taking Sides: Clashing Views on Educational Issues*. 16th edn. New York: McGraw Hill, pp. 86–95.

Nye, J. & Wang, J. (2009) 'Hard decisions on soft power: Opportunities and difficulties for Chinese soft power' in *Harvard International Review*, 31(2), pp. 18–22.

Ofsted. (2011) *Summerhill School Inspection Report* (inspection 29th – 30th November, 2012), Manchester HMSO. Available at: reports.ofsted.gov.uk/provider/files/2151659/urn/103854.pdf [accessed 27 February 2016].

Sahlberg, P (2011) *Finnish Lessons: What Can the World Learn from Educational Change in Finland?* New York: Teachers College Press.

Simola, H (2005) 'The Finnish miracle of PISA: Historical and sociological remarks on teaching and teacher education' in *Comparative Education*, 41(4), pp. 455–470.

Stronach, I. (2012) '(B)othering education: An autobiography of alternatives' in *Other Education: The Journal of Educational Alternatives*, 1(1), pp. 171–174.

Stronach, I. & Piper, H. (2008) 'Can liberal education make a comeback? The case of "Relational touch" at Summerhill School' in *American Education Research Journal*, 45(1), pp. 6–37.

Summerhill General Policy Statement (Community Life) (2014) Available at: www.summerhillschool. co.uk/downloads/Policy%20statement%20community%20life.pdf [accessed 1 March 2016].

Summerhill School. (n.d) Available at: www.summerhillschool.co.uk [accessed 1 March 2016].

Winnicott, D. W. (1990) *Deprivation and Delinquency*. London: Routledge.

8 Perspectives on accountability in education

Local democracy versus national regulation

Jenny Gilbert, Pentti Moilanen & Sakari Saukkonen

Introduction

Neoliberal forms of accountability favour evaluation of schools and privilege ranking through performance indicators. A key international indicator is PISA (Programme for International Students Assessment; http://www.oecd.org/pisa/). It records the performance of 15/16-year-olds in mathematics, reading and science and produces league tables of countries. Finland's PISA scores were high in 2009; although they dropped in 2012, they are well above OECD average. Scores for England, incorporated in UK figures, have remained at OECD average. Consequently, Finland has been held as an exemplar for English education, referenced frequently in the UK White Paper *The Importance of Teaching* (DfE, 2010). We should note that the population of England is roughly ten times that of Finland and the demographics of the two countries differ considerably: England is multi-ethnic and multicultural, while Finland has a homogenous culture.

For our adopted methodology, we drew upon our experience of education as teacher educators in England and Finland. We exploited secondary sources to identify and explore factors holding teachers and schools to account in each national education system. We compared England's policy and practice with that of Finland. In the English case, we explored the types and governance of schools, the *National Curriculum*, the testing and inspection regime and the status of teachers. In the Finnish case, we investigated evaluation, national and local curricula and tests, the role of parents and the responsibility of the teaching profession. Following this analytical method, we adopted a synergistic approach to compare the two educational systems holistically (Checkland, 1981).

In Finland, there is strong focus on the self-evaluation of schools and education providers, together with national evaluation of learning outcomes. There is an annual student test, either in the mother tongue/literature or mathematics. The Ministry of Education and Culture evaluates other subjects and cross-curricular themes. Municipalities and schools receive their results for development purposes. In contrast, the inspection of English schools follows an approximately three-year cycle, with poorly performing schools receiving annual inspections and schools judged against regularly modified inspection criteria. Schools are

94   *Jenny Gilbert et al.*

graded on the basis of classroom observations, staff meetings and prescribed data, including test scores. Results are made public. Inspectors are not expected to take a developmental role, although reports include recommendations for action.

Perspectives on accountability in England

To understand accountability in England, we explore three features: the educational structure, the curriculum with its associated testing regime and thirdly, the inspection process. The educational structure, the school organisation, its funding and governance form the landscape on which the accountability regime of testing and inspection is erected. Since the 1988 UK Education Reform Act (ERA), the structure of the English education system has experienced regular modification plus sporadic seismic shifts in direction, as a consequence of government directives. In England, one will find selective grammar schools, from the 1944 Education Act, comprehensive high schools dating from the 1960s and many academies established within the last five years. The academy project has radically changed the nature of the English system. As Finn (2015:5) says with regret:

> No more would English education, as it had been since 1870, be a national system locally administered.

Students are registered for qualifications that are constantly adjusted and occasionally transformed, making comparison of 16-year-olds' performance between year groups difficult. Nevertheless, schools' examination results are compared across regions, between schools and over time. These statistics alongside schools' inspection outcomes are used, ostensibly, to provide parents with the market information to make choices. This appears to be evidence of democratic process.

School structure and organisation

Until 1993, all maintained schools, primary and secondary, were controlled by the local authority (LA), funded and overseen locally. The prevalent model was the comprehensive secondary school, with 164 selective grammar schools remaining from the previous 'tripartite' system (Eleven plus exams, 2016). Under ERA legislation, the Local Management of Schools allowed schools to manage aspects of their budget or to convert to Grant Maintained status and opt out of LA control. Few schools converted to this status, and the new Labour Government abolished them in 1998. A similar Conservative Government initiative, City Technology Colleges, was sponsored by private companies; few sponsors came forward, and only 15 remained when the government changed in 1997. The legislation, however, endured and was used by the Labour Government to establish City Academies (Chitty, 2014). These sponsored academies were replacements for failing schools; by 2010, there were 203 (BBC News:

Perspectives on accountability in education 95

Education and family, 2015a). The incoming Conservative/Liberal Democrat Coalition Government of 2010 embraced the term academy and modified the character slightly (Chitty, 2014), claiming them as the schools of the future. Any school can now elect to become a convertor academy, although priority is given to those graded 'outstanding'. In June 2015 (BBC News: Education and family, 2015a), there were 4,676 academies, with several hundred more anticipated; currently more than half of secondary schools are academies. They are funded directly from central government and have certain freedoms not awarded to maintained schools. They need not teach the *National Curriculum* or appoint qualified teachers, though most choose to do so (DfE, 2016). They can set their own term dates and teaching day and can determine some admission criteria. Under the academy model, it is also possible to establish a new 'free' school, normally founded by parents or faith groups.

LAs retain the responsibility for the remaining maintained schools within their area and for managing school admissions. Given the powers devolved to academies, the LA has limited control over school numbers and cannot influence the location of a new free school. This has led to mismatches between the supply and demand of school places in some regions. Financial cuts after 2010, together with the reduction in maintained schools, has resulted in the disappearance of LA subject advisors. Despite the appointment in September 2014 of Regional School Inspectors to monitor academy performance and support poorly performing academies, the House of Commons Public Accounts Committee (2015:3) expressed concerns that the Department for Education (DfE) '…presides over a complex and confused system of external oversight.'

While exploring the state system of education, one cannot omit the influence of the independent (fee-paying) sector that includes prestigious English public schools. While the proportion of children attending independent schools is small, 5.3 percent (the Independent, 2015), their alumni are more likely to attend elite universities. The high proportion of members of parliament with a public school education and an Oxbridge degree is testament to the conundrum at the heart of the British widening participation project.

The case for the creation of academies is threefold: increased autonomy for the school, school improvement and increased market choice for parents. While academy status does afford greater autonomy, many schools are nervous about changing status, for they are still measured by the same performance indicators as maintained schools. For example, they tend to adopt the *National Curriculum*. It is too early to judge whether the change of status does lead to school improvement. While parents have a 95 percent chance of gaining a school place at one of their first three school choices, their first choice cannot be guaranteed. In 393 schools, pupils will only be accepted if they live within 500 metres of the school (BBC News: Education and family, 2015c). It is not uncommon, particularly when families move, for their children to attend different primary schools. The rhetoric of market choice does not match up to the reality and the transfer of schools' accountability from the LA to the state has attenuated the local democratic process (West et al, 2011).

96   *Jenny Gilbert et al.*

Curriculum

The *National Curriculum*, also introduced under the 1988 ERA, provided the platform upon which accountability through inspection could be constructed. Kelly (1994:1) describes the preceding report that spells out the aims of a common curriculum to:

> ... develop the potential of all pupils and equip them for the responsibilities of citizenship and for the challenges of employment in tomorrow's world.
>
> (DES, 1987a:2)

A common curriculum aimed to raise standards, match competitor countries, ensure that all pupils experienced a broad and balanced curriculum and have equal access to a '... good and relevant curriculum' (Chitty, 2014:2). Crucially, it would ensure that schools were accountable and parents could judge the progress of their children against national targets. The ERA also set up a Task Group on Assessment and Testing that recommended criterion based assessment to serve multiple purposes (DES, 1987b). It would be formative and diagnostic, enabling teachers to judge the next steps for pupils; be summative to record pupils' progress systematically; and be evaluative. Teachers were already using assessment for such purposes, but crucially, a national testing regime allowed the comparison of schools and LAs across the country.

The *National Curriculum* was accompanied by many documents and directives, generating a new language: key stages, attainment targets, levels of attainment, SATs. Pupils were tested at ages seven, 11, 14 and 16, using Standard Attainment Tests (SATs), with the final stage judged by General Certificate of Secondary Education (GCSE) examination. Initially, tests were held and reported at all four stages, but in 2008, a fiasco with outsourcing the marking of the age 11 SATs led to the re-marking of many of the papers (Chitty, 2014) and was a factor in the abolition of SATs for 14 year olds. SATs for seven-year-olds were replaced with teacher testing, though recently, there have been intimations of reinstatement. The *National Curriculum* was introduced under a Conservative Government, and the Labour Government (1997) intervened further and launched *the National Strategies for Numeracy and Literacy*. With these initiatives, we see a shift from defining what will be taught to determining how it will be taught. Perhaps the most radical example is the obligation, introduced in 2010, to teach reading using Systematic Synthetic Phonics (SSP; Childs, 2013), a prescriptive method accompanied by several competing commercial reading schemes. This initiative has been policed through Ofsted inspection of primary schools and initial teacher training providers. In 2010, one university was given a fail grade and one of the recommendations was to ensure that all trainee teachers could teach effectively using SSP.

Alongside the *National Curriculum*, there have been constant changes within the national secondary examination system. Students are often 'guinea pigs' as new qualifications are introduced. Comparison of performance across cohorts

Perspectives on accountability in education 97

becomes problematic. A recent development is the judgement of a school's performance using the English Baccalaureate (Ebacc) that measures the percentage of 16-year-olds obtaining grades A*- C in English, Mathematics, Science, a foreign language and a humanity. Ebacc is not a qualification, '... merely an additional device for measuring and ranking school performance' (Burn, 2015:55). Not only has this led to ranking of subjects, but it can generate prudent selection of pupils to study Ebacc subjects, denying those unlikely to achieve a C grade access to the subject.

Inspection

Until the early nineties, inspection of schools was carried out in a low key manner by Her Majesty's Inspectorate (Chitty, 2014). Inspection was privatised under the Education (Schools) Act 1992 and Ofsted was created as an independent body to inspect schools (Earley, 1998). Secondary schools were the first to be inspected in 1993 (West, Mattel and Roberts (2011). From the outset, the initial Chief Inspector of Schools, Chris Woodhead, assumed a high profile in the media, making statements that were not greeted well by teachers (Earley, 1998). The current Chief Inspector, Sir Michael Wilshaw, appointed in 2012, also courts attention and can be critical of teachers, although he is currently stating that there is problem with teacher supply, hence disagreeing with Department for Education statements (The Guardian: education, 2015). Until recently, inspections were outsourced; however, in September 2015, this was brought in-house. In the process, only 60 percent of the 3,000 inspectors were re-appointed (BBC News: Education and family, 2015b). This led to cries of a purge, suggestions that inspectors had been substandard and Ofsted inspections unsound.

In 2012, the Ofsted framework for inspection of schools, further education and initial teacher training was radically changed with a shift to a risk-based approach. The previous 'satisfactory' grade was reclassified as 'requires improvement', thus joining 'inadequate' as a fail grade. Associated with this were tougher conditions: teacher training providers graded 'requires improvement' are re-inspected the following year and de-accredited if they are not graded good or outstanding (Gilbert, 2013). This has resulted in the closure of several universities' teacher training provision. Meanwhile, 'outstanding' providers are inspected less frequently, though a poor performance indicator can trigger inspection. Adjustments to judgment criteria and shorter notice of an inspection visit have accompanied this change. Schools are informed the day before the visit, and universities are informed on Thursday for an inspection the following week. In just over a working day, the university must set up meetings of university and school staff and contact placement schools to arrange for students to be observed. This visit does not form the sole judgement of the university. During school inspections, newly qualified teachers are observed and their performance is linked to the university that trained them: this can impact on the grade and timing of the university's next inspection. School performance

98 *Jenny Gilbert et al.*

tables and Ofsted grade are published online and most estate agents link each house to the local schools, an indicator of the importance of school location in England. While heads of academies have greater autonomy than their colleagues in maintained schools, their choices are still guided by these 'powerful external mechanisms' (Harris & Burn, 2011). The panopticon of accountability and inspection operates under the guiding principle that regular revision of procedures and standards will lead to school improvement. The result is that schools and universities spend a high proportion of their time responding to the bureaucracy associated with new rules.

From 2016/17, secondary schools will be judged by a new accountability measure, entitled Progress 8. It is a value-added method whereby pupils' performance, from entering to leaving secondary school, is compared. A 33-page booklet (DfE, 2016) describes a complex system that allows each school to generate a grade. The new indicator aims to encourage schools to offer a broad and balanced curriculum, but it may produce unintended side effects when combined with existing indicators. The individual student can suffer in the pursuit of overall school success. Through Progress 8, the UK seeks to rise up the PISA tables, seen as an important indicator of global economic standing. England has moved from the meritocracy of a post-war binary, selective education with an elite university system to a widening participation agenda accompanied by mass higher education. The purpose of education will always be contested, but there is no doubting the primacy of the economic demands of the workforce and the emphasis on '. . . harnassing knowledge to wealth creation' (Chitty, 2014:208).

Teacher professionalism, parents and school councils

In Finland, the element of trust in teachers' judgement is writ large, although Hannus and Simola (2010) argue that national-level control over teachers is emerging in the form of a centralised national curriculum. The status of teachers in England is lower than those in Finland and many other countries. Teachers' individual autonomy has diminished over the years with the advent of a national curriculum and a constricting inspection regime. Its lowest ebb was the period (2010–2015) when Michael Gove was Secretary of State for Education. Teachers were regularly criticised and blamed for most of the social ills of the country. Gove reserved his most severe criticism for the group he labelled the 'Blob' and 'enemies of promise': it included so-called militants within the teaching unions and academics running teacher training courses in universities (Simons, 2015).

Under the 1997–2010 Labour government, there was a growth in policy agencies (Hodgson & Spour, 2006). One of these agencies, the General Teaching Council for England, was the professional body for teaching from 1998. It required teachers in maintained schools to register and it awarded Qualified Teacher Status. It was abolished in 2012 and many of its responsibilities transferred to the Teaching Agency, an executive agency of the DfE (Lightman, 2015). Shortly afterwards, a set of professional standards for teachers was introduced

Perspectives on accountability in education 99

that includes expectations of trainee teachers. These designated standards allow the university and school training a student teacher to judge their ability to teach. Unlike most European countries, including Finland, where graduates register for a two-year master's programme in order to become teachers, English graduates take a one year Post-Graduate Certificate in Education, two-thirds of which is spent in school placement, giving limited opportunity to engage with educational theory or pedagogical development. In 2012, 'School Direct', a new system to train teachers was introduced: applicants are recruited to a school and the school selects a university with which to work. This is a continuing move away from university-trained teachers to school-trained teachers.

We complete this section on accountability in English education by considering parental influence. School Governing Bodies have a strategic role that includes monitoring and evaluating schools. They have been part of the educational landscape for many years and include teacher, parent and community representatives. The Education and Inspection Act 2006 introduced Parent Councils, but they have not been popular and remain similar to long-standing Parent Teacher Associations, mainly fundraising bodies. School Councils that include elected student representatives are commonplace even in primary schools and are a useful way to encourage students to engage in the democratic process.

Perspectives on accountability and evaluation in Finland

The neoliberal reform wave includes accountability and assessment practices. The majority of industrialised nations carry out school inspections. They form the core of integrated education policies in several countries: the OECD reported in 2011 that inspections are implemented in 24 of 31 countries (Rönnberg, 2014). The state of Texas was a pioneer in using school measurement and incentive devices, and many European countries, such as England, have followed this path (Christophersen et al, 2010). Finland, however, has taken a different route. Until the early 1990s, school inspection in Finland was administered by regional authorities; then, municipalities were given more autonomy and responsibility. This led to the current situation, where schools have considerable freedom in determining curriculum content and employing distinctive pedagogical practices. An ethos of autonomy and trust has replaced the shadow of inspection (Salhberg, 2011). However, following the perceived collapse of the PISA results in 2012 (Sahlberg, 2015), there have been demands for more direct control of schooling (Hannus & Simola, 2010). However, no new educational policy has emerged, but there have been public funding cuts and increasing stress on competiveness and excellence (Simola, 2005).

A decentralised Finnish school system does not mean a lack of quality assurance, performance evaluation and accountability. While no overall body holds responsibility, the Finnish Education Evaluation Center is an independent government agency responsible for the national evaluation of education (http://karvi.fi/en/). It carries out large-scale evaluation studies and case studies

100 *Jenny Gilbert et al.*

focused on different fields. In addition, many municipalities carry out their own evaluations, and there is a marginal market for consultancy firms assessing the current state of schooling. Additionally, the National Board of Education and the Ministry of Education and Culture have much to say. There has never been standardised large-scale testing in Finland, with the exception of the traditional matriculation examination at the end of upper secondary school. Over the decades, trust has been invested in the country's highly qualified teachers, judging them effective professionals capable of ensuring that pupils reach learning goals without the imposition of national inspection procedures. It is often stated that Finnish schooling as a whole is based on trust (Sahlberg, 2011; 2015).

Alternative mechanisms of accountability

While the neoliberal inspection and testing culture has not reached the shores of Finland, there are accountability mechanisms in place. The World Bank recently published a country report on school autonomy and accountability in Finland (World Bank, 2012); it identified five different aspects of autonomy and accountability. The five categories are interdependent and form three composite categories: participation of the school council in school governance, assessment of school and student performance and school accountability. These categories describe the landscape of Finnish evaluation systems and accountability processes.

Parents have access to school management *via* school councils. While theoretically, this gives them the potential to evaluate and influence schooling, the report states, and we Finns know well, that school councils have a minor role. They do not track and evaluate schools or teachers. From an accountability perspective, the school council seldom interviews the teachers or principals. The council is more like a discussion forum for those rare parents willing to take part in school governance.

With regard to assessment, the *World Bank Report* (2012) states that Finland has well-organised and well-functioning systems for assessing school and student performance based on trust. Individual schools and teachers have considerable freedom to choose appropriate methods to assess their students. This freedom is set within a framework of national and municipal protocols and instructions. Nonetheless, there is variation in assessment practice, and this is accepted. The National Core Curriculum outlines performance criteria for each grade and subject, but there is no common test taken by students. Student and teacher discuss how a student might meet these criteria, and sometimes, parents are involved. In this kind of evaluation climate, it is unsurprising to find that only 15 percent of schools are annually inspected (World Bank, 2012).

Evaluation mechanisms do have an effect on Finnish schooling; there is a tradition of periodic sampling of learning outcomes. Evaluations are carried out nationally by the National Board of Education and the Finnish Education Evaluation Center. Meanwhile, the Finnish Institute for Educational Research has developed its profile as 'the home of PISA-studies'. In the Finnish domestic debate over education, the 'PISA card' is frequently played, and PISA evaluations influence the way schools position themselves. Official national statistics are gathered, and municipalities have their own mechanisms for evaluating schools. So according to the *World Bank Report*, schools' accountability to stakeholders is well established in Finland (World Bank, 2012). Nevertheless, competition and a market approach have arrived. Parents are showing interest in a school's status, and when they can choose a school for their children, then we see greater differentiation of performance, ethnicity and socio-economical background in schools (Hannus & Simola, 2010).

Teachers perceive their work as wide-ranging, set within the context of the Finnish welfare state, a relatively homogenous population and an isolated and oddly self-sufficient culture. This span embraces collective nation building, includes pride over achievements in the fields of technology, sports and culture and, perhaps most importantly, the idea of 'leaving no Finn behind'. Our actions are not only for individual success but for the success of all Finns: that is why every child, pupil and student really does matter. As competition and demand for excellence are on the rise, the question is: how long can this ethos persist?

National core curriculum and local curricula

The Finnish Board of Education is legally responsible for establishing the common foundation for Finnish schooling. We have a National Core Curriculum for all stages, from pre-school to upper secondary education. Most of the key aspects of schooling, like the subjects taught, minimum and maximum number of school hours and general guidelines for pedagogy, are prescribed. However, there is freedom for local municipalities to refine that curriculum. Basic education in Finland is organised along comprehensive lines: it comprises grades one to nine, with a slight distinction between primary level (grades one to six) and lower secondary level (grades seven to nine) (Ministry of Education and Culture, 2013). This distinction is diminishing and is not as clear and straightforward as it was once. After basic education, almost all students apply either for a general upper secondary school or a vocational school. Because of the nature of the National Core Curriculum, every municipality, and normally every school, needs to produce a local curriculum, and many schools join forces and produce a joint curriculum with limited variation to satisfy different needs and abilities in the schools involved in the co-production. This local curriculum is based on each community's premise, needs and resources. Theoretically, there can be significant variation in the translation of subject content into pedagogical action. In practice, the National Core Curriculum is followed for many aspects.

High-quality academic teachers: fact or fantasy?

Pupils in grades one to six are taught mainly by class teachers whose major subject at university is educational science; meanwhile, grade seven to nine pupils are taught by subject teachers who have majored in their teaching subject. Subject

102 *Jenny Gilbert et al.*

teacher qualifications to teach grades seven to nine and general upper secondary school include a master's degree incorporating at least 60 European Credit Transfer and Accumulation System (ECTS) credits of pedagogical studies and a thesis (Räihä et al, 2012). While comprehensive schoolteachers in all grades belong to the same academic profession and claim to share the same concepts and theories of education as their professional foundation, Räihä et al. (2012) claim that teachers are often unable to define what is meant by the ambiguous concept of theory, let alone explain how it underpins their work. Although Finnish teachers form an integrated academic profession, this does not mean that Finnish teaching is always based on educational theory. Practical didactics and everyday wisdom play a significant part in teaching (Räihä et al, 2012). We have a paradox: in Finland, we rely heavily on the competence of teachers, and this is the main reason for the culture of trust. However, this confidence may arise from a strong tradition of school and teacher involvement in nation building (Simola, 2005) rather than being grounded in teachers' academic expertise.

Accountability: a relevant concept in Finland

To conclude our brief journey into accountability in Finnish schooling, we reach some tentative conclusions. In the light of the Finnish welfare state and the political constellation surrounding the school system, we contest the notion of accountability. More suitable concepts could be responsibility and trust. Accountability in the Finnish context relies heavily on our welfare state heritage. We have built a culture based on the collective perception that we are all in this together. In principle, all Finns are rowing in the same direction. This is enabled by the homogenous population and culture, and we Finns tend to obey laws and feel safe within hierarchies (Simola, 2005). In this context, we believe that we are taking action for ourselves and for society. If, as teachers, we take responsibility, it is because we believe it is for the best, for the children, for us and for the nation. In a school culture where trust is a central pillar, teachers can feel pride and joy when acting as responsible citizens.

During the last few decades, evaluation and ranking systems have been introduced in Finland, as in many other OECD and EU countries. This 'Big Brother' mentality is lurking around the corner and may even have entered the halls of education. However, we contend that in Finnish schooling the notion of accountability has a soft, even tender, interpretation. There may be change as political power and balance fluctuates, but we do not see a rapid change in the basic assumptions underlying Finnish schooling. It is possible to do a good job, to have high-quality teaching and learning, without inspecting each small aspect, without large-scale standardised testing and without centralised, in many cases ritualistic, quality assurance and accountability systems.

Comparative views from Sweden, Norway and Australia

Finland's Scandinavian neighbours have chosen different paths in terms of accountability mechanisms. In Sweden, school inspection was reintroduced in

Perspectives on accountability in education   103

2003, after a period of soft self-evaluation. Since 2008, inspection has been carried out by a separate agency, the Swedish Schools Inspectorate (Lindgren, 2015). Inspection activities consist of four processes: regular supervision, thematic quality audits, licences and applications and certification of complaints. In the Swedish case, the usage and production of knowledge is seen as a high-stakes matter for schools. Reputation and economy are at risk, and credibility in inspection activities is crucial. It is evident that policy makers place confidence in inspection as an instrument of government (Rönnberg, 2014). In contrast, the Norwegian attitude towards accountability is more familiar to Finns. Turbulence surrounds Norway's policy, with pressure to adopt more intensive accountability procedures. Norway has been a reluctant reformer, but during the early 2000s accountability tools emerged in education, including tests, value-added indicators, publication of school results and decentralisation of governing body responsibility (Christophersen et al, 2010). Accountability systems have not been approved for the Norwegian education sector, but accountability devices are in operation through Norway's local quality assurance systems. As a whole, the Finnish accountability system with decentralised bodies of responsibility is much closer to Norway than to Sweden.

Australia's legacy as a British colony leads to similarities between the Australian and English education systems. However, in Australia, there are more fee-paying schools, including Catholic independent schools that are heavily subsidised by state and federal government (Australian Education Union, 2015). Australia's 2012 PISA scores ranked higher than the UK, though lower than Finland. However, the PISA data for Australia also reveal very poor performance by one particular group: the indigenous Aboriginal and Torres Straight Islanders (Dreise & Thompson, 2014). Australian education has been shaped by neoliberalism and market choice, though it is some way behind the UK. The Australian Curriculum, Assessment and Reporting Authority (ACARA, 2015) developed the national curriculum in 2008 (O'Meara, 2011), together with the national assessment programme and national tests that include the National Assessment Program – Literacy and Numeracy. Since 2010, outcomes from these sources have been reported alongside socio-economic data about schools on the My School website (ACARA, 2015). These data are publicly available: parents can refer to them to aid selection of a school for their child. In cities, this has resulted in the enlargement of school catchment areas and some secondary pupils traveling long distances to school. However, schools are no longer inspected. Surprisingly, in 2009, Australian teacher unions (The Australian, 2009) proposed a return to the earlier system of state-level inspection, asserting that the compilation of a league table alone stigmatises schools.

Conclusions

In comparing Finland and England, we have identified contrasting approaches to accountability. On the one hand, in Finland, we have a devolved approach to curriculum development and evaluation, with local autonomy and democracy. Teaching is a high-status profession warranting a high degree of trust; teachers

104 *Jenny Gilbert et al.*

receive a longer education, with more emphasis on theoretic and pedagogic study. Finland has greater social cohesion and social justice. On the other hand, in England we have a prescriptive, centralist approach to curricula with instances of government intervention. We have national testing and high-stakes inspection processes alongside publication of performance indicators. As a result of these factors, exacerbated by changing models for teacher education, we have a lower-status workforce and difficulty recruiting to certain subjects and posts.

Governments like to 'cherry pick' aspects from countries scoring highly in PISA and add them to their solutions. This approach generates unintended consequences because the system is not considered holistically. One method of acknowledging the importance of an integrated system is to adopt a metaphor to describe it. One metaphor that illustrates the two education systems is likening the English system to the mass production of widgets and the Finnish system to craft manufacturing. To ensure consistency in English mass production, the product is strictly specified, with routine quality control measures; faulty goods are melted down and recycled. The workforce receives adequate training for repetitive conveyor belt production and there is a resulting high turnover of staff. Most of the population buy the mass-produced product, but a small percentage buy a product elsewhere. Meanwhile, in the artisan craft practice of Finland, the professionals are well trained and well paid; they input on the design of products, and they self-evaluate and constantly improve their outputs. Their product is inevitably more expensive but customers recognise the quality of a local artefact created by an experienced, professional expert.

England represents the epitome of the global education reform movement, stressing testing of literacy and numeracy, competition between schools and market mechanisms in education (Lingard, Martino & Rezai-Rashti, 2013; Sahlberg, 2010), whereas Finland has contrasting policies. Education systems comprise multiple components and stakeholders; causal mechanisms are difficult to discern, the key outputs that emerge at the level of the whole system, the emergent properties (Checkland, 2000; Lingard & Sellar, 2013) are often unintended consequences. There are anecdotes of English schools turning down less able pupils on the ground that 'this isn't a suitable school for them' when the school wishes to maintain its high performance indicators. Goal displacement, teaching to the test and cheating are other side effects (Lingard & Sellar, 2013; Wolf & Janssens, 2007). The nature of the indicators is of crucial importance. When funding and reputation are tied to performance measures there can be perverse results (Lingard & Sellar, 2013). Although public performance indicators aim to guarantee educational quality, poor school grades result in mediocre reputations and cause those parents who can to avoid the school. Under right-wing market mechanisms this is encouraged; parents lacking social and cultural capital are much less likely to be in a position to move their children, enabling 'sink schools' to emerge.

West, Mattel and Roberts (2011) propose a typology of accountability comprising professional, hierarchical and market. Other writers use similar models

Perspectives on accountability in education   105

contrasting comparative, top–down, one-dimensional (hierarchical), account-ability with horizontal (professional) accountability of schools to their communities and *vice versa*. Professional accountability considers the wider community context and the purpose of schooling, while hierarchical accountability focuses narrowly on what happens within schools and denies the impact of structural inequality, laying all responsibility at the feet of teachers (Lingard et al, 2013). Market accountability, based on test scores and inspection grades, has replaced more educative, professional accountability in many countries (Hardy, 2015; Lingard et al, 2013).

There are, of course, unwanted systemic side effects in the Finnish case. The quality of evaluations within municipalities varies and national evaluations are not always followed up (Committee for Education and Culture of the Finnish Parliament, 2002 cited in Simola et al, 2013). Lapiolahti (2007) states that municipalities have different starting points and there is inadequate support for their evaluations. The provision of in-service teacher training and encouragement for pedagogical development demands additional resources. Unsurprisingly, education officers within municipalities wish to retain autonomy over schooling in their district (Rannisto & Liski, 2014). However, most municipal education strategies focus on curriculum content and knowledge transmission; pedagogical development and the learning experience are scarcely mentioned (Rannisto & Liski, 2014). These critical comments imply that good results in international evaluations are not the result of the pedagogy of Finnish schools. According to Sahlberg (2010), it is the emphasis on social justice and the moral purpose of schooling that influences the outcomes of education. Social justice includes having high educational expectations of all children.

Finally, we should ask what level and type of accountability is appropriate to a democratic society. The government of a nation state is held to account through the ballot box. However, key public services should also be accountable. In a neoliberal society, many of these public services are privatised, but nevertheless, these services must still be accountable. In England the education system is strictly held to account through performance indicators and inspection, league tables and 'naming and shaming'. Teachers and school management, held to account, spend much time calculating how best to manipulate their performance indicators in a competitive system, resulting in unwanted side effects for their students. Meanwhile, the Finnish system respects local democracy and uses evaluation to feed back to individual schools so that they can use the data to formulate actions. The English system is transparent, yet focuses on employing 'the stick rather than the carrot'. The Finnish system yields much better PISA results. 'Cherry picking' odd elements of the Finnish system, as proposed in the UK White Paper (DfE, 2010), assumes cause and effect without evidence to support the relationship. Instead, by taking a systems approach, exploring means of accounting to the citizens within two entirely different cultures, we reveal one based on professionalism and trust and the other relying on transparent, repetitive quality control. If the English wish to emulate the Finns, it will demand a culture change.

106 *Jenny Gilbert et al.*

References

ACARA (2015) Australian Curriculum, Assessment and Reporting Authority. *My School factsheet, March 2013*. Available at: http://www.myschool.edu.au [accessed 5 December 2015].

BBC News: Education and Family. (2015a) *Academies – Old and New Explained, 3rd June 2015*. Available at: http://www.bbc.co.uk/news/education-13274090 [Accessed 5 January 2016].

BBC News: Education and Family. (2015b) *Ofsted Purges 1,200 'Not Good Enough' Inspectors, 19th June 2015*. Available at: http://www.bbc.co.uk/news/education-33198707 [accessed 5 January 2016].

BBC News: Education and Family. (2015c) *Shrinking Distances for School Admissions, December 5th 2015*. Available at: http://www.bbc.co.uk/news/education-34996387 [accessed 5 January 2016].

Burn, K. (2015) 'The Gove Legacy in the Curriculum: The Case of History' in Finn, M. (Ed.) *The Gove Legacy: Education in Britain After the Coalition*. Basingstoke: Palgrave Macmillan, pp. 47–62.

Checkland, P. (1981) *System Thinking: Systems Practice*. London: Wiley.

Checkland, P. (2000) 'Soft systems methodology: A thirty year retrospective' in *Systems Research and Behavioural Science*, 17(1), pp. S11–S65.

Childs, A. (2013) 'The work of teacher educators: An English policy perspective' in *Journal of Education for Teaching: International Research and Pedagogy*, 39(3), pp. 314–328.

Chitty, C. (2014) *Education Policy in Britain*. 3rd edn. Basingstoke: Palgrave Macmillan.

Christophersen, K. A., Elstad, E. & Turmo, A. (2010) 'Is teacher accountability possible? The case of Norwegian high school science' in *Scandinavian Journal of Educational Research*, 54(5), pp. 413–429.

Department for Education. (2010) *The Importance of Teaching: The Schools White Paper 2010*. London: The Stationery Office.

Department for Education. (2016a) *Progress 8 Measure in 2016, 2017 and 2018: Guide for Maintained Secondary Schools, Academies and Free Schools*. London: The Stationery Office.

Department for Education. (2016b) *Types of School*. Available at: https://www.gov.uk/types-of-school/academies [accessed 27 December 2015].

Department of Education and Science. (1987a) *The National Curriculum 5–16: A Consultation Document*. London: The Stationery Office.

Department of Education and Science. (1987b) *Task Group on Assessment and Testing*. London: The Stationery Office.

Dreise, T. & Thomson, S. (2014) Unfinished business: PISA shows Indigenous youth are being left behind. *Australian Council for Educational Research*, occasional essay February 2014. Available at: https://www.acer.edu.au/occasional-essays/unfinished-business-pisa-shows-indigenous-youth-are-being-left-behind [accessed 13 February 2016].

Earley, P. (1998) *School Improvement After Inspection? School and LEA Responses*. London: Paul Chapman Publishing.

Eleven plus exams. (2016) *What-is-11-plus?* Available at: http://www.elevenplusexams.co.uk/advice/what-is-11-plus [accessed 1 January 2016].

Finn, M. (2015) *The Gove Legacy: Education in Britain After the Coalition*. Basingstoke: Palgrave Macmillan.

Gilbert, J. (2013) *Preparing for and Managing Short Notice Inspections: Advice Based on the 2012 Ofsted Inspection Framework*. London: University Council for Education of Teachers.

Perspectives on accountability in education 107

The Guardian: Education. (2016) *Ofsted Clashes with Ministers Over Extent of Teacher Shortages,* 2nd *January, 2016.* Available at: http://www.theguardian.com/education/2016/jan/02/ofsted-row-ministers-extent-teacher-shortages-michael-wilshaw [accessed 6 January 2016].

Hannus, S. & Simola, H. (2010) 'The effects of power mechanisms in education: Bringing Foucault and Bourdieu together' in *Power and Education,* 2(1), pp. 1–17.

Hardy, I. (2015) 'Data, numbers and accountability: The complexity, nature and effects of data use in schools' in *British Journal of Educational Studies,* 63(4), pp. 467–486.

Harris, R. & Burn, K. (2011) 'Curriculum theory, curriculum policy and the problem of ill-disciplined thinking' in *Journal of Education Policy,* 26(2), pp. 245–261.

Hodgson, A. & Spours, K. (2006) 'An analytical framework for policy engagement: The contested case of 14–19 reform in England' in *Journal of Education Policy,* 21(6), pp. 279–296.

House of Commons Committee of Public Accounts. (2015) *School Oversight and Intervention: Thirty-Second Report of Session 2014–15.* London: The Stationery Office.

The Independent. (2015) *Number of Pupils Attending Independent Schools in Britain on the Rise, Figures Show: 30th April, 2015.* Available at: http://www.independent.co.uk/news/education/education-news/number-of-pupils-attending-independent-schools-in-britain-on-the-rise-figures-show-10215959.h [accessed 5 January 2016].

Kelly, A.V. (1994) *The National Curriculum: A Critical Review.* 2nd edn. London: Paul Chapman Publishing.

Lapiolahti, R. (2007) The Evaluation of Schooling as a Task of the Communal Maintainer of Schooling: What Are the Presuppositions of the Execution of Evaluation in One Specific Communal Organization. *Jyväskylä Studies in Education, Psychology and Social Research* 308. Jyväskylä: University of Jyväskylä.

Lightman, B. (2015) 'The Gove Legacy in State Education' in Finn, M. (Ed.) *The Gove Legacy: Education in Britain after the Coalition.* Basingstoke: Palgrave Macmillan, pp. 14-33.

Lingard, B., Martino, W. & Rezai-Rashti, G. (2013) 'Testing regimes, accountabilities and education policy: commensurate global and national developments' in *Journal of Education Policy,* 28(5), pp. 539–556.

Lingard, B. & Sellar, S. (2013) 'Catalyst data': Perverse systemic effects of audit and accountability in Australian schooling' in *Journal of Education Policy,* 28(5), pp. 634–656.

Lindgren, J. (2015) 'The front and back stages of Swedish school inspection: Opening the black box of judgment' in *Scandinavian Journal of Educational Research,* 59(1), pp. 58–76.

Ministry of Education and Culture. (2013) *Education System.* Available at: http://www.minedu.fi/OPM/Koulutus/koulutusjaerjestelmae/?lang=en. [accessed 1 December 2016].

O'Meara, J. (2011) 'Australian teacher education reforms: Reinforcing the problem or providing the solution?' in *Journal of Education for Teaching: International Research and Pedagogy,* 37(4), pp. 423–431.

Räihä, P., Rautiainen, M. & Nikkola, T. (2012) 'Critical Integrative Teacher Education (CITE): Breaking Loose from Empty Theory and Blinkered Practice' in Malalinska-Michalak, J., Niemi, H. & Chong, S. (Eds.) *Research Policy, and Practice in Teacher Education in Europe.* Lodz: University of Lodz, pp. 277–290.

Rannisto, P. H. & Liski, A. (2014) *Municipalities as Developers of Education: An Investigation in the Visibility of the Education Sector in Municipal Strategies and the Impact of Pedagogical Expertise in the Municipal Governance.* Helsinki: Opetushallitus.

Rönnberg, L. (2014) 'Justifying the need for control: motives for Swedish national school inspection during two governments' in *Scandinavian Journal of Educational Research,* 58(4), pp. 385–399.

108 *Jenny Gilbert et al.*

Sahlberg, P. (2010) 'Rethinking accountability in a knowledge society' in *Journal of Educational Change*, 11(1), pp. 45–61.

Sahlberg, P. (2011) *Finnish Lessons: What Can the World Learn from Educational Change in Finland?* New York: Teachers College Press.

Sahlberg, P. (2015) *Finnish Lessons 2.0: What Can the World Learn from Educational Change in Finland?* 2nd edn. New York: Teachers College Press.

Simola, H. (2005) 'The Finnish miracle of PISA: Historical and sociological remarks on teaching and teacher education' in *Comparative Education*, 41(4), pp. 455–470.

Simola, H., Rinne, R., Varjo, J. & Kauko, J. (2013) 'The paradox of the education race: How to win the ranking game by sailing to headwind' in *Journal of Education Policy*, 28(5), pp. 612–633.

Simons, J. (2015) 'The Gove Legacy and the Politics of Education After 2015(1)' in Finn, M. (Ed.) *The Gove Legacy: Education in Britain After the Coalition.* Basingstoke: Palgrave Macmillan, pp. 116–128.

The Australian (2009) *Bring back school inspectors, says national teachers union* Available at: http://www.theaustralian.com.au/news/nation/bring-back-school-inspectors-says-national-teachers-union/story-e6frg6nf-1225809983607(Accessed: 11 February 2016)

West, A., Mattel, P. & Roberts, J. (2011) 'Accountability and sanctions in English schools' *British Journal of Educational Studies*, 59(1), pp. 41–62.

Wolf, I. & Janssens, F. (2007) 'Effects and side effects of inspections and accountability in education: an overview of empirical studies' in *Oxford Review of Education* 33(3), pp. 379–396.

World Bank. (2012) *Finland. School Autonomy and Accountability: Saber country report 79946.* Available at: http://saber.worldbank.org/index.cfm?indx=2&ctrn=FI. [accessed 3 February 2016].

9 Inclusion and democracy in England and Finland

Cathal Butler & Aimo Naukkarinen

Introduction

This chapter will explore how concepts of democracy and modern neo-liberal policy have acted to support, and act as a barrier to, the successful inclusion of students in mainstream settings, in England, Finland, and internationally. Basic elements of democratic practice will be explored to explain the development of practices to support the education of all children – including those with special educational needs (SEN) – which have generally moved to take greater consideration of the diversity of needs of all students, and to allow for greater opportunities for them to participate, and succeed in mainstream educational settings. This will be followed by a more in-depth focus of how modern educational policy considerations impact on inclusive practice. Considerations outside of political elements will also be summarized, to give a broader view of current issues facing countries, schools, and staff, in meeting an inclusive agenda.

Definition of main concepts

There are a range of definitions of democracy, depending on whether the focus is on the pure concept, or democracy as a form of governance. Democracy is both an ideal and a process. Cambridge Dictionaries Online (2015) defines democracy as '. . . the belief in freedom and equality between people, or a system of government based on this belief, in which power is either held by elected representatives or directly by the people themselves'. In democratic education, the students should have equal access to school and to the curriculum, and have the opportunity to attend heterogeneous learning environments in school, i.e., learning environments should be socially representative of the national community (e.g., García-Huidobro & Corvalán, 2009). Grossman (2008) emphasizes citizenship rights, participation, and pluralism (for instance, in relation to race, gender, and ethnicity) in order to deal with diversity. In sum, key elements within democracy are equality in general, as well access and participation, all of which are relevant to the concept of inclusion.

There are a number of potential definitions for inclusion. This is a point that will be returned to, but for now, it is worth focusing on the index of inclusion

(Booth & Ainscow, 2002), which provides a range of different potential definitions of the term inclusion. Major ideas include that every individual should be valued equally, and everyone should have the ability to participate in the culture, curricula, and community of schools. These clearly match the description of democracy in the previous paragraph. Individuals with disabilities should be valued rather than seen as having problems to overcome. School policies should respond to the diversity of needs of students. A final important element of the index of inclusion is the recognition that inclusion is both an ideal and a process that requires continuous updating to ensure that barriers to participation and learning are reduced or removed.

Similar ideas in relation to inclusion are espoused in the Salamanca Statement (UNESCO, 1994), which states that every child has a right to education, and that countries should set out education systems whereby the diverse characteristics, abilities, and learning needs of children should be taken into account, so that all children can be educated in mainstream schools. It is also noted that an inclusive education system should be more cost-effective.

The concept of neo-liberalism is harder to pin down, as is evident from other chapters in this book. Mitchell (2005) identifies a number of elements of neo-liberalism which impact on inclusive policy. These are the importance of free-market processes, competition, and accountability through standard setting and high-stakes exams. Notions of accountability will be the most important theme related to neo-liberalism, which will be a focus later in the chapter.

Methodology

Following discussion between the authors, it was decided to split the chapter into the following sections:

- Policy and practice in relation to SEN in Finland and England up to 1994
- Contemporary policy and practice in Finland, England, and internationally, post-1994, in response to the Salamanca Statement
- Factors that act to support or as barriers to inclusive education
- Conclusions

In every section, discussion will be focused on the major similarities and differences between England and Finland and the reasons for them.

Historical policy

In both England and Finland, attempts to educate individuals with special educational needs and disabilities can be traced back to the early 1800s (Kivirauma, 2015; Warnock, 1978)). This provision was mainly supported by religious and charitable organizations. These 'special schools' predate the beginnings of universal education in both countries.

Inclusion and democracy in England and Finland 111

In Finland, the state got involved in the education of people with disabilities in the 1860s. The interest in educating children with disabilities stemmed from a civilizing and control project of the people that was manifested in the originating of a nationwide public education system (Kivirauma, 1989), e.g., the 1866 *Primary School Decree*. *The Foster Act* (1870) in the UK set out a similar process, developing universal access to primary education under the oversight of local education authorities.

Access to primary education did not extended to those with SEN at this time, with the *Idiots Act* (1886) and the *Mental Deficiency Act* (1913) covering the rights of these individuals in England. In Finland, in 1892 the *Decree for Schools for Sensory Impaired* paved the way for people with certain types of disabilities, transferring the responsibility of students with hearing and visual impairments to the state, while in England, the *Elementary Education (Blind and Deaf Children) Act* (1893) transferred the responsibility of students with sensory impairments to local authorities long before other categories of need. Looking back, the lack of opportunity and access for learners with and without disabilities in this era can easily be described as undemocratic.

From the 1900s to the 1930s, in Finland, there were a few auxiliary schools for students with learning difficulties in bigger cities (Kivirauma, 1989) alongside schools for those with sensory impairments and reform schools for students with maladjusted behavior. Access to education was strongly promoted in 1921 by the *Compulsory Education Act*. However, children who needed more support could still be legally exempted. In England in the early 20th century, the *Warnock Report* (1978) indicates that there was a debate over whether children considered 'mentally defective' should be catered for at all educationally. The democratic ideals of equal access to school and to the curriculum, as well as pluralism in relation to intellectual diversity, were far from coming true.

In 1944, in England, the *Butler Act* (Education Act 1944) conceded that the mainstream school environment was likely to be the appropriate setting for the education of most children. This seems consistent with democratic ideals. This marked the beginning of the turning away from segregated settings, for all but the most severely disabled children. However, until 1970, those with the most severe impairments were still deemed 'ineducable', so access to education was still impossible for some. This shift to access to education for all children did not occur in Finland until 1997 (*Amendment to Comprehensive School Act 1368/1996*).

The need for special education services grew in Finland between 1940 and 1960, as primary school and grammar school education expanded (Kivirauma, 1989). In 1952, the *Auxiliary School Decree* and in 1958, *the Primary School Act* strengthened the status of both auxiliary schools and observation classes (for students with maladjusted behavior), the latter imposing that once transferred to any form of special education setting, the student cannot participate in regular education setting. Finnish special education teacher training began in 1958. Separate special education placements for citizens regarded as deviant were seen as modern and signs of progress (Kivirauma, 2015).

112 *Cathal Butler & Aimo Naukkarinen*

In Finland, integration and mainstream class placement in the education of students with SEN was first mentioned in 1966 in the *Rehabilitation Committee report* (Saloviita, 2006). In 1968, the *Comprehensive School Act* ascertained the move from a parallel school system to a nine-year comprehensive school system in 1972–1977. Comprehensive school provides all citizens equal access to education with free support systems. This policy change – accompanied by the development of social services – has been very important to the development of democratic education and inclusion in Finland. The amount of students receiving special education grew from two to 15 percent between the mid-1960s and the end of the 1970s (Kivirauma, 1989). The principle of integration was introduced, but it was then based on 'readiness' of the student (Saloviita, 2009). Part-time special education (elaborated on below) became a central means of support in Finnish basic education.

In the UK, the 1978 *Warnock Report* can be seen as key in the movement towards a modern vision of inclusion. The report challenged the simple distinction made between the disabled and the non-disabled. The discourse was subtly altered, with the term 'Special Educational Need' being coined, suggesting that they had different or more complex educational needs, moving away from previous negative labels. This was an attempt to ensure equality in the perception of these learners. A similar shift occurred in Finland in the mid-1980s.

The 1981 *Education Act* (Great Britain 1981), following the *Warnock Report*, officially adopted the term 'special educational needs' and revised the categories of need instituted in 1944. A formal assessment process with statements was established for those with learning difficulties, setting out entitlements of therapy and/or support. A key aim for the act was that children with SEN should be integrated into mainstream schools wherever possible, matching the language of integration also being used in Finland at this time. However, in both countries, this was qualified: children were only integrated in mainstream schools if their needs could be reasonably met there with appropriate resources and without detriment to their classmates.

In Finland, the *Basic Education Act* abolished tracking, streaming, exemption, auxiliary schools, and observation classes. Differentiated and individualized instruction was emphasized. The law promoted equal access by decreasing segregation and increasing individual support. Municipalities were given the autonomy to categorize special education services. According to some critics (e.g., Kivirauma, 2001), local authorities began developing new medicalization-oriented categories for special education students, and special teacher education programs were named after disability-based categories.

Inclusive policy post-Salamanca

The Salamanca Statement (UNESCO, 1994) has been hugely influential in shaping international policy in the last 20 years, shaping the discourse around SEN and accentuating access and child-centered pedagogy to meeting needs. Participation is highlighted in the *Salamanca Framework of Action* (1994). In

Inclusion and democracy in England and Finland   113

many ways, inclusive education appears to support democratic ideals within educational settings. In this section, we will look specifically at the responses from Finland and England before looking briefly at international responses.

In Finland, the assessment of SEN in the mid-1990s (Blom et al, 1996) meant special schools and classes. The knowledge, attitudes and practices of teachers, schools, and municipalities were segregation-orientated. Based on this, the educational management system aimed to support the integration of municipal service systems and the development of inclusive school culture (Halinen & Järvinen, 2008). In the assessment document, the Salamanca Statement was not discussed, which can be seen as an indication of slow Finnish inclusive development.

In contrast, the influence of the Salamanca Statement impacted quickly in England. The principle of inclusion can be identified in documents such as *Excellence for All Children* (DfEE, 1997*), Every Child Matters* (DfE, 2003), and *Removing Barriers to Achievement* (DfE, 2004). Common principles recur across policies, including targeted early intervention, the need for high expectations and aspirations for children, and the desire to improve children's outcomes. The latter two strongly overlap with the more general educational policy of the New Labour Government to drive up standards in schools. This can be interpreted as a drive towards a more equitable and democratic education system.

In England, the 2001 *Special Educational Needs and Disability Act* (Great Britain 2001) further strengthened the position of those with SEN and disability, stating that educational settings could not discriminate against individuals due to their needs. They were expected to provide reasonable adjustments to support individuals in order to support them to achieve their democratic right of participation in education.

Finnish legislation (the *Basic Education Act* 1998; the *National Core Curriculum for Basic Education* 2004) stated that, whenever possible, the student should attend regular class in the neighbourhood school. The effect of *Salamanca Statement* can be seen in the banning of policies based on disability categories in both education and teacher education and in the emphasizing of IEP, multiprofessional collaboration, and learning environment development as ways of continuous support (Halinen & Järvinen, 2008).

Similar ideas emerged in England in the *SEN Code of Practice* (DfE, 2001; 2014). The document, which all schools must follow, provides centralized guidance on expectations for all schools, detailing policy in relation to identification, assessment, and provision in early years, primary, and secondary phases. The importance of schools and teachers (as well as other professionals) working in partnership with parents is highlighted. Children should also be able to participate and voice their opinions when important decisions are being made in relation to them (e.g., setting their educational goals, choice of school, etc.). The 2001 *Code of Practice* highlights the important role of teachers and school in achieving inclusion. Every teacher, through good planning and differentiation, should be able to support the learning needs of a diverse group of pupils in one classroom.

114   *Cathal Butler & Aimo Naukkarinen*

A revised version of the *Code of Practice* was published in 2014, following updates to policy in the Child and Families Act (2014), explicitly covering the age range 0–25 to ensure that learning opportunities for SEN children do not stop after 18 years of age. 'The youth guarantee' in Finland is similar. Everyone under the age of 25 is offered a study place or place for on-the-job training or rehabilitation within three months from unemployment (Ministry of Culture And Education, 2012).

In Finland, one major development in the last 20 years has been that part-time special education (PTSE) has become a central type of support. PTSE does not label students, as attending a special school or class does. An official referral is not needed and the placement is temporary. PTSE secures the uninterrupted functioning of a classroom, is cheap compared to special class teaching, and is better for sparsely inhabited rural areas. The most dominant form of PTSE has been the clinic type, in which two to four students study, usually independently, with one special education teacher in his/her classroom. The other type, co-teaching, has been used much less (Saloviita & Takala, 2010). Although PTSE temporarily interrupts the student attending his/her regular education group, it can enable the student's access to curriculum.

Realizing the ideals of equal access and participation can be assessed in relation to the volume of separate special education. According to Statistics Finland (2015), the number of SEN-categorized basic education students grew in the 2000s to 8.5 percent by 2010. In 2014, roughly half of SEN-categorized students attended regular education, with 28 percent attending special class and 12 percent special school full-time. The number of students attending PTSE between 2002–2014 was 20–23 percent. Placement of students in separate special education settings has not been the exception, but a rather typical. In England, Black and Norwich (2014) note that after three decades of downward trends in special school population, there has been slight increases from 2007 onwards. The most striking trend is the high proportion of secondary school-aged pupils attending special schools in England – the implication is that mainstream schools may be less able to deal with the needs of these learners. In addition, special schools increasingly cater for children with a range of 'complex' needs.

The Special Education Strategy (Finland, 2007) introduced ideas for increasing support in Finnish regular education. Since 2004, Finland has funded special education, school welfare, and student guidance and counseling development programs (Halinen & Järvinen, 2008), anticipating the legislation of the 2010s. The *National Core Curriculum for Pre-primary Education* (Finland, 2010a) and the *National Core Curriculum for Basic Education* (2014) contain a three-tiered organization of support. The principle of early intervention is central to three categories of support: general support that every student is entitled to, intensified support, and special support.

Intensified support and special support both involve careful assessment and planning of students' learning pathways involving multiprofessional teams, parents and students. If general support is insufficient, pedagogical assessment resulting in a plan for intensified support is completed in the school's student

Inclusion and democracy in England and Finland 115

welfare group. If this support is inadequate, a more extensive pedagogical assessment will be done. The municipality education officer makes an official decision concerning special support, after which the student's Individualized Education Program (IEP) is completed. For the first time in Finnish basic education, the curricula strongly promote the development of school culture (Halinen, 2015), giving school communities new possibilities for inclusive development in a social model framework (Booth & Ainscow, 2002).

The Salamanca Statement's aim of cost effectiveness has been hard to achieve in Finland, since the percentage of students receiving expensive separate special education has constantly been high. To decrease both the identification of pupils with SEN and separate special education, in 2010, the funding system was changed from being based on the number of students with SEN (pupil weight funding) into one based on total enrollment (census-based funding). Pulkkinen and Jahnukainen (2015) found that principals and local authorities in the new system pay more attention to early identification, which can eventually decrease costs. For students needing special support, small special education groups were seen as effective learning environments, and regular education teaching groups were seen as financially most effective. It was felt that more resources for PTSE were needed to promote inclusion. English policy documents express the rhetoric of inclusion being cost effective, e.g., in *Excellence for All Children* (DfEE, 1997). However, there is no research directly commenting on the cost effectiveness of the English education system, particularly given the range of different initiatives and elements of government spending supporting inclusive education.

Looking beyond Finland and England, many countries have responded to the Salamanca Statement by adopting an inclusive policy (Johansson, 2014). In countries like Australia, for example, the ability for mainstream schools to reject students with disabilities has been restricted. However, it is still felt that the extent to which inclusive education is put into practice is limited (Hunt, 2011). In Malaysia, Lee and Low (2013) note that inclusion exists in government policy but is not fully implemented. Research from a number of countries suggests that teaching staff may not be able to support inclusion in mainstream classrooms. (Fraser, 2014; Malak, 2013). For Ainscow and Cesar (2006), the millions of children who do not have access to education in developing countries are a more prominent policy focus than students with SEN.

Inclusive policy development can also be hampered by competing political policies. Berhanu (2011), for example, mentions the conflict in Sweden between inclusive policy recommending that all children attend mainstream schools, and the policy of allowing parents a choice of settings, which includes a special setting if that is their choice. Engsig and Johnstone (2015) also highlight recent changes in policy in Denmark. They talk of a new law requiring at least 96 percent of students with disabilities to attend mainstream schools. They anticipate a tension between this and an increasing standards agenda which expects schools to be improving in proficiency, evidenced by academic testing, year on year. This issue will be returned to in relation to England in the next section.

Two key American policies highlighted by Husband and Hunt (2015) are the *No Child Left Behind Act* (NCLB, 2002), and the *Individuals with Disabilities Education Acts* (IDEA, 1997). The NCLB focuses on raising academic achievement, with accountability a strong element – testing is used to ensure that there are increases in academic achievement for all students. This mirrors ideas which we will return to when discussing current English policy. A key element of the *IDEA act*, aligning with NCLB, is that there should be high expectations for children with disabilities, and that they should access the general curriculum in the general classroom to the maximum extent possible. While the policy, focusing on high expectations, aspirations, and access, is laudable, it would seem that these policies in the USA have not been successful. Husband and Hunt (2015) note that NCLB has not as a whole been successful in raising standards, with many states not achieving the proficiency rates required, with a new policy expected in the near future to replace it.

Factors that act to support and factors that act as barriers to inclusion

The previous section has shown that in both countries, close attention has been paid to the cause of inclusion in the last 20 years. Concurrently, there have been a growing use of ICT and assistive technologies to support learners' engagement with education (BECTA, 2003). The exposure of events such as the Special Olympics can help to foster more positive attitudes (Li & Wu, 2012). Higher visibility in the local community has also led to more positive attitudes to people with learning disabilities, though it is worth noting that exclusionary practice and prejudice, undermining access, participation, and pluralism, are still experienced by those with disabilities (Aiden & McCarthy, 2014).

Referring largely to PISA results, Mitchell (2014:322) summarizes five factors that are behind the good reputation of Finland's basic education system in educating all students:

> [1] The balance between centralized and decentralized control of education, [2] High quality teachers, [3] Philosophy of education for all in comprehensive schools, [4] Quality early childhood provisions, and [5] Comprehensive support for students with special educational needs.
>
> (Mitchell, 2014:322)

Comprehensive support consists of IEPs, learning pathway plans, PTSE, student welfare support, teacher assistants, small groups, special classes, special schools, and, as a combination of all above, three-tiered multiprofessional support. PTSE has been considered crucial especially in supporting literacy skills and offering support flexibly within regular education. Whether all forms of comprehensive support in Finland promote inclusive education will be discussed below.

In the following subsections, we will look at a range of factors and discuss whether they have acted to assist or impede the progress of inclusion in England and Finland.

Marketization

In England, perhaps the largest barrier to the successful implementation of inclusive policy is a broader policy shift within education towards a more competitive, market-driven philosophy that can endanger the ideal of equal access to school and to the curriculum. Tomlinson (2005) dates this philosophy back to the Conservative governments of the 1970s and 1980s which placed schools within league tables, based on pupils' examination results. Parents are expected to use league tables for school selection. Given that children with SEN are likely to fare poorly in national assessments, their inclusion in schools can lead to a drop in a school's standing within the league table. This could lead to a drop in parents applying to send their children to the school, and therefore a drop in income for the school. More generally, it has also been stated that the competitive atmosphere engendered by league tables is incompatible with the basic tenets of inclusion (Davies et al, 1998). The situation in Finland is quite different. According to Sahlberg (2011), the early 1980s Global Educational Reform Movement's (GERM) efforts to improve student learning has increased testing of rote learning, over-focused on literacy and numeracy, decreased creativity through outcome-based teaching, become market-oriented, controlled, and accountability-driven. Sahlberg then notes that Finland has chosen a different way: none of the GERM elements above have been accepted in Finland in the ways they have been adopted elsewhere. Instead, from the 1980s, Finland has built a culture of trust within the educational system.

In Finland, the *Basic Education Decroo* Finland (1998b; 2004) abolished school districts, allowed school specialization and competition to some extent, and gave parents restricted opportunities to choose their child's school (Ahonen, 2002). According to Seppänen and Rinne (2015), until the 2010s, the basis of comprehensive school and neighborhood school prevailed, but recently the state has voiced fear of unequal fragmentation of comprehensive schools. The state has not used its regulative powers, but has supported troubled schools by positive discrimination. The absence of a powerful private basic education sector makes marketization effects in Finland different from those of England.

Standards and inclusion

A broader 'standards' agenda strongly promoted in the UK by the Labour government of the 1990s and 2000s, focusing in particular on basic competences in literacy and numeracy, has also proven incompatible with the inclusion agenda. This is because students must be shown to be making measurable progress within subjects, an element that can prove problematic, especially to students with certain special educational needs (Department for Children, Schools, and Families, 2010). Schools wishing to include students with a range of needs need a higher level of resources and support to achieve measurable achievements, making those students 'less attractive' to schools, which may lead to denial of access for them. This may help to explain the slow progress towards inclusion,

118 Cathal Butler & Aimo Naukkarinen

as reported by Norwich (2002) and Ofsted (2004). A similar issue has already been identified in the USA and Denmark in this chapter.

In Finnish basic education, standardized testing is uncommon. Reflecting the culture of trust, teachers are the main organizers of assessment procedures (Peruskoulun opetussuunnitelman perusteet, 2014:48–60).

How inclusion is conceptualized

Another key political influence has been the lack of clarity around the concept of inclusion and its definition. Armstrong and Barton (2008) claim that successive British governments have failed to truly engage with the concept of inclusive education, and retain the view that special schools have an important role, particularly Pupil Referral Units catering for students with severe emotional and behavioral difficulties, who are the most likely to be excluded from mainstream settings. Mary Warnock (2005), who had a significant impact on the development of inclusive policy through the *Warnock Report* (1978), has raised questions about inclusion and has now questioned the current policy. The simple idea that all children can be educated under one roof seems problematic.

Returning to the shared understanding of the concept of inclusion, it is worth highlighting that the Salamanca Statement discusses ALL children, so is not exclusive to children with SEN. The concept of inclusion can be interpreted very broadly and can be applied to diverse groups, based on disadvantage and marginalisation due to their gender, socio-economic status, language, ethnicity, and geographic location (Mitchell, 2005). While research can be used to identify issues for the inclusion of these groups in England (e.g., Dyson et al, 2009), it would certainly appear that when discussing the concept of inclusion, both in research and in policy, in England, the focus is still very much on those with SEN. In Finland, the focus on inclusion is also very much on students with SEN, which can partly be explained by the powerful role of special education professionals, both academic and in the field, in shaping the concept, policy, and practices of inclusion. Indeed, there is a view that trying to coalesce a large range of groups under a 'one-size-fits-all' inclusion policy, stating that one form of provision can universally meet all needs is likely to be counter-productive (e.g., CESI, 2002).

Finnish conception and practices of inclusive education emphasize equity in learning at the expense of equity in participation (Naukkarinen, 2010:188), based on the idea of the least restrictive environment. Students with disabilities are educated in a regular classroom with other students or in the placement option as close as possible to that. 'How teaching is done and what happens in the classroom is more important than what kind of classroom it is and where it is' (Savolainen, 2009:128).

Participation in heterogeneous learning environments is watered down in the legislation. The amendment (642/2010, 17§) to the *Basic Education Act* states that '. . . [s]pecial-needs education is provided . . . in conjunction with other instruction or partly or totally in a special-needs classroom or some

Inclusion and democracy in England and Finland 119

other appropriate facility'. Although proposed, primacy of regular education placement was not included in the legislation. A clear definition of inclusion is missing in the *National Core Curriculum for Basic Education* (Peruskoulun opetus-suunnitelman perusteet, 2014), although many characteristics of inclusion are mentioned. These escape clauses have given room for non-inclusive organization of education.

The unsatisfactory socio-emotional well-being of Finnish students is partly a sign of insufficient emphasis on student participation. Too many students do not like school and too many classrooms are restless; more learner-centeredness and joy of learning are needed (e.g., Ahtola & Niemi, 2014; Kupari et al, 2012; Välijärvi, 2015). Ahtola and Niemi (2014, 140) argue that Finland '. . . has not shared the international interest in the possibilities and responsibilities of school communities to advance the well-being of children and youth'.

Also, the Finnish mindset has an effect on the appreciation of participation. Traditional agrarian characteristics of authoritarianism, obedience, coping on one's own, not reflecting on one's feelings, overall conformity, and rejection of people regarded deviant might have discouraged community building in classrooms and schools (for descriptions of Finnish identities, see Ahtola & Niemi, 2014; Saloviita, 2009; Simola, 2005).

Other factors impacting inclusive practice

A number of other factors touch on schools' abilities to give students and children opportunities to participate in mainstream settings. The first area of focus is regional variation, noted by Armstrong (2005). Some local authorities favor inclusive placement where possible, with others maintaining an approach of sending more students to special schools. The term 'postcode lottery' applies, with a child likely to have different access and opportunities depending on where s/he lives. There are also troubling provincial differences (e.g., Statistics Finland, 2015). A key factor relevant to this issue is funding. The Salamanca Statement noted that inclusion is a cost-effective approach. However, the additional resources and support added in both countries' educational policies to support inclusion in the last 20 years have not always been supported by country's education budgets (Pulkkinen & Jahnukainen, 2015).

Another major factor is parental attitude. Glazzard (2011) has provided evidence relating to parental resistance to inclusion within English schools. In this instance, the resistance arises from parents whose children do not have special educational needs. Parents were concerned about being children with social, emotional and behavioral difficulties being in the same class as their children. Parents resist inclusion if they think it may impede their own child's education. This is an interesting point, as it potentially involves a contest between the democratic rights of children with disabilities and those without. In Finland, there is also resistance toward inclusion from the politically powerful teacher union.

Teacher attitude towards inclusion is also identified as an important aspect in research. Teacher attitudes are generally more positive for less serious forms of

SEN in both countries (Avramidis & Norwich, 2002; Moberg, 2001). Part of the reason for negative attitudes towards inclusion may be the lack of inclusive placements or informative input on inclusion within teacher training courses (EADSNE, 2010). Hodkinson (2005) has raised concerns that in England, final-year teacher trainees have limited understanding of implementing inclusive pedagogy in classroom settings. In Finland, teacher education is divided into teacher education and special teacher education; this adds to the challenge of achieving inclusive teacher education (Naukkarinen, 2010).

In English policy, the role of the pupils' voice is prominent. However, Lewis and Porter (2004) report issues in providing equivalent opportunities for children with learning difficulties. Research has shown that students are given little or no say in important meetings that decide their future (Carnaby et al, 2003; Smart, 2004). Indeed, it was noted by De Matteo et al. (2012) that students may not be given the support to be able to engage with transition meetings. The latest Finnish basic education legislation aims to improve the opportunities of students to have their voices heard. This can be seen as a twofold problem of students holding neither direct power nor representational power through participation. The opportunities for the student to have a say in matters concerning him/herself should be improved, as well as the channels of representational power in student communities.

Conclusions

A three-stage democratic, inclusive process for developing equity in education in England and Finland has been identified (Halinen & Järvinen, 2008 UNESCO, 2007). The first stage, 'access to education', was advanced by the *Compulsory School Act* of 1921 in Finland and achieved in 1997 as students with severe and profound mental disabilities were granted access, and in 1870 and 1970 in England.

The second, 'access to quality education', refers to curricula, teacher training, and learning material. PISA standings from the 2000s show that quality learning outcomes have become a reality for the majority of Finnish basic education students. Research shows that an essential part of quality inclusive education, student participation, still has to be promoted more in the Finnish school system. England's standing in PISA tables is not as impressive, though the idea of improving quality and standards is explicit within educational policy. However, student participation seems to be supported in English policy, though the research discussed raises questions about whether practice matches policy.

The issue of whether England can simultaneously have a successful inclusive policy whilst maintaining a specific standards agenda is open to debate. Indeed, Hodkinson (2014:250) broadly asks:

> Is inclusion as a global initiative even possible given the unrelenting moves towards increased accountability, standards and economic prosperity which are necessarily folded into the neoliberal globalisation of the education product?

Inclusion and democracy in England and Finland 121

It is too soon to evaluate the most recent changes in policy in relation to SEN in England. However, it would appear that as long as a standards agenda is maintained, the success of any inclusive policy is questionable, as is whether the current inclusive policy can be considered cost effective, as the Salamanca Statement claims.

Returning to Finland, the third stage in developing equity in education, 'access to success in learning', emphasizes '. . . removing learning obstacles and adequately supporting all students to facilitate their learning, healthy growth, and development' (Halinen & Järvinen, 2008:81) with the support of flexible learning environments, professional collaboration, and inclusive pedagogies. These ideas were clearly set out as goals in the policy document *Every Child Matters* in England. As learning outcomes assessed by PISA, the third stage has been achieved well in Finland. However, it can be argued that participation with peers in regular education learning environment is part of successful learning, healthy growth, and development. Based on the strong emphasis on inclusion in mainstream settings in England, this can be deemed to be largely achieved. However, developing access to successful learning in Finnish basic education also means that the number of students in small groups, special classes, and special schools should be reduced, conservative pedagogies (Simola, 2005) should be transformed into inclusive ones, and students' well-being in school should be addressed.

Segregated practices based on rehabilitation do not sufficiently enable democratic virtues of access, pluralism, active participation, and belonging in everyday life. Therefore, more efforts should be put in transforming segregated practices into ones based on support. One way to proceed could be the adoption of social-psychological and organizational-psychological mindsets in school reforms (e.g., organizational learning, communities of practice, professional learning communities; see Naukkarinen, 2010).

An important area for consideration for inclusive policy is the extent to which it is evidence based. Lindsay and Dockrell (2014) note that there are a number of barriers that inhibit research having a strong impact on how policy is developed. In order to arrive at a more nuanced position on how inclusion should be defined in policy, it is likely that further research in natural circumstances, particularly using ethnographic and action research approaches, will be necessary.

References

Ahonen, S. (2002) 'From an industrial to a post-industrial society: Changing conceptions of equality in education' in *Educational Review*, 54(2), pp. 173–181.

Ahtola, A. & Niemi, P. (2014) 'Does it work in Finland? School psychological services within a successful system of basic education' in *School Psychology International*, 35(2), pp. 136–151.

Aiden, H. & McCarthy, A. (2014) *Current Attitudes Towards Disabled People*. London: SCOPE.

Ainscow, M. & César, M. (2006) 'Inclusive education ten years after Salamanca: Setting the agenda' in *European Journal of Psychology of Education*, 21(3), pp. 231–238.

122 Cathal Butler & Aimo Naukkarinen

Armstrong, D. (2005) 'Reinventing inclusion: New labour and the cultural politics of special education' in *Oxford Review of Education*, 30(1), pp. 135–152.

Armstrong, F. & Barton, L. (2008) 'Policy, Experience and Change and the Challenge of Inclusive Education: The Case of England' in Barton, L. & Armstrong, F. (Eds.) *Policy, Experience and Change: Cross-Cultural Reflections on Inclusive Education*. London: Springer, pp. 5–18.

BECTA (2003) *What the Research Says About ICT Supporting Special Educational Needs (SEN) and Inclusion* [Online]. BECTA briefing. Available at: http://webarchive.nation alarchives.gov.uk/20130401151715/http://www.education.gov.uk/publications/eOrderingDownload/15009MIG2791.pdf. [accessed 15 February 2016].

Berhanu, G. (2011) 'Inclusive education in Sweden: Responses, challenges, and prospects' in *International Journal of Special Education*, 26(2), pp. 128–148.

Black, A. & Norwich, B. (2014) *Contrasting Responses to Diversity: School Placement Trends 2007–2013 for all Local Authorities in England*. Bristol: CSIE.

Blom, H., Laukkanen, R., Lindström, A., Saresma, U. & Virtanen, P. (Eds.). (1996) *Erityisopetuksen tila*. Helsinki: Opetushallituksen julkaisuja 2.

Booth, T. & Ainscow, M. (2002) *Index for Inclusion: Developing Learning and Participation in Schools*. 2nd edn. Bristol: Centre for Studies on Inclusive Education.

Cambridge Dictionaries Online. (2015) Available at: http://dictionary.cambridge.org/dictionary/english/ [accessed 13 February 2016].

Carnaby, S., Lewis, P., Di Martin, P., Naylor, J. & Stewart, D. (2003) 'Participation in transition review meetings: A case study of young people with learning disabilities leaving a special school' in *British Journal of Special Education*, 30(4), pp. 187–193.

Centre for Economic and Social Inclusion (CESI). (2002) Social Inclusion. Available at: www.cesi.org.uk/kbdocs/socinc.do [accessed 8 August 2015].

Davies, J. D., Garner, P. & Lee, J. (Eds.). (1998) *Managing Special Needs in Mainstream Schools: The Role of the SENCO*. London: David Fulton Publishers.

DeMatteo, F. J., Arter, P. S., Sworen-Parise, C., Fasciana, M. & Paulhamus, M. A. (2012) 'Social skills training for young adults with autism spectrum disorder: Overview and implications for practice' in *National Teacher Education Journal*, 5(4), pp. 57–65.

Department for Children, Schools, and Families. (2010) *The Salt Review: An Independent Review of Teacher Supply for Pupils with Severe, Profound and Multiple Learning Difficulties*. Nottingham: DCSF Publications.

Department for Education and Employment. (1997) *Excellence for all Children: Meeting Special Educational Needs*. London: HMSO.

Department for Education and Skills. (2001) *The SEN Code of Practice*. London: HMSO.

Department for Education. (2003) *Every Child Matters*. London: HMSO.

Department for Education. (2004) *Removing Barriers to Achievement*. London: HMSO.

Department for Education. (2014) *The SEN Code of Practice*. London: HMSO.

Dyson, A, Jones, L. & Kerr, K. (2009) *Inclusion and Social Disadvantage in the English Education System: The Role of Area-Based Initiatives*. Paper presented to the international research forum 'A Comparative Analysis of Equity in Inclusive Education'. Stanford University, Palo Alto, California, U.S.A., 2–4 February 2009.

Engsig, T. & Johnstone, C. (2015) 'Is there something rotten in the state of Denmark? The paradoxical policies of inclusive education – lessons from Denmark' in *International Journal of Inclusive Education*, 19(5), pp. 469–486.

European Agency for the Development of Special Needs Education (EADSNE). (2010) *Teacher Education for Inclusion: International Review of Literature*. Odense, Denmark: EADSNE.

Inclusion and democracy in England and Finland   123

Finland. (1998a) *Basic Education Act 628/1998*. Helsinki: National Board of Education. Available at: http://www.finlex.fi/en/laki/kaannokset/1998/en19980628.pdf [accessed 15 February 2016].

Finland. (1998b) *Basic Education Decree 852/1998*. Helsinki: National Board of Education. Available at: http://www.minedu.fi/export/sites/default/OPM/Koulutus/yleissivistaevae_koulutus/Liitetiedostoja/basicedu_decree.pdf [accessed 15 February 2016].

Finland. (2004) *The National Core Curriculum for Basic Education*. Helsinki: National Board of Education. Available at: http://www.oph.fi/english/curricula_and_qualifications/basic_education [accessed 15 February 2016].

Finland. (2007) *Erityisopetuksen Strategia*. Opetusministeriön työryhmämuistioita ja selvityksiä 2007:47. Helsinki: Opetusministeriö.

Finland. (2010a) *Amendments and Additions to the National Core Curriculum for Basic Education*. Helsinki: National Board of Education. Available at: http://www.oph.fi/download/132551_amendments_and_additions_to_national_core_curriculum_basic_education.pdf [accessed 15 February 2016].

Finland (2010b) *The National Core Curriculum for Pre-Primary Education*. Helsinki: National Board of Education. Available at: http://www.oph.fi/download/153504_national_core_curriculum_for_pre-primary_education_2010.pdf [accessed 15 February 2016].

Fraser, S. (2014) 'Removing the hurdles: A brief highlight of inclusion challenges in Guyana' in *Journal of the International Association of Special Education*, 15(2), pp. 48–55.

García-Huidobro, J.E. & Corvalán, J. (2009) Barriers that prevent the achievement of inclusive democratic education in *Prospects* 39, pp. 239–250.

Glazzard, J. (2011) Perceptions of the barriers to effective inclusion in one primary school: Voices of teachers and teaching assistants in *Support for Learning*, 26(2), pp. 56–63.

Great Britain. (1886) *Idiots Act*. London: HMSO.

Great Britain. (1893) *The Elementary Education (Blind and Deaf Children) Act*. London: HMSO.

Great Britain. (1913) *Mental Deficiency Act*. London: HMSO.

Great Britain. (1944) *Education Act*. London: HMSO.

Great Britain. (1981) *Education Act*. London: HMSO.

Great Britain. (2001) *Special Educational Needs and Disability Act*. London: HMSO.

Great Britain. (2014) *Children and Families Act*. London: HMSO.

Grossman, D. L. (2008) 'Democracy, citizenship education and inclusion: A multi-dimensional approach' in *Prospects*, 38, pp. 35–46.

Halinen, I. (2015) 'Perusopetuksen toimintakulttuurin uudet suuntaviivat', in Salo, O.-P. & Kontoniemi, M. (Eds.) *Kohti uutta: 100 vuotta koulun kehittämistä Jyväskylän normaalikoulussa*. Jyväskylä: Jyväskylän yliopisto, pp. 39–60.

Halinen, I. & Järvinen, R. (2008) 'Towards inclusive education: The case of Finland' in *Prospects*, 38, pp. 77–97.

Hodkinson, A. (2005) 'Conceptions and misconceptions of inclusive education one year on – a critical analysis of newly qualified teachers' knowledge and understanding of inclusion' in *Research in Education*, 76, pp. 43–55.

Hodkinson, A. (2014) 'Inclusion 'All present and correct?' A critical analysis of new labour's inclusive education policy in England' in *Journal for Critical Education Policy Studies*, 11(4), pp. 242–262.

Hunt, P. (2011) 'Salamanca statement and IDEA 2004: Possibilities of practice for inclusive education' in *International Journal of Inclusive Education*, 15(4), pp. 461–476.

Husband, T. and Hunt, C. (2015) 'A review of the empirical literature on no child left behind from 2001 to 2010' in *Planning and Changing*, 46(1), pp. 212–254.

124 Cathal Butler & Aimo Naukkarinen

Individuals with Disabilities Education Act (IDEA 1997), 20 U.S.C. §§ 1400 et seq (2006 & Supp.V. 2011).

Johansson, S. (2014) 'A critical and contextual approach to inclusive education: Perspectives from an Indian context' in International Journal of Inclusive Education, 18(12), pp. 1219–1236, DOI: 10.1080/13603116.2014.885594.

Kivirauma, J. (1989) Erityisopetus ja suomalainen oppivelvollisuuskoulu vuosina 1921–1986. Turun yliopiston julkaisuja C 74. Turun yliopisto.

Kivirauma, J. (2001) 'Erityispedagogiikka, normaalisuus ja medikalisaatio' in Murto, P., Naukkarinen, A. and Saloviita, T. (Eds.) Inkluusion haaste koululle. Oikeus yhdessä oppimiseen. Jyväskylä: PS-Kustannus, pp. 167–183.

Kivirauma, J. (2015) 'Erityisopetuksen historialliset kehityslinjat' in Moberg, S., Hautamäki, J., Kivirauma, J., Lahtinen, U., Savolainen, H. & Vehmas, S. (Eds.) Erityispedagogiikan perusteet. Jyväskylä: PS- Kustannus, pp. 25–45.

Kupari, P., Sulkunen, S., Vettenranta, J. & Nissinen, K. (2012) Enemmän iloa oppimiseen. Neljännen luokan oppilaiden lukutaito sekä matematiikan ja luonnontieteiden osaaminen. Kansainväliset PIRLS- ja TIMSS-tutkimukset Suomessa. Jyväskylän yliopisto, Koulutuksen tutkimuslaitos and Opetus- ja kulttuuriministeriö.

Lee, L.W. & Lo, H. M. (2013) "Unconscious' inclusion of students with learning disabilities in a Malaysian mainstream primary school: Teachers' perspectives' in Journal of Research in Special Education Needs, 13(3), pp. 218–228. DOI: 10.1111/j.1471–3802.2012.01250.

Lewis. A. & Porter, J. (2004) 'Interviewing children and young people with learning disabilities: Guidelines for researchers and multi-professional practice' in British Journal of Learning Disabilities, 32, pp. 191–197.

Li, C. & Wu, L. (2012) 'A survey study on attitudes of special Olympic Games volunteers toward the inclusion of individuals with intellectual disabilities in China' in European Journal of Adapted Physical Activity, 5(1), pp. 28–38.

Lindsay, G. & Dockrell, J. (2014) Evidence Based Policy and Practice: The Better Communication Research Programme in Norwich, B. (Ed.) Research in Special Needs and Inclusive Education: The Interface with Policy and Practice. SEN Policy Research Forum: Policy Paper 30, March 2014, pp. 37–43.

Malak, S. (2013) 'Inclusive education reform in Bangladesh: Pre-service teachers' responses to include students with special educational needs in regular classrooms' in International Journal of Instruction, 6(1), pp. 195–214.

Ministry of Culture And Education. (2012) The Youth Guarantee in Finland Provides Employment, Training and a Customized Service. http://www.minedu.fi/export/sites/default/OPM/Julkaisut/2013/liitteet/The_Youth_Guarantee_in_Finland.pdf?lang=en [accessed 4 December 2016].

Mitchell, D. (2005) 'Introduction: Sixteen Propositions on the Contexts of Inclusive Education' in Mitchell, D. (Ed.) Contextualising Inclusive Education: Evaluating Old and New International Perspectives. London: Routledge, pp. 1–21.

Mitchell, D. (2014) What Really Works in Special and Inclusive Education. 2nd edn. London: Routledge.

Moberg, S. (2001) 'Opettajien näkemykset inklusiivisesta opetuksesta' in Murto, P., Naukkarinen, A. & Saloviita, T. (Eds.) Inkluusion haaste koululle: Oikeus yhdessä oppimiseen. Jyväskylä: PS-Kustannus, pp. 82–95.

Naukkarinen, A. (2010) 'From discrete to transformed? Developing inclusive primary school teacher education in a Finnish teacher education department' in Journal of Research in Special Educational Needs, 10(1), pp. 185–196.

NCLB (2002) No Child Left Behind Act of 2001, 20 U.S.C. §§6301 et seq (2006 & Supp.V. 2011).

Inclusion and democracy in England and Finland   125

Norwich, B. (2002) *LEA Inclusion Trends in England 1997–2001, Statistics on Special School Placements and Pupils with Statements in Special Schools*. Bristol: CSIE.

Norwich, B. & Avramidis, E. (2002) 'Teachers' attitudes towards integration/inclusion: A review of the literature' in *European Journal of Special Needs Education*, 17(2), pp. 129–147.

Ofsted. (2004) *Special Educational Needs and Disability: Towards Inclusive Schools*. London: Office for Standards in Education.

Peruskoulun opetussuunnitelman perusteet 2014. (2014) Helsinki: Opetushallitus. Available at: http://www.oph.fi/download/163777_perusopetuksen_opetussuunnitelman_perusteet_ 2014.pdf [accessed 15 February 2016].

Pulkkinen, J. & Jahnukainen, M. (2015) 'Finnish reform of the funding and provision of special education:The views of principals and municipal education administrators' in *Educational Review*, 68(1), pp. 1–18.

Sahlberg, P. (2011) 'The 4th way of Finland' in *Journal of Educational Change*, 12(3), pp. 173–185.

The Salamanca Statement. (1994) *The Salamanca Statement and Framework for Action on Special Needs Education: Excess and Quality. Salamanca, Spain, June 7–10, 1994.* Salamanca, Spain: UNESCO and Ministry of Education and Science of Spain.

Saloviita, T. (2006) 'Paradigms of Disability Services in Finland' in Gustavsson, A., Sandvin, J.,Traustadottir, R. & Tössebro, J. (Eds.) *Resistance, Reflection and Change: Nordic Disability Research.* Lund: Studentlitteratur, pp. 47–57.

Saloviita,T. (2009) 'Inclusion in Finland: A thwarted development' in *Zeitschrift fur Inclusion*, 3(1). Article is retrieved from: http://www.inklusion-online.net/index.php/inklusion-online/article/view/172/172/29.

Saloviita,T. & Takala, M. (2010) 'Frequency of co-teaching in different teacher categories' in *European Journal of Special Needs Education*, 25(4), pp. 389–396.

Savolainen, H. (2009) 'Erilaisuuden huomioimisesta hyviin oppimistuloksiin' in *Kasvatus*, 40(2), pp. 121–130.

Seppänen, P. & Rinne, R. (2015) 'Suomalainen yhtenäiskoulu ylikansallisen koulutuspolitiikan paineissa' in Seppänen, P., Kalalahti, M., Rinne, R. & Simola, H. (Eds.) *Lohkoutuva peruskoulu – Perheiden kouluvalinnat, yhteiskuntaluokat ja koulutuspolitiikka.* Tutkimuksia 68. Jyväskylä: Suomen Kasvatustieteellinen Seura, pp. 23–58.

Simola, H. (2005) 'The Finnish miracle of PISA: Historical and sociological remarks on teaching and teacher education' in *Comparative Education*, 41(4), pp. 455–470.

Smart, M. (2004) 'Transition planning and the needs of young people and their careers:The alumni project' in *British Journal of Special Education*, 31(3), pp.128–137.

Statistics Finland. (2015) *Special Education Statistics.* Available at: http://www.stat.fi/til/erop/ index_en.html [accessed 15 February 2016].

Tomlinson, S. (2005) *Education in a Post-Welfare State.* 2nd edn. Maidenhead, Berks: Open University Press.

UNESCO. (1994) *Final Report – World Conference on Special Needs Education: Access and Quality.* Paris: UNESCO.

UNESCO. (2007) *IBE-UNESCO Preparatory report for the 48th ICE on inclusive education "International workshop on inclusive education, Andean and Southern Cone regions".* Preparatory activity of the 48th session of the international conference on education Buenos Aires, Argentina, 12–14 September 2007. Available at: http://www.ibe.unesco.org/fileadmin/ user_upload/COPs/News_documents/2007/0709BuenosAires/Argentina_IE_Final_ Report.pdf [accessed 15 February 2016].

Välijärvi, J. (2015) 'Peruskoulun rakenteet ja toiminta' in Välijärvi, J., Kupari, P., Ahonen, A., Arffman, I., Harju-Luukkainen, H., Leino, K., Niemivirta, M., Nissinen, K., Salmela-Aro, K., Tarnanen, M., Tuominen-Soini, H., Vettenranta, J. & Vuorinen, R. (Eds.) *Millä eväillä osaaminen uuteen nousuun? PISA 2012 tutkimustuloksia.* Helsinki: Opetus- ja kulttuuriministeriön julkaisuja 2015:6, pp. 179–231. Available at: http://www.minedu.fi/export/sites/default/OPM/Julkaisut/2015/liitteet/okm6.pdf?lang=fi [accessed 15 February 2016].

Warnock. M. (2005) *Special Educational Needs: A New Look.* London. Philosophy of Education Society of Great Britain.

Warnock Report. (1978) *Report of the Committee of Enquiry into the Education of Handicapped Children and Young People.* London: HMSO.

10 Educational research for democracy

Josephine Moate, Sarah Cousins, Wendy Cunnah & Maria Ruohotie-Lyhty

Introduction

The chapter adopts a broad conception of democracy, one that goes beyond recent conceptualisations that align democracy with 'the freedom of individuals [or governments] to decide on their own on actions to pursue their own purposes' (Nikolakaki, 2016:87). Dewey (1922) suggested that democracy is more than the pursuits of individuals or governments. It is also a process whereby individuals and government partner with each other as they work toward optimal conditions for societal growth. As such:

> A democratic society is precisely one in which the purpose of education is not given but is a constant topic for discussion and deliberation ... [however] the current political climate in many Western countries has made it increasingly difficult to have a democratic discussion about the purposes of education.
>
> (Biesta, 2007:18)

Accordingly, educational research should contribute to the common democratic process by advancing understanding through thought and action (Biesta & Burbules, 2003; Dewey, 1922). Democracy, however, is not the only philosophical position that influences educational research. Beder (2008) questions whether market values of competition, salesmanship and deception interfere with notions of democracy. According to DuRand (1997), such values are far removed from the historical core of democracy. Further, some authors (Freire, 2004;Nikolakaki, 2016) suggest that market forces contradict the normative practices of education and educational research. Kemmis (2014:31) adopts the Aristotelian view that education should strive 'to form people so that they can live well in a world worth living in'.

In this chapter, educational research for democracy is understood as research that is conducted through interactions with people and in particular the educational community. This definition resists the notion that educational research can or should be conducted in a vacuum, purely or primarily concerned with the advancement of science. This does not suggest that educational research

128 *Josephine Moate et al.*

automatically advances democracy; yet, a positive societal impact should be visible in the formulated aims of the research as well as the sharing of research findings. At its best, educational research should support democracy, lead to deeper understandings of education and educational practices, arrive at recommendations for practice, and generate models that contribute to citizenship and societal participation.

At a European level, the Magna Charta Universitatum (1988) defines academic freedom as 'the foundation for the independent search for truth and a barrier against undue intervention for both government and interest groups' (http://www.magna-charta.org/marga-charta-universitarium). Other organizations (European Council: Recommendation 1762; 2006) have highlighted the role of research in solving the fundamental and long-term problems of society. However, it is not possible to fulfill this societal mission without 'strong public funding' (EHEA ministerial conference, 2015) directed at long-term research projects with a societally relevant focus. Hence, it is important to look at the ways in which the societal mission of research is perceived and supported through policies and national strategies and what possibilities and channels of communication are available for the dissemination of research. Indeed, different European nations have responded to the Magna Charta Universitatum in different ways. In Spain, for example, educational researchers compete for funding in response to national or regional calls. The centralizing tendency in Hungary, however, has ended national calls and competitive bids for research funding. The focus of this chapter considers how educational research is constructed in Finland and England as a framework for critical thinking about wider European research environments.

A three-dimensional model

Educational research has increasingly been transformed into *schooling* research, which potentially reduces the scope and humanizing potential of education and undermines connections with rich educational heritages (Kemmis, 2014). For example, superficial notions of democratic research focus on individuals and efficacy, rather than individuals-in-relation and critical understanding. Such notions risk undermining the conditions that enable participation in democratic research communities. According to Kemmis and Smith (2008), these conditions may be conceptualized as shared 1) *cultural-discursive understandings*, 2) *material-economic arrangements*, and 3) *social-political commitments*. These categories are referred to as 'sayings', 'doings', and 'relatings'. The sayings, then, are shared ways in which language is used within and about education. The doings relate to mutual actions and resources that belong to and are available for education. Finally, the relatings are the mechanisms that surround and connect education as a practice and that influence the provision and normative function of education and educational research.

This chapter applies these three dimensions to educational research in the contemporary democracies of Finland and England. Research policies and

Educational research for democracy 129

frameworks are drawn on to discuss the ways in which educational research aligns with notions of democracy. Using the three dimensions outlined above, it is possible to construct an overview of and identify synergies between what is said and done in the two contexts, as well as the relationships that enable or disable educational research for democracy. Each of the different dimensions is presented in turn before considering to the wider implications for educational research for democracy.

Research 'sayings' in Finland and England

Many universities in both Finland and England belong to the Magna Charta Universitatum (1988), as well as national policies and priorities relating to educational research. Governments, boards of education, and national funding bodies, such as the Academy of Finland or the Economic and Social Research Council (ESRC) in England, issue statements regarding the purpose and practice of educational research. In addition, local research policies are published by universities and funding organizations. Scrutiny of these documents provides an overview of what is *said* about educational research within particular national contexts. It is possible, for example, to establish how research is directed at universities in general, how money is distributed and funding applications evaluated. These 'sayings' are considered in this section in order to identify research priorities and funding streams and to evaluate notions of democracy in research practice.

Educational research in Finland is regulated on several different discursive levels. The University Law (FINLEX, 2009) provides a broad vision of the mission of Finnish universities and the role of research, stating that universities are:

> . . . to advance free research and scientific and artistic education, to give research-based higher education and to raise the students to serve their home country and humankind. By taking care of these tasks the universities should promote lifelong learning, act in active interaction with the whole society and promote the societal impact of the scientific and artistic activities.
>
> (FINLEX, 2009, trans. Ruohotie-Lyhty)

This goes back to the historical origins of Finnish universities as part of the nation-building project in the mid-nineteenth century. The welfare state project that began in the 1950s aimed to develop services and well-being across the nation. As part of the welfare state project, universities were required to serve different regions of Finland in order to improve the quality of the lives of communities and the nation as a whole (Välimaa, 2004). These democratic aims remain current today. However, a neoliberal discourse has emerged that couches education in terms of commercialization, digitalization and efficacy. Education is constructed in a utilitarian sense, whereby it prepares individuals to make a contribution to the economy (Ministry of Education and Culture,

130 *Josephine Moate et al.*

2012). The commercial value of Finnish educational research is recognized; its role, however, in attaining the outlined democratic goals remains less clear. Nevertheless, the policy of Finnish universities partnering with the government in the formation of the goals for education continues today (FINLEX, 2009).

This vision has been interpreted at a regional level as a mandate 'to rapidly recognise and respond to new research and education needs arising in society' (University of Jyväskylä, 2015). The University of Jyväskylä's strategy (2015–2020) states that:

> . . . through education and research, the University participates in solving national and global problems. Global responsibility and sustainable development are emphasised in all activities.
>
> (University of Jyväskylä, 2015, https://www.jyu.fi/hallinto/strategia/en/strategy-of-the-university-of-jyvaskyla-201520132020).

These discourses acknowledge the visionary ideals of universities as nation builders with global responsibilities and democratic values. Such open-ended frameworks provide educational researchers with freedom and opportunities to develop initiatives that uphold these values (e.g., CITE: Critical Model of Integrative Teacher Education, Osaava Verme: Peer Group Mentoring network). Although policy documentation provides space for these initiatives, the more restrictive doings of funding potentially compromise this rather ideal environment.

Whereas Finnish educational research comes under the rubric of the Finnish University Law, English educational research is subject to the *Research Excellence Framework* (REF). As a system of expert review that assesses the quality and impact of research in UK universities for the allocation of funding and driving up standards, what the REF says with regard to educational research is of the greatest significance to academics in the UK. The assessment criteria of the REF states that 'quality, significance and rigour' (REF, 2014:4) are of the utmost importance, with research impact judged according to 'any social, economic or cultural impact or benefit beyond academia . . . underpinned by excellent research produced by the submitting institution within a given timeframe' (REF, 2014:4). Arguably, the aims of making a contribution to economic prosperity, national well-being, and the expansion and dissemination of knowledge are the conditions of democracy adopted within this framework.

In England, both the government (Department for Education, DfE) and academics (e.g., *The Cambridge Primary Review*: Alexander et al, 2010) emphasize the importance of educational research for democratic development. The DfE (2013), for example, says that the aim of social research is to provide high-quality evidence to inform policy development and delivery. It states that:

> . . . building evidence into our services is crucial to improving the education and children's services we provide. We have . . . set out research priorities and questions . . . for the research community . . . we hope these papers

Educational research for democracy 131

will encourage researchers ... to discuss research needs and contribute to the development of policy and practice.

(DfE, 2013)

Furthermore, government research priorities cover a wide range of topics: academies, assessment, curriculum and qualifications, and capital funding for schools. Government priorities also incorporate children in care, early education and childcare, funding for disadvantaged children ('pupil premium'), school behavior and attendance, special educational needs and disability, teachers and teaching, and educational governance. In a similar vein, academics, as represented by the Cambridge Primary Review Trust (2013), explicitly state the importance of a more democratic approach to education, giving voice to all stakeholders and addressing issues of inequality, poverty, and social deprivation. Significant differences exist, however, between the *sayings* of the DfE and academics with regard to who *does* the research that is to inform policy and educational development and the purpose of educational research. The *doings* of educational research are the focus of the next section.

Research 'doings' in Finland and England

A recent national evaluation of educational institutions in Finland highlighted a disjuncture between the *sayings* and the material-economic arrangements or practical *doings* of research at the University of Jyväskylä:

> ... it is in praxis visible in the fact that the societal impact is seen to emerge as part of the research and teaching activities, but the evaluation indicators of these activities do not include the aspect of societal impact. In addition the staff feels that the model for distributing resources does not support engaging in and developing the aspect of societal impact, because these activities are not directly given money.
>
> (Seppälä et al, 2015, trans. Ruohotie-Lyhty)

This seeming contradiction between the vision and realization can be better understood when looking at the national funding bodies and the competitive processes Finnish universities engage in to receive research funding.

Finnish universities became independent in 2010, adopting a financial model based on potential and demonstrable productivity (Ministry of Education and Culture, 2015a, 2015b). Two primary national bodies, the Ministry of Education and the Academy of Finland, exist to provide this funding. The Ministry of Education provides basic funding for universities, with thirty-four percent of the distributed money based on research, including funding for doctoral degrees, international publications, and securing external funding for research. There is no expectation, however, that research activities address wider societal needs. The Academy of Finland (2015) states that:

> ... in principle, a project to be funded *must in some way* contribute to Finnish research and society *or* international collaboration. The review process

132   *Josephine Moate et al.*

in calls by the Strategic Research Council includes reviewing the proposed projects both for their societal relevance and impact and for their scientific quality.

(Academy of Finland, 2015, italics added, http://www.aka.fi/en/
review-and-funding-decisions/how-applications-are-reviewed/
review-criteria/)

The criteria used to review and evaluate applications in Finland are based on the merits of the applicant, the research team, and the scientific innovativeness of the project. There is no reference to societal impact. One possible interpretation is that these criteria are more aligned with the priorities of the current government, with its commercial, economic priorities. It is also common practice for individual researchers to compete with each other and to build strategic alliances, focusing on journal publications and meeting university funding criteria as outlined in the publication forum (Publication forum, 2015) rather than prioritizing the core values as articulated in the University Law.

There are some examples, however, of funded projects and programs in Finland that are deemed to be of societal relevance and go beyond the competitive strictures outlined above. These projects include Education for Global Responsibility (2007), the LUKIMAT project (Ronimus & Lyytinen, 2015) designed to develop reading skills and strategies, and the Osaava Verme project (Korhonen et al, 2015) for teacher mentoring. Whether these projects can establish themselves as permanent features of the Finnish educational landscape once funding has ceased remains unknown, thus highlighting the problematic nature of short-term funding projects.

There is an abundance of research in teacher education contexts in both England and Finland. Student teachers conduct research during their undergraduate and postgraduate studies supervised by academics and professionals. In Finland, educational research conducted within or beyond the vicinity of the university campus feeds back into teacher education and the ongoing development of education. In England, there is an emphasis on practitioner research, and universities play an increasing role in supporting teachers in schools with this aspect of their work.

The *sayings* of educational research within the English context are largely prescribed by the *Research Excellence Framework* (REF, 2014). This promotes a much closer alignment between what is *said* and what is *done* within the English context. The REF exercise, conducted every seven years, judges the overall quality of research submissions and determines funding for UK universities. In addition to funding provided via the REF, educational researchers bid for competitive research funding from large organisations, such as NFER and ESRC in England and the EEC at a European level.

Although Finnish researchers also compete for national and international funding opportunities, for the most part, Finnish researchers design and implement their own research projects based on their interests and expertise. In England, however, the emphasis on evidence-based research tends to favor quantitative approaches carried out by teams on a large scale, applied to policy

Educational research for democracy 133

and disseminated widely. This position has been emphasized in a series of papers written by the DfE (2013) explicitly promoting a greater focus on quantitative evidence in areas where gaps in research have been identified.

This pressure arguably limits the democratic participation of educational researchers to contribute to the development of education. The participation of educational researchers is further limited in the English context, as incentives are offered to educational practitioners to engage in research in their own contexts (Goldacre, 2013) bypassing university-based educational researchers. While from a democratic perspective, it would seem to be of great importance to include educational practitioners as partners in educational research and development, to exclude academic educational researchers from this process carries negative connotations. The approach restricts rather than enables conceptions of democracy. It is these social-political arrangements, often experienced in terms of power or powerlessness, that are the focus of the *relatings* in the section below.

Research 'relatings' in Finland and England

When higher education was part of the welfare state project in Finland, the most important relations were regional. The expectation was that the university would serve the region in which it was placed, supporting the overall development of the nation (Välimaa, 2004). However, the situation in reality is not so straightforward. It could be perceived that internationalization of research was part of the democratic aims of the nation-building project. However, it was also possible to perceive this as an attempt to facilitate competition in a global market for research funding.

Although educational researchers in Finland enjoy a significant amount of freedom and responsibility, the democratic ideals of educational research outlined in the opening of the chapter, particularly in relation to societal impact, are little discussed. Whereas in England, the REF data exist to highlight the impact of educational research, in Finland, ideals of responsibility seem to have been transformed or reduced to the notion of recognition. University researchers are concerned with how to gain international funding, develop international research partnerships, and achieve international publications, as listed in the Academy of Finland funding criteria (Academy of Finland, 2015).

This need for recognition is also reflected in the University of Jyväskylä's commissioned audit published as the Research Assessment Report in 2011. The aim of the audit was to strengthen the reputation of the university as an international, research-based institution, with talented and creative scientists, and efficient infrastructures. This in turn would make it more attractive to potential investors and sponsors (Research Assessment Report, 2011:144).

The assessment criteria include:

1. Scientific quality of the unit's research
2. Quality of the scientific impact (only in terms of international success)
3. Quality of research collaborations

134 *Josephine Moate et al.*

4. Quality and quantity of the research funding
5. Quality of the research environment.

It is interesting that the notions of relating to and addressing societal needs are absent from these criteria. Nevertheless, according to the University of Jyväskylä Faculty of Education:

> The societal impact of the research conducted in the Faculty of Education is evident in many respects. The Faculty of Education offers teacher education (from kindergarten teachers to adult educators) that is based on research . . . In the key research areas the faculty does internationally high standard research and produces on this basis quality education. These research activities form a strong foundation for the continual development of the internationally top quality education and training system in Finland.
>
> (Faculty of Education, 2015, trans. Ruohotie-Lyhty)

One possible interpretation is that these two texts highlight the conundrum faced by educational researchers in Finland: on the one hand, the requirement for socially meaningful research exists and is enshrined in the University Law. On the other hand, this research is funded and justified through other means. Funding for this research is gained through competition and evaluated according to criteria that does not necessarily value or recognize socially meaningful research. The absence of strong guidelines with regard to educational research enables individual researchers to determine what is important in response to what is happening in schools and to develop educational activities within the university.

The ramifications of these diverse drivers for research are visible in the strategic recruitment and use of fixed-term or part-time contracts for academic staff in higher education in both countries. In order to keep up with the demands of increasingly neoliberal policies, educational researchers have to publish in internationally recognized journals, teach, compete for funding, be sensitive to local needs, responsive to global demands, and build international networks. In Finland, if educational researchers are able to meet these demands, the social-political arrangements of educational research provide them with the freedom to develop projects, trial initiatives, and engage with different partners. In England, researchers have currency if they are well published and win bids for significant funding opportunities.

The recent curriculum reform process in Finland (Perusopetuksen opetussuunnitelman perusteet, 2014) as well as a recent working report to reform teacher development (Heikkinen et. al, 2015) are indicative of the ways in which educational researchers continue to be valued partners in the broader development of education in Finland. Although there are no specific mechanisms in place for sustaining these relationships, these *relatings* are nevertheless sustained by the current social-political arrangements of Finland.

Educational research for democracy 135

The prevailing agenda of the government in England views higher education institutions as costly and research outputs as not necessarily adequately linked to effective schooling. There are also conflicting interests between research stakeholders. Student researchers relate to supervisors and examiners, researchers to participants, whether practitioners, children, or people who are vulnerable. Researchers also relate to publishers, and publishers to potential audiences, and markets as well as to governments and governing bodies. It is perhaps unsurprising that 'there is a significant tension between researchers and policy makers . . . [As t]he two parties have conflicting interests, agendas, audience, timescales, terminology and concern for topicality' (Levin, 1991 cited in Cohen et al, 2000:44).

Educational researchers face difficult choices and may be inclined to focus on government-stated priorities, significantly limiting the possibilities of educational research to contribute to the democratic development of society. Findings from large-scale quantitative studies on what works from commissioned research projects may not be relevant to specific educational contexts or the individuals educational researchers are working with. Research questions may be reduced to questions about effectivity and effectiveness obscuring the complexity of education and educational research as democratic practices. As Biesta notes:

> The extent to which a government not only allows the research field to raise this set of questions (i.e. what is educationally desirable) but actually supports and encourages researchers to go beyond simplistic questions about 'what works' may well be an indication of the degree to which a society can be called democratic. From the point of view of democracy, an exclusive emphasis on 'what works' will simply not work.
>
> (Biesta, 2007:20)

Educational researchers working within the qualitative research paradigm may also choose 'interpretivist/constructivist' approaches rather than 'critical theory/emancipatory' paradigms with more explicitly democratic agendas. These choices not only risk reducing the scope of educational research (Albrecht et al, 2001:149), but also impoverish the quality and range of participation within educational research (Cunnah, 2015;Liamputtong, 2007)) and the democratic potential of educational research (Biesta, 2007).

It is perhaps in the *relatings* around educational research that the most significant differences exist between Finland and England. Within the English context, educational researchers are cajoled, arguably required to take certain approaches in response to given questions seeking particular answers with mechanisms in place to reward compliance with official policy. This is within the context of regulatory research priorities of the time. Within the Finnish context, on the other hand, educational researchers still benefit from a well-established tradition that favors equality and autonomy, a system that requires educational researchers to be able to act independently and responsibly.

136　*Josephine Moate et al.*

These differences arguably stem from the *sayings* outlined at the beginning of the chapter. Finnish ideals are given voice in the University Law. In England, on the other hand, the impact of research goals is judged by the DfE and the evaluative framework of the REF. Of course, research in Finland and England cannot in reality be reduced to simple statements and categories: it is a complex process that grows out of disparate societal, political, and cultural discourses.

Concluding discussion

The aim of this chapter was to look at the ways in which educational research is constructed as a practice in two contemporary democracies, Finland and England, and to see what possibilities the existing structures provide for educational research to serve democratic development within these contexts.

Arguably, a democratic society is a society in which social research can perform both a technical and a cultural role (De Vries, 1990, as cited in Biesta, 2007). Furthermore, a democratic society should be distinguished by open and informed debate about the definition of educational problems and the aims and outcomes of educational undertakings. It could be perceived that the Finnish model with its open-ended mission for educational research creates a more fertile basis for this kind of debate, and the model in England is limited by more direct political guidance. However, the results of the REF show significant social impact of research in England.

The results of the 2014 REF, for example, demonstrate the high quality and enhanced international standing of research conducted in UK universities. The expert panels, which included international members of the research community, found a significant improvement across a broad range of universities in the UK. Outstanding impacts on the economy, society, culture, public policy and services, health, the environment, and quality of life within the UK and internationally were found. Impact, in the context of the REF, refers to any effect on, change, or benefit to the economy, society, culture, public policy or services, health, the environment, or quality of life, beyond academia. These domains of impact reflect universities' productive and democratic engagement in a wide range of public and private fields in the UK and beyond.

To support equality and diversity, each university applies a code of practice on the fair and transparent selection of staff and conducts an equality impact assessment. However, access to these panels is restricted to highly successful and experienced academics and scholars, rather than educational practitioners and other stakeholders, or novice and aspiring scholars. Inevitably, questions arise in relation to the REF. *Who* can be part of this panel of experts? When experts make judgments on outputs submitted, how can researchers defend their work? Is there room for the voice of the researcher? Are democratic practices applied? Nevertheless, the significant impact on social change ensuing from the REF exercise is in accordance with democratic principles.

Regardless of the freedom offered in Finland for open-ended discussion about the methods and goals of education, the discussion has not been particularly animated in recent years. As the model of the Finnish university changes

Educational research for democracy 137

in response to international evaluations and expectations, researchers may recognize the threat to the existing freedom they enjoy.

Educational research that is restricted to a mere technical role without responding to larger questions of societal structures, human rights, and the possibility for change cannot be considered as educational research for democracy. Ignoring or weakening the role of university-based educational research and coercing researchers to conform to a particular educational approach in England may serve short-term political goals but risks undermining future development, as it impoverishes participation in and around educational research. However, the REF evidence in England does suggest a positive societal impact. The Finnish model, in which societal impact of research remains largely unrecognized and unmotivated by the funding bodies, is problematic. Although educational researchers in Finland have the freedom to participate in educational research for democracy, the focus of research lacks reference to the societal mission that was formerly a keystone in the development of Finnish society.

In order for optimum knowledge and learning to be generated by diverse educational research stakeholders and society at large, constructive relationships 'between research, policy and practice that allow reciprocal learning to occur' (Darling-Hammond, 1996:11) are vital. If a democratic society is distinguished by open and informed debate about the definition of educational problems and the aims and outcomes of educational undertakings, research relationships should be carefully nurtured with time given for deliberation (Robertson, 2009) around research questions, paradigms, purposes, policies, and implications. It is not only deliberation *within* the research process that is necessary, but also *around* educational research. Ongoing discussion is needed with regard to the purpose of educational research and the responsibilities of educational research within a democratic society. It is this ongoing discussion and the ensuing action that unites participants within a democracy.

In this chapter, we used the theory of practice architectures (Kemmis & Smith, 2008) to examine the practices of educational research in Finland and in England. We suggest that this model can significantly contribute to the scrutiny of education and educational research in other European and global contexts as well. The model of practice architectures draws attention to different conditions that comprise any practice as well as revealing a-synergies in the *saying*, *doings*, and *relatings* that enable or disable development. This model is sensitive enough to capture different starting points and national situations beyond apparent similarities, serving as a basis for learning from each other rather than making generalizations about apparent differences. It is this kind of approach that we hope will strengthen educational research for democracy.

Acknowledgements

With grateful thanks to those who provided feedback and insights along the way, including Professor Jussi Välimaa, Dr. Tamás Szabo, Professor Carmen Sanchidrián, Dr. Elvira Barrios, Dr. Matti Rautiainen, and Dr. Andrea Raiker.

138 *Josephine Moate et al.*

References

Academy of Finland. (2015) *Decision Criteria.* Available at: http://www.aka.fi/en/review-and-funding-decisions/funding-decisions/decision-criteria/ [accessed 2 December 2015].

Albrecht, G. L., Seelman, K. D. & Bury, M. (Eds.) (2001) *Handbook of Disability Studies.* London: Sage.

Alexander, R., Armstrong, M., Flutter, J., Hargreaves, L., Harrison, D., Harlen, W., Hartley-Brewer, E., Kershner, R., MacBeath, J., Mayall, B., Northen, S., Pugh, G., Richards, C. & Utting, D. (2010) *Children, Their World, Their Education: The Final Report and Recommendations of the Cambridge Primary Review.* London: Routledge.

Beder, S. (2008) 'The corporate assault on democracy' in *The International Journal of Inclusive Democracy*, 4(1). Available at: http://www.inclusivedemocracy.org/journal/vol4/vol4_no1_beder.htm [accessed 2 March 2016].

Biesta, G. (2007) Why "what works" won't work: Evidence-based practice and the democratic deficit in educational research' in *Educational Theory*, 57(1), pp. 1–22.

Biesta, G. & Burbules, N. C. (2003) *Pragmatism and Educational Research.* Lanham, MD: Rowman and Littlefield.

Cohen, L., Manion, L. & Morrison, K. (2000) *Research Methods in Education.* 5th edn. London: Routledge Falmer.

Cunnah, W. (2015) 'Disabled Students: Identity, inclusion and work-based placements' in *Disability and Society*, 30(2), pp. 213–226.

Darling-Hammond, L. (1996) 'The right to learn and the advancement of teaching: Research: Policy and practice for democratic education' in *Educational Researcher*, 25(6), pp. 5–17.

DeVries, G. H. (1990) *De Ontwikkeling van Watenschap [The Development of Science].* GroningenWolters: Noordhoff.

Dewey, J. (1922) 'Human Nature and Conduct' in Boydston, J. A. (Ed.) *The Middle Works 1899–1924 (vol. 14),* Carbondale: Southern Illinois University Press, pp. 1–227.

DfE. (2013) *The DfE Analytical Review: Research Priorities for Education and Children's Services.* Available at: http://www.gov.uk/government/publications/department-for-educationanalystical-review [accessed 6 November 2015].

DuRand, C. (1997) 'The Idea of Democracy' in University of Havana, October 21, Conference, *Socialism Toward the 21st Century*, pp. 1–3. Havana, Cuba: University of Havana.

EHEA Ministerial conference. (2015) *Yerevan communiqué.* Available at: http://www.ehea.info/Uploads/SubmitedFiles/5_2015/112705.pdf [accessed 2 December 2015].

European Council. (2006) *Recommendation 1762 Academic freedom and University Autonomy.* Parliamentary Assembly, European council. Available at: http://assembly.coe.int/nw/xml/XRef/Xref-XML2HTML-en.asp?fileid=17469&lang=en [accessed 15 December 2015].

Faculty of Education. (2015) *Research.* Available at: https://www.jyu.fi/edu/tutkimus [accessed 12 January 2016].

FINLEX. (2009) *Universities Act.* Available at: http://www.finlex.fi/fi/laki/alkup/2009/20090558 [accessed 2 December 2015].

Freire, P. (2004) *Pedagogy of Indignation.* Boulder, CO: Paradigm.

Goldacre, B. (2013) *Building Evidence into Education.* Available at: http://www.media.education.gov.uk/assets/files/pdf/b/520goldacre520paper.pdf. Last [accessed 2 December 2015].

Heikkinen, H. L. T. Aho, J. & Korhonen, H. (2015) *TEACHER LEARNS NOT: Development of Teacher Education Continuum.* University of Jyvaskyla. Finnish Institute for Educational Research.

Kemmis, S. (2014) 'Education, educational research and the good for humankind' (pp. 15–68) in Heikkinen, H. L. T., Lerkkanen M-K. and Moate, J. (Eds.) *Enabling Education: Proceedings of the Annual Conference of Finnish Educational Research Association FERA 2013.* FERA.

Educational research for democracy 139

Kemmis, S. & Smith, T. (2008) 'Praxis and praxis development' in S. Kemmis & T. Smith (Eds.) *Enabling Praxis: Challenges for Education*, pp. 3–13. Rotterdam: Sense Publishers.

Korhonen, H., Heikkinen, H. L. T. & Kiviniemi, U. (2015) 'Peer-group mentoring in Finland' (pp. 122–146) in Heikkinen, H. L. T. Swachten, L. & Akyol, H. (Eds.) *Bridge Over Troubled Water: New Perspectives on Teacher Induction*. Ankara: Pegem Akademi.

Levin, H. M. (1991) 'Why isn't educational research more useful?' in Sanderson, D. S. & Biddle, B. J. (Eds.) *Knowledge for Policy: Improving Education through Research*. London: Falmer, pp. 70–80.

Liamputtong, P. (2007) *Researching the Vulnerable*. London: Sage.

The Magna Charta Universitatum. (1988) *Rectors of European Universities*. Available at: http://www.magna-charta.org/magna-charta-universitatum [accessed 21 January 2016].

Ministry of Education and Culture, Finland. (2012) *Education and Research 2011–2016: A development plan*. Available at: http://www.minedu.fi/export/sites/default/OPM/Julkaisut/2012/liitteet/okm03.pdf [accessed 2 February 2016].

Ministry of Education and Culture. (2015a) *Financing of Education*. Available at: http://www.minedu.fi/OPM/Koulutus/koulutuspolitiikka/rahoitus/?lang=en [accessed 12 December 2015].

Ministry of Education and Culture. (2015b) *Productivity and Impact of Finnish University Research: Report by the Profile Working Group of the Ministry of Education and Culture*. Reports of the Ministry of Education and Culture: 5.

Nikolakaki, M. (2016) 'Critical Pedagogy and Democracy (Greece)' in Darder, A., Mayo P. & Paraskeva, J. (Eds.) *International Critical Pedagogy Reader*. London: Routledge, pp. 86–96.

Perusopetuksen opetussuunnitelman perusteet [Principles for planning the core curriculum]. (2014) Helsinki: National Board of Education. Available at: http://www.oph.fi/download/139848_pops_web.pdf [accessed 7 November 2015].

Research Evaluation Framework. (2014) Available at: http://www.ref.ac.uk/panels/assessment criteriaandleveldefinitions/ [accessed 9 December 2015].

Research Assessment Report (2011) *Evaluation of Research Activities 2005–2009*. Jyväskylä, Finland: University of Jyväskylä.

Robertson, E. (2009) 'Public Reason and the Education of Democratic Citizens: The Role of Higher Education' in Katz, M. S., Verducci, S. & Biesta, G. (Eds.) *Education, Democracy and the Moral Life*. London: Springer, pp. 113–126.

Ronimus, M. & Lyytinen, H. (2015) 'Is School a Better Environment than Home for Digital Game-Based Learning?: The Case of GraphoGame' in *Human Technology*, 11(2), pp. 123–147.

Seppälä, K., Björkroth, J., Karjalainen, P., Keränen, H., Levä, K. & Hiltunen, K. (2015) *Audit of the University of Jyväskylä*. Jyväskylä: Finnish Education Evaluation Center.

University of Jyväskylä. (2015) The University of Jyväskylä's strategy (2015–2020). Available at: https://www.jyu.fi/hallinto/strategia/en/strategy-of-the-university-of-jyvaskyla-201520132020 [accessed 3 December 2015].

Välimaa, J. (2004) 'Nationalisation, localisation and globalisation in Finnish higher education' in *Higher Education*, 48(1), pp. 27–54.

11 Fighting against the flow in theorizing education

Olli-Pekka Moisio, Andrea Raiker & Matti Rautiainen

Introduction

This chapter explores the role theory plays in the field of educational research and classroom practice and how conceptions of educational theory can provide insights into the democratic processes at work in English and Finnish teacher education. In Chapter 1 of this book, it was argued that differences in conceptions of educating for democracy would arise because of the differing historical, political, social and economic contexts in the two countries. Discussions in previous chapters have shown that educational practice and approaches to research are not the same in the two countries. By considering the way theorizing education is constructed in England and Finland, we will demonstrate a fundamental epistemological difference focused on conceptions of education as a discipline in its own right and as an amalgam of facets of contributing disciplines. We will show how these conceptions reflect underlying political ideologies, and their combined impact on teacher education and classroom practice.

'What is theory?' is a contentious question. 'What is theory meant to do?' invites greater agreement: theory informs research. So, educational theory informs educational research. According to Biesta (2006), educational research is scientific and wide-ranging, based on paradigms and involving a variety of methodological approaches and data collection methods to investigate educational processes and practices. Consequently, there are diverse theories based on ontological positions underpinning educational research. Since the nineteenth century and the advent of mass primary education, a response to the development of Germany as a political and military presence, English education has been regarded as a necessary but subservient discipline serving capitalist and, more recently, neo–liberalist agendas. It is not surprising, therefore, that education in England is not perceived as a discipline in its own right but as embedded within other disciplines, such as philosophy, anthropology, history, sociology and in particular, psychology. Thus, educational theory is taken from, and amalgamated with, theories from the 'dominant' disciplines. For example, theories currently in vogue in English research include Engeström's activity theory (historical/sociological), Kemmis's ecologies of practice (philosophical/anthropological) and Vygostsky's social constructivism (psychological). Such a

Fighting against the flow in theorizing education   141

many-faceted approach to theory in education results in complexity and creativity, but also has the potential for conflict and confusion. In contrast, Finnish educational theory is influenced by German ideas and approaches to education. The notion of *Erziehung* underpins educational theorizing which, as developed by Biesta (2006), relates to the current context of education by focusing on the processes and productions involved in the development of the emancipated individual associated with contemporary and future social life. Such a theoretical approach indicates that education is a discipline in its own right and, centered as it is on the individual and his/her relationship to society, suggests a direct connection with ethics and democracy.

This chapter will now discuss theorizing education and democratic process by discussing the relationship between education, theory and democracy in Finland and England, and the influence Calvanistic doctrine has had on the approach to educating for democracy in the two countries. Finally, the impact of this comparison on democratic practices within teacher and school education will be assessed.

The Finnish perspective

For this discussion on the Finnish perspective on theorizing education, it is essential to use as a theoretical frame the concepts of Max Weber because Protestantism has had a profound influence on the development of Finnish thought. Despite Western Europe's focus on industry and business, teaching has always been thought of as a calling as well as a profession in Finland. Lutheran Protestantism is regarded as one of the reasons why social and political factors, including theory drawn from the social sciences, have had so little impact on teacher education in Finland (Sitomaniemi-San, 2015). The data we are using are varied, including official documents concerning education and educational policy, but also empirical data from Finland. We have interviewed professors who worked at the Department of Teacher Education at the University of Jyväskylä when teacher education became academic in Finland (1970s–1990s).

Finnish teacher education has been called 'research-based' since the late 1970s, when the Finnish education system, including teacher education, was undergoing substantial reform. Of significance to this discussion were changes to teacher qualifications. All prospective teachers had to attain master's degrees. This was considered to be radical, particularly for primary school teachers. Also, subject teacher education, which included a pedagogical studies element of what is currently measured as 60 ECTS, was transferred to departments of teacher education.

Was there also a significant change concerning the theorizing of teacher education? Yes and no. Master's degrees in education have strong theoretical bases and include students' own research; the former required qualification for teacher education, the bachelor's degree, did not. This is not to say that there was no research in teacher education before the 1970s. From the early days of teacher education in colleges (the first such college being established at

142 *Olli-Pekka Moisio et al.*

Jyväskylä in 1863), some lecturers carried out research even if it was not part of their working plans. Their focus was on didactics and educational psychology, which remain important and popular areas for research in Finnish education. However, the impetus for educational research was given in 1934 through the foundation of the first college for educational sciences in Jyväskylä. This not only improved the output of research in education throughout Finnish colleges of education: Jyväskylä became the center for Finnish educational research, and today, the Finnish Institute for Research in Education is situated on the campus of the University of Jyväskylä (Valtonen & Rautiainen, 2013.) Increased emphasis on educational research resulted in many philosophers being drawn to contribute to discussions concerning educational philosophy, for example, Professors Erik Ahlman, J. A. Hollo J. E. Salomaa and Reijo Wilenius. The Finnish philosopher Johan Wilhelm Snellman, who was also for a short period a professor of pedagogy at the University of Helsinki in the 1850s, emphasized the importance of the relationship between practice and theory. His idea was to combine subject teacher training with the professorial teaching of pedagogy in training schools (*normaalilyseo*). He also thought universities should control and train teachers in the *normaalilyseo* (see, for example, Heinonen, 1987). It could be assumed that from such a positive starting points, teachers' theoretical understanding and identity as 'teachers as researchers' should be strong, but according to studies, it is not. New teachers do not recognize theoretical knowledge and understanding to be useful in their everyday work (Rautpuro et al, 2011).

Snellman's ideas were never realized. Teacher education developed in a practical direction; theoretical studies were separated from training. In the late 1970s, as part of the new academic teacher education resulting from the reforms outlined above, Snellman's ideas were resurrected as providing sound principles on which to base the new conception of teacher education. However, interaction between theory and practice remained tenuous. Why? According to professors working currently at the University of Jyväskylä, the main reason was tension between the new conception and tradition. The majority of teacher educators and students were against the reforms. According to them, the profession of teaching was practically, not academically, based. They did not resist the inclusion of theory in teacher education courses; on the contrary, theories on learning, didactics and educational psychology were respected. Despite this, there was no understanding that their own research and methodological studies could have significant roles in their studies to become teachers.

The model of academic teacher education, which was mostly copied from other social sciences, was also problematic. Methodological studies stressed quantitative methods, and students' research projects were often far removed from the everyday work of teachers. Research groups studying the development of schools and teacher education were rare. Qualitative methods did not become accepted until the 1990s. Also, attitudes towards research in authentic environments were unusual in teacher education.

These problems were well known among teacher educators and other stakeholders, as they remained into the early 2000s (Opettajankoulutus 2020, 2007).

Fighting against the flow in theorizing education 143

On the other hand, alternative teacher education programs were established. There were new experimental groups at the Universities of Helsinki and Jyväskylä, groups that had strong theoretical bases behind their programmes. Educational psychology was an experiment started in Helsinki as part of the prospective teacher education program. It was based on constructivism and was developed together with students, an approach which was considered to be radical (http://blogs.helsinki.fi/educationalpsychology/). An innovative program called Critical Integrative Teacher Education was begun at Jyväskylä in 2003. In this program, psychodynamic theories and learner's experiences are used as starting points to underpin the learning processes involved in teacher education (https://www.jyu.fi/edu/laitokset/okl/integraatio/en).

At the same time, critical pedagogy challenged teacher education from a different perspective. Finnish teacher education has always been based on psychological and didactical theories; content from the social sciences was rare. It might be argued that critical pedagogy in Finland, and maybe in the world in general, is in theoretical, methodological and practical senses 'a book to be written' (Suoranta & Moisio, 2009). In 2001, Tapio Aittola and Juha Suoranta edited in Finnish a book which contained texts from the work of Henry Giroux and Peter McLaren. Paolo Freire's *Pedagogy of the Oppressed* was released in Finnish in 2005, and bell hooks's selected writings followed in 2007. It has been noted that, during the last two decades, many doctoral dissertations and other studies have found their theoretic structures from the field of critical pedagogy (see, for example, Bedford, 2009; FitzSimmons, 2004; Hannula, 2001;Moisio, 2009;; Saurén, 2008);).

Currently, the relationship between teacher education and theory is in flux. On the one hand is the classic Finnish ideal of the teacher established by Uno Cygnaeus, the founder of the teacher education movement. This approach does not construct teachers' professionalism around theories, but on cultural beliefs and assumptions of what a teacher should be. On the other hand, there are teacher educators and students who are interested in developing teacher education through a range of projects, which are not only adapting theories but also creating them. In a sense, this might be seen to be a venture towards what Zygmunt Bauman (2000:204) meant when he wrote about sociology as '. . . a third current, running in parallel with those [history and poetry] two. Or at least this is what it should be if it is to stay inside that human condition which it tries to grasp and make intelligible'. Theorizing, in education especially, is a way to search for possibilities to understand the human condition, be it in a learning environment or as life in general, from the inside.

The changes and processes described above are important from the viewpoint of democracy. Education has been traditionally constructed from top to bottom; the new experimentation in education is changing the direction of influence, coming from bottom to up. This direction is especially strong at the Department of Education at the University of Jyväskylä, which is the only teacher education unit in Finland which has a phenomenon-based curriculum both in primary and secondary teacher education. According to the new

144   *Olli-Pekka Moisio et al.*

curriculum, phenomena should be studied from a multidisciplinary perspective (from the points of view of history, philosophy, psychology and sociology), not by separate courses based on each discipline like earlier. In this new curriculum, the understanding of theory is also in a process of change towards the experiential, where research carried out by the students can be seen as 'ending at the colon', that is, an open-ended process. As in life, student research needs to have a certain amount of mystery so that, to paraphrase C. Wright Mills, the 'educational imagination' can be ignited.

Is there any place for theories concerning democracy and education for democracy in teacher education? Compared with earlier times, the content of 'democracy' has grown during the last decade. At the same time, the operational culture of departments of teacher education have become more democratic. However, students are still mostly on their own if they want to develop their own understanding of democracy and education for democracy (Rautiainen et al, 2014). The biggest difference compared with earlier times is that students have possibilities to develop and study theories from their own interests and needs, and develop new and in a sense more authentic questions and insights from their own encounters with theories and experiences in the learning process.

The English perspective

In order to understand the concept of theorizing education and its relationship with democratic practice in the English context, it is necessary to provide, albeit briefly, essential historic and political background so that the cultural underpinnings to the argument are clear. As was outlined in Chapter 1 of this volume, notions of democracy in England are deep-rooted: they can be traced back to the Anglo-Saxon era (410–1066) and their legal system, which formalized the relationship between 'folkright' and privilege. Folkright is the accumulation of shared, debated and voted ways of behaving, articulated and overseen by the local communities themselves in association with the shire moots, the assemblies or courts controlling larger administrative areas. Although the Norman Conquest of 1066 and the feudal organization of society it imposed dispensed with folkright both as a word and in practice, the fundamental societal concept that 'folkright' signified in the everyday life of the people remained, eventually to re-emerge during the next century as 'common law', aspects of which survive in English legislation to this day. Consequently, the democratic processes centered on the right of ordinary people to debate issues governing the relationship between individuals and society with a show of hands to signify the outcome is deeply embedded in English culture. This right is in conflict with the dominant neo-liberalist ideology, a legacy of empire that reflects the beliefs and interests of the socially elite governing class. The aim of this elite class is to create wealth so that the standard of living of the populace improves, while at the same time, the elite's position in society is maintained. The purpose of education is thus to produce more effective workers to improve the country's

Fighting against the flow in theorizing education   145

global competitiveness and hence wealth, while at the same time keeping them in their relative social position. Consequently, the role of educators is to legitimize and propagate the existing cultural hegemony, and the role of education policymakers is to create rules and processes to ensure educators' compliance.

It is to be expected that knowledge and understanding of the theory of education are neither prized highly by education policymakers nor emphasized in teacher training courses; they are not. The word used to describe a student teacher in England, 'trainee', supports this. Students who are teachers attending master's courses in education generally have little knowledge and understanding of theory. The reason is, arguably, that policymakers in the Department for Education believe that engagement with theory might encourage critical thinking and the undermining of compliance. As argued above, English educators have within them, to varying degrees, the heritage of folkright, of grassroots participation in determining the acceptable behaviours that direct everyday life. They also have within them the legacy of humanism, a philosophy that focuses on individual endeavor for the public good. It might be expected that teacher educators would press to have theory recognized as necessary and equal to practice, and essential for teacher professionalism and individual personal development.

But professionalism has been eroded as effectively as the managerialism of education has been established. Today, learning is outcome based, teachers teach to meet SMART targets and career progression is tied to performance management procedures.

However, from the start of the de-professionalism process initiated by Margaret Thatcher's Conservative government, English educational thinkers were proposing ways that teachers could maintain and develop their professionalism themselves at grassroots levels. For example, Lawrence Stenhouse (1981) proposed that teachers should engage in action research to take back control. He believed that it was not politicians but '. . . teachers who in the end will change the world of the school by understanding it' (Stenhouse, 1981:46); that developing professionalism involved being active by studying the work of teaching and researching it oneself, not passively leaving it to others. He was convinced that involvement in research would restore in teachers a sense of democratic professionalism and power in the sense of teachers having a voice. His work was taken up in the 1990s by the renowned British educationalist Professor David Hargreaves. He criticized the quality of educational research produced by academics in universities at the time for what he saw as its lack of rigor. 'One alternative . . . ', he wrote, '. . . is to treat practitioners themselves as the main (but not only) source for creation of professional knowledge' (Hargreaves, 1999:125). Stenhouse, Hargreaves and others said that teachers should be the subjects and the users of educational research – that is, for their own and their schools' development – and to generate educational knowledge and theory on teaching and learning for a wider, public audience. This provoked debate and tension. Should teachers be engaged with research and theory for self-improvement, to put political agendas into practice, for school improvement or

146 *Olli-Pekka Moisio et al.*

to generate educational knowledge and theory on teaching and learning for a wider, public audience? As theory informs research and this book is concerned with educating for democracy, a further question could be asked: what theories should be advocated to promote and research educating for democracy? As theory is time and context specific, it appears that theories should be in the process of being created by teachers acting as researchers to reflect twenty-first-century issues and interests.

Some years ago, Carr and Kemmis (1986:221), in their work integrating Habermas's conceptions of communicative action with teacher education, proposed that teachers could '. . . organise themselves as communities of enquirers, organising their own enlightenment'. Enlightenment involves insight, the result of personal and purposeful critical reflection and evaluation. In another volume, we argue that insight in higher education involves growing awareness and understanding of the epistemological and ontological underpinnings of pedagogy (Raiker, 2011). At first glance, this appears to resonate with the definition of professional development given by the Department of Education's Teaching Agency (TA):

> Professional development consists of reflective activity designed to improve an individual's attributes, knowledge, understanding and skills. It supports individual needs and improves professional practice.
>
> (TA, 2012 online)

However, 'reflective activity' takes place in an education system controlled by government through imposed standards, inspection and competition stimulated by the publication of league tables. The outcome is that higher education courses for teachers, focused on improving their professional practice through 'reflective activity', become aligned with and conform to government neoliberalist ideology. Being a government agency, the TA's role is to encourage improvement through conformity. This does not resonate with improvement construed as the deepening of personal insight into the epistemological and ontological underpinnings of pedagogy, which are the bases of understanding and creating theory. Indeed, the TA's definition of professional development does not even include the terms 'pedagogy' or 'theory'. A conclusion can be drawn that the TA does not consider knowledge, understanding and creation of theory as important in improving practice. Because of this approach, the one-year postgraduate course that prospective secondary school teachers undertake to achieve Qualified Teacher Status contains little theory. This top-down repression contrasts with the bottom-up investigations taking place in Finnish teacher education.

Consequently, we were inspired to research Carr and Kemmis's proposal that teachers working in communities of practice could organize their own enlightenment in terms of generating theory. In 2012, we worked with academics and practicing teachers from five European countries on an action research project combining seminars in traditional university locations with online collaborative

Fighting against the flow in theorizing education   147

software (Raiker, 2014). According to Kemmis and McTaggart (1992:16), action research involves '. . . changing individuals, on the one hand, and, on the other, the culture of the groups, institutions and societies to which they belong'. Furthermore, action research is '. . . a form of collective self-reflective inquiry undertaken by participants in social situations in order to improve the rationality and justice of their own social or educational practices . . . ' (*ibid.*:5). Although we undertook the research in the spirit of 'teachers-as-researchers', as advocated by Stenhouse (1975) and Whitehead (1985), and 'researchers-as-participators' (Weiskopf & Laske, 1996), the democratic process was enhanced by colleagues being consulted and included throughout the project. This conception of action research would surely promote educating for democracy and be the stimulus for theory creation. Indeed, one aim of the project was to investigate if a blended physical/virtual environment enabled teachers, through reflection on practice in collaboration on a task, to create educational theory as a step towards questioning and potentially opposing ideological conformity. We saw the community of enquirers established virtually, in the digital habitat, as Wenger, White and Smith (2009) term it, as a 'public sphere' for communicative action (Habermas, 1991). The findings from two action research cycles indicated that although that the teachers in the project could, with the support of the academics, establish agendas for the practice of collecting data, there was evidence neither for the use of educational theory in creating agendas nor even the beginnings of creating educational theory. Furthermore, there was no evidence of knowledge and understanding of *existing* educational theory. This was disappointing, as we were persuaded by Freire (1978) in his proposal that the professional as agent must forge together *theory and practice* to create 'praxis'. Praxis is a high-level mode of professional operation where the practitioner possesses skills and deep knowledge and understanding of the theories that underpin practice. This can lead to a profound change in teachers' understanding of their professional identity, giving them the power to democratize their profession further through taking control as Stenhouse advised and intended. This was clearly not an outcome of the action research described above.

Three key issues arise from the discussion so far. The one-year postgraduate secondary teacher course is not long enough for meaningful engagement with theory; knowledge and understanding of theory take time to develop; for theory to be created, teachers must understand that the role of theory in praxis and professional development. How is this to be achieved? It appears that in England, the decades-old educational policy of separating theory and practice, and constructing courses focused on the latter, is bound to continue. The government is moving initial teacher education out of universities, with Ofsted-approved training schools taking a greater role. Unlike Finland, this is not because teachers and teacher educators are against theory. Research by Procter (2014) showed that teachers wanted to know more about research and theory, but were constrained by time, workload and lack of financial and school leadership support. It appears that, with the dirth of theory in Initial Teacher Education (ITE) courses, master's and doctoral programs will become

148 *Olli-Pekka Moisio et al.*

increasingly important in ensuring the survival and generation of educational theory. This view is supported by recent governments *not* showing any indication that they intended, or indeed intend, to reverse the cutting of funding for teacher-as-researcher projects, exemplified by the Best Practice Research Scholarships (BPRS) of the late 1990s and early 2000s. BPRS holders worked with university-based academics so that the essentials of improved knowledge of subject, practice and educational theory and understanding of research methodologies in education were achieved. No more. In Finland, the relationship between teacher education and theory is in flux; in England, it is becoming extinct.

This is despite increasing evidence in the UK on the impact of teachers' research and their experience of being involved in research and inquiry. A systematic review of the literature by McLaughlin et al. (2004) showed that the research experience:

- reminded teachers of their intellectual capability and the importance of that capability to their professional lives;
- reconnected many of the teachers to their colleagues and to their initial commitments to teach;
- encouraged teachers to develop an expanded sense of what teachers can and ought to do.

Although aspects of democratic practice can be seen here, there is nothing that can be identified as theory and its creation. More recently, last year, the British Education Research Association published its final report on *Research and the Teaching Profession; Building the capacity for a self-improving education system* (2014). The report states, 'The evidence gathered by the inquiry is clear about the positive impact that a research literate and research engaged profession is likely to have on learner outcomes' (*ibid.*:6). The report also calls for 'commissioners of education research [to] build teacher engagement into commissioning processes, so that wherever possible teachers are involved in the democratic process of being active agents in research, rather than passive participants' (*ibid.*:8). However, nothing was said about theory and its creation. University master's courses contain content on educational theory, but as a general rule, these have to begin at a level of basic or no knowledge because of the lack of theoretical content in initial teacher training courses. It appears that in England, the creation of theory remains in doctoral work and universities, not in teachers-as-researchers and schools.

Some further thoughts on the theorizing of education

In this chapter, albeit in a brief and very general sense, we have discussed the changing situations and fates of educational theory in two different countries. Now it is time to consider whether in the different theoretical and methodological works of different times we might find from the old something new and

Fighting against the flow in theorizing education 149

useful for this book in terms of critical pedagogy and the theory of democratic teaching practices.

Over the previous 20 years, in most parts of the developed world, educational systems have been facing a problem, a problem which we have not fully addressed in our discussion of educational theory. It is the problem of the diminishment of the promise of hope, which is at the core of the whole endeavor of education. Hope underpins all action that is intended to promote change, hope that change will make things better. Change is at the core of all educational practice, and as we have seen throughout this volume, educational change is the result of social, cultural, political and economic forces manifested in the life of every individual. Young adults in schools, colleges and universities face reality, possibly with more purpose and interest today they were in earlier decades, that following graduation they may not get work commensurate with their level of education. It used to be the case that the central promise of education was that education was the best and most efficient way to gain social and economic status: this promise has been profoundly betrayed. Education is still one of the key factors predicting the future of the individual, but this factor has become and is becoming weaker.

Industry, commerce and many different educational policy think tanks have rushed to offer a solution to the situation. Let's raise the level of education! This argument is based on the fantasy that the problem facing the educational world is that the educational system is functioning poorly when seen from the viewpoint of different vocational requirements of the work life. When the level of education is fundamentally linked to the needs of industry and commerce, it is believed that the skilled person is more valuable and usable in the labor market. This kind of thinking demolishes one of the key levels in the project of education: *Bildung*, i.e., education itself! This project of changing the educational system to the functionary of industry and commerce, throws education completely upside down and leaves individuals alone without a way to rise above the immediate requirements of their society.

In this situation, there is one intractable problem at hand if the assumption is made that a society should produce young people capable of evaluating and appreciating their personal understanding of the good, the meaning of life and the things making life meaningful. We argue that education in the form it has taken over the previous 20 or so years has actually marginalized those things that young people cherish as valuable and meaningful in general and particularly for themselves. How well, for example, do schools prepare young people for the main events in their lives, for example, how they express love? In many families, young people face the situation after school where, instead of further education, they choose to leave without considering what tomorrow may bring or the income needed to balance what is consumed. This will impact on the structure of society as a whole. When life can be taken into one's own hands, young people will take it completely.

The overpowering influence of the economical viewpoint in educational policy today is an example of the impact of ideology over educational thought.

150   *Olli-Pekka Moisio et al.*

If the end product of education is seen as an asset or property, it is simple to perceive the impact of neo-liberalism on education. In the ethics of Calvinism, assets or property are not considered to be bad in themselves; quite on the contrary, they were seen as an indicator of the value of the person. Calvin advocated a combination of democracy and aristocratic hegemony. Following Calvinistic thought, both John Milton and John Locke advocated that politics could and should protect the liberties of all and there should be a system of checks and balances to protect these liberties and freedoms. It is clear that education was one of them. In both Finland and England, it was accepted that those who worked hard and profited from that work should enjoy their gains. However, there was the danger that those who acquired economic riches through inheritance or had too much surplus would succumb to laziness and enjoyment. The words of the Paul from the Bible, 'If a man will not work, he shall not eat', were not directed against the poor but also against the rich. Instead, he instructed, 'Such people we command and urge . . . to settle down and earn the bread they eat'. Paul's instruction regarding those who preferred not to work was to 'keep away from every brother who is idle and does not live according to the teaching you received from us' (2 Thessalonians 3:12). There is a paradox here: although profit seeking was criticized, the lauded compulsion to austerity promoted the development of capital and hence, it can be argued, the current neo-liberalistic hegemony.

As has been argued above, it appears that the goals and practices of education today promote the already privileged social groups. For them the salvation that education can bring is already given. We might ask the question: are our educational systems in any way Calvinistic? The objective sign that Calvin looked for was submission to the goals and requirements of society, to be able to act according to the ordained requirements of schools in particular and the educational system in general. In this sense, schools and other educational establishments become a way to licentiate and in a sense give learned people blessing for their social status. So the elite groups are blessed and those less privileged are struggling. This is hardly educating for democracy.

Concluding thoughts

To summarize this chapter, the most important point behind theorizing education is the core idea of democracy. Before we can make any decisions, we have to understand the phenomena under discussion and debate. Theory is the key towards understanding education and its latent constructions. However, in England, there is little theory or theorizing in ITE courses. University master's courses contain content on educational theory, but as a general rule, these have to begin at a level of basic or no knowledge because of the lack of theoretic content in initial teacher training courses. It appears that in England, the creation of theory remains in doctoral work and universities, not in teachers-as-researchers and schools. Epistemologically, theorizing education is not considered as a necessary pre-requisite for effective pedagogy. In Finland, compared

Fighting against the flow in theorizing education 151

with earlier times, the content of 'democracy' has grown during the last decade. At the same time, in Finland, the operational culture of departments of teacher education have become more democratic. However, students are still mostly on their own if they want to develop their own understanding of democracy and education for democracy (Rautiainen et al, 2014). The biggest difference compared with earlier times is that students have possibilities to develop and study theories from their own interests and needs, and develop new and in a sense more authentic questions and insights from their own encounters with theories and experiences in the learning process. Epistemologically, the Finnish approach is experiential and individualistic. However, social and political theories have no major role in teacher education. This means that knowledge and understanding of democracy and democratic issues in education is superficial. In England political ideology controls education, but we have argued that democracy is understood and enacted by educators because of centuries of engagement with local, if not national, democratic practices. The place of theory in English teacher education should be to support the externalization and investigation of such practices, how they have developed and where they might lead in the future. In the absence of political will in this direction, particularly in England, we are fighting against the flood. We conclude with the proposal that without understanding political and social connections in education, our understanding of education for democracy is one way or another incomplete, perhaps even nonexistent.

References

Bauman, Z. (2000) *Liquid Modernity.* Cambridge: Polity Press.

Bedford, T. (2009) Promoting Educational Equity through Teacher Empowerment: Web-Assisted Transformative Action Research as a Counter-Heteronormative Praxis. *Acta Universitatis Ouluensis E Scientiae Rerum Socialium 103.* Oulu: University of Oulu.

Biesta, G. J. J. (2006) *Beyond Learning: Democratic Education for a Human Future.* Boulder Col: Paradigm Publishers.

British Educational Research Association. (2014) *Research and the Teaching Profession; Building the Capacity for a Self-Improving Education System.* Available at: https://www.bera.ac.uk/wp-content/uploads/2013/12/BERA-RSA-Research-Teaching-Profession-FULL-REPORT-for-web.pdf?noredirect=1 [Accessed 6 November 2015].

Carr, W. & Kemmis, S. (1986) *Becoming Critical.* London: Falmer Press.

FitzSimmons, R. (2004) *Toward a Critical Revolutionary Pedagogy: Inquiries into Karl Marx, Vladimir Lenin, Mao Tse-Tung and Fidel Castro. Acta Universitatis Lapponiensis 71.* Rovaniemi: University of Lapland.

Freire, P. (1978) *Pedagogy in Process.* New York: Seabury.

Habermas, J. (1991) *The Structural Transformation of the Public Sphere: An Inquiry into a Category of Bourgeois Society.* Cambridge, MA: MIT Press.

Hannula A. (2001) Tiedostaminen ja muutos Paolo Freiren ajattelussa. Systemaattinen analyysi Paolo Freiren ajattelusta. *Helsingin yliopiston kasvatustieteen laitoksen julkaisuja 168.* Helsinki: University of Helsinki.

Hargreaves, D. H. (1999) 'The knowledge creating school' in *British Journal of Educational Studies,* 47(2), pp. 122–144.

152 Olli-Pekka Moisio et al.

Heinonen, R. E. (1987) *Aineenopettajakoulutus kulttuuripolitiikan ristivedossa. Koulutussuunnitelman synty, toteutus ja uudistus Normaalikoulun alkuvaiheissa 1860–1880–luvuilla.* Jyväskylä: Gummerus.

Kemmis, S. & McTaggart, R. (Eds.) (1992) *The Action Research Planner.* 3rd ed. Geelong, Victoria, Australia: Deakin University Press.

McLaughlin, C., Black-Hawkins, C. & McKintyre, D. (2004) *Researching Teachers, Researching Schools, Researching Networks: A Review of the Literature.* Cambridge: University of Cambridge.

Moisio, O.-P. (2009) Essays on Radical Educational Philosophy. *Jyväskylä Studies in Education, Psychology and Social Research 353.* Jyväskylä, Finland: University of Jyväskylä.

Opettajankoulutus 2020. (2007) *Opetusministeriön työryhmämuistioita ja selvityksiä 2007:44.* Available at: http://www.minedu.fi/export/sites/default/OPM/Julkaisut/2007/liitteet/tr44.pdf?lang=fi [Accessed 6 January 2016].

Procter, R. (2014) *Teaching as an Evidence Informed Profession: Knowledge Mobilisation with a Focus on Technology.* PhD Dissertation, University of Bedfordshire.

Raiker, A. (2011) 'Developing a Framework for Postgraduate Education' in Nygaard, C., Holtham, C. & Courtney, N. (Eds.) *Postgraduate Education: Form and Function.* Faringdon: Libri Publishing, pp. 9–26.

Raiker, A. (2014) 'Using Computer Supported Collaborative Learning to Enhance the Quality of Schoolteacher Professional Development' in Nygaard, C., Courtney, N. & Batholomew, P. (Eds.) *Quality Enhancement of University Teaching and Learning.* Faringdon: Libri Publishing, pp. 103–122.

Rautiainen, M., Vanhanen-Nuutinen, L., & Virta, A. (2014) Demokratia ja ihmisoikeudet: Tavoitteet ja sisällöt opettajankoulutuksessa. Opetus- ja kulttuuriministeriön työryhmämuistioita ja selvityksiä, 18. Opetus- ja kulttuuriministeriö: Helsinki.

Rautopuro, J., Tuominen, V. & Puhakka, A. (2011) 'Vastavalmistuneiden opettajien työllistyminen ja akateemisten taitojen tarve' in *Kasvatus,* 42(4), pp. 316–327.

Saurén, K.-M. (2008) Asiantuntijavalta – koulutettu mielikuvitus. Systemaattinen analyysi Ivan Illichin tuotannossa esitetystä köyhyyden modernisoitumisesta kulutusyhteiskunnassa. *Acta Universitatis Lapponiensis 147.* Rovaniemi: University of Lapland.

Sitomaniemi-San, J. (2015) Fabricating the Teacher as Researcher. A Genealogy of Academic Teacher Education in Finland. Acta Universitatis Ouluensis E Scientiae Rerum Socialum 157. Oulu: University of Oulu.

Stenhouse, L. (1975) *An Introduction to Curriculum Research and Development.* London: Heinemann Educational Books.

Stenhouse, L. (1981) 'What counts as research?' in *British Journal of Educational Studies,* 29(2), pp. 103–114.

Suoranta, J. & Moisio, O-P. (2009) 'Ensimmäinen vuosikymmen' in Moisio, O-P., & Suoranta, J. (Eds.) *Kriittisen pedagogiikan kysymyksiä 3.* Tampere: University of Tampere, pp. 9–25.

Teaching Agency. (2012) *Continuing Your Professional Development.* Available at: http://webarchive. nationalarchives.gov.uk/20111218081624/http://tda.gov.uk/teacher/developing-career/professional-development.aspx [accessed 3 February 2016].

Valtonen, H. & Rautiainen, M. (2013) 'Jyväskylän seminaari ja opettajankoulutuksen akatemisoitumisen ensioireet' in: Rantala, J. & Rautiainen, M. (Eds.) *Salonkikelpoiseksi maisterikoulutukseksi. Luokanopettaja- ja opinto-ohjaajakoulutusten akatemisoitumiskehitys 1970-luvulta 2010-luvulle. Kasvatusalan tutkimuksia (64).* Helsinki: Suomen kasvatustieteellinen seura, pp. 17–31.

Weiskopf, R. & Laske, S. (1996) Emancipatory Action Research: A Critical Alternative to Personal Development or a New Way of Patronising People? In Zuber-Skerritt, O. (Ed.) *New Directions in Action Research.* London: Falmer, pp. 173–182.

Fighting against the flow in theorizing education 153

Wenger, E., White, N. & Smith, J. D. (2009) *Digital Habitats: Stewarding Technology for Communities.* Portland, OR: CPsquare.

Whitehead, J. (1985) 'An Analysis of an Individual's Educational Development: The Basis for Personally Orientated Action Research' in Shipman, M. (Ed.) *Educational Research: Principles, Policies and Practices.* Lewes: Falmer, pp. 97–108.

12 Towards the future

Matti Rautiainen & Andrea Raiker

To see what the future might hold for the concept of educating for democracy, it is clear from all the chapters that we must first consider the past, as it provides the principles and the platform on which developments are based. In Chapter 1 of this volume, we have acknowledged the struggles and hardships endured by men and women over the centuries to obtain universal suffrage, but have argued that democratic citizenship is more than a duty to vote on polling day. For us, the Socratic ontology that to be human involves constant engagement with deliberations on the constitution and achievement of the 'good life' still holds. Democratic practices are manifested through what Habermas terms communicative action in the public sphere, in other words, the sayings, doings and relatings of individuals in the social and cultural contexts. So as well as participating in politics, for example, through the ballot box, democracy is an essential part of human life and humanity and cannot be separated from everyday life. We have taken Dewey's perspective that individuals have the propensity for critical evaluation and the capacity to act upon their judgements if empathetic environments are established for democratic life. Schools and systems under which they operate and the institutions that produce the teachers that work with them should be empathetic environments. As Dewey would agree, the fundamental work of schools is not just to impart and instill the knowledge and understanding required by society for economic growth and profit; it is also to develop communality and communal life, the stuff of democratic living.

Our discussion in Chapter 1 concluded with the proposition that schools and teacher education institutions in England were more concerned with enforcing compliance on teaching and learning for competitive reasons, such as improved performance in international tests such as the PISA exercise, than developing environments where citizens' abilities to engage effectively with democracy and its processes could be developed. In contrast, Finland, with its background in social democracy and belief in the paramount importance of teachers and their autonomy, seemed to provide greater potential for promoting and developing democracy. Clearly, England is the more neo-liberal of the two countries, wielding greater control over its education system, its teachers and their 'voice'. However, intimations that in fact the picture was more complex were beginning to reveal themselves. In England, pupil and student representation on councils at schools and universities are common, thus providing fora where the learners' voices could join those of their teachers and lecturers in establishing collaborative action; in contrast, in Finland pupils' unions have little influence on decision-making. Whereas group work is an established and encouraged pedagogy in England, supporting the utilization of individuals' skills and knowledge in collaborative projects and the emergence and development of the potential for leadership, Finnish schools prefer didactic class teaching and increasing individual attainment through teacher/child interaction. It seemed that Finnish schools, despite being more successful in international tests such as PISA, could be creating passive subordinates as teachers enforce their own views of democracy rather than giving pupils the opportunity to experiment with 'democracy in action' from their own perspectives.

The discussions in all chapters have been directed at identifying the key elements in developing democratic practices through comparing the similarities and differences in educating for democracy in England, Finland and, where relevant, other nations also. The purpose of this was to enable us to come to some conclusions on how democratic practices could be developed as a basis for encouraging shared understanding and an agreed direction for Europe and beyond in the future.

The nature of education as well as debate concerning education is always future-oriented, even if the contents of debate arise from contemporary analysis of schooling. New kinds of debate began in Finland in December 2013. The most recent PISA results were released then, and Finland's ranking position fell from sixth place to twelfth in mathematics, from third to sixth in literacy and in science from second to fith. Even though rankings in the PISA exercise have never held a significant role in the developmental work of Finnish schools, many stakeholders, including politicians, became concerned. This led to intense debate concerning the state of the Finnish comprehensive school and its future. Core questions in this debate have been: what are the skills needed in the future? What kind of pedagogy is needed to acquire these skills? In response, the Finnish government reacted in a number of ways. The Ministry of Education and Culture created a project called *Basic education of the future – Let's turn the trend*. The final report of the project was released in 2015 and highlighted nine broad themes to develop Finnish basic education. One theme is directed at developing the operating culture of the school and the structure of the school day:

> The operating culture and structures of the school must support the pupils' learning, wellbeing and participation. The school will be developed as an ethical and a learning community where pupils have a voice and a choice, and also responsibility for their own learning.
>
> (Oukrim-Soivio et al, 2015:8.)

At the same time, the National Board of Education published a new National Core Curriculum for basic education in 2014 (to come into force on August 1, 2016). The new curriculum emphasizes active learning processes, new learning environments and cooperation between other stakeholders in society. Of importance, teachers are encouraged to teach their subjects through phenomenon-based learning. This includes participation in, and development of, the democratic culture. However, as chapters in this book have demonstrated, there has always been a gap between aims based on theory and school practice on issues concerning participation in, and educating for, democracy. Will the aims described above be only new failed attempts or the beginning of a new era – even a third educational reform in Finland?

Finland has had two important educational reforms in basic education. Uno Cygnaeus's vision to establish a folk school system was realized in the 1860s. Schools were opened for boys and girls. A hundred years later, the introduction of a new nine-year comprehensive school system equalized education radically. Continuing studies after basic education were guaranteed through the security provided by the Finnish welfare state. The last reform did not encourage the emergence of pupil voice in school, even if this was a firm promise in the new curriculum for basic education issued in 1970. However, the 21st-century vision for Finnish education is based more than previously around the ideas of democracy, pupil's participation and voice, including pupil-centered learning methods. These will be achieved *via* different approaches based on cooperation between teachers and other stakeholders. The difference compared with earlier reforms is significant, because the development is based on 'bottom-up' direction and experimental work in schools instead of centralized models imposed by the government. The nature of the new reforms is for them to be introduced in an evolutionary, rather than a revolutionary, manner.

The discussion above highlights several fundamental differences underlying recent educational reforms in Finland with those introduced in England. Firstly, in England, decreasing achievement was placed firmly at the door of teachers, their knowledge and their expertise. Pupil's participation and voice, including pupil-centered learning methods, were already embedded in teachers' pedagogic approaches, in part through the influence of progressive schools such as Summerhill (see Chapter 7) and the battery of reforms speedily introduced by the Labour government post-election victory in 1997, outlined in Chapter 3. The principle of increasing democratic involvement was not considered. Rather, also argued in Chapter 3, an assumption was made and published in the *Teachers' Standards* that teachers' understanding of 'democracy' was a given; what teachers had to demonstrate was that they were not undermining democracy and 'fundamental British values' in their professional and personal lives.

There is some evidence that this assumption, that democratic practices are embedded in English culture, has some truth. For example, recent successive British governments have extended the range of types of schools. Whereas in Finland, all schools are comprehensive, England has a diverse range of schools, ranging from council-controlled state schools following the *National Curriculum* and employing teachers with Qualified Teacher Status (QTS) to academies that are independent of the local council, can choose their own curriculum and can employ non-qualified teachers; from community schools controlled by the local council and that are not influenced by business or religious group to faith schools associated with a particular religion; from schools that are funded by the state to private schools that charge fees. The diversity in English culture is substantial, and this can be cited as an example of growing democracy in that parents have greater choice of schools for their children and teachers with QTS have a greater choice of schools in which to teach. However, as parents' choice of school is principally determined by proximity to home and the time needed to transport the children to school, a technical 'choice' can be no choice at all.

Another indicator of increasing democracy in English schools is choice of curriculum, depending on the type of school. State schools have to follow the *National Curriculum*, but even here there has been loosening of prescription. The current *National Curriculum* came into force in 2014 (apart from curricula for mathematics and English in September 2015 and science for older pupils in September 2017). However, the English government's usual speed in implantation has meant that pupils are still being taught to the existing curriculum and teachers are struggling with integrating old and new content. At the same time, reforms to the national academic tests for pupils aged 16 and 18, and to vocational qualifications, were being brought in the system. Michael Gove, the then Secretary of State for Education, in his speech to the First Education Reform Summit in London in July 2014, stated that:

> One of the most encouraging trends in English education – which helps the cause of reform worldwide – is the way in which those leading the debate and driving evidence-based change in our schools are teachers.
>
> (2014a: online)

However, the teaching unions maintain that teachers have not had a part of in redrafting the new curriculum. It appears that the 'teachers' referred to by Gove were individuals who had taught had some time in their careers but were not the 'grassroots' teachers who worked with pupils every day. In contrast with the Finnish experience, this cannot be designated 'bottom-up' reform.

Nevertheless, teachers have been given more control over what and how they teach and how they assess attainment. The curriculum documents are brief, compared to earlier versions, and the attainment targets are no longer defined year on year. At the end of a given key stage, pupils are simply '. . . expected to know, apply and understand the matters, skills and processes specified in the programme of study' (DfE, 2014b:82). Published league tables that rank schools' success in pupil attainment in national tests at age 16 are to take into account the socio-economic background of individual school's intake as well as success in examinations. In democratic terms, this is of great importance because of the wide socio-economic disparity between regions in England, and between urban and rural localities in those regions.

What will drive educating for the future in England is the acknowledgement of, and the management of diversity, at all levels of the education system. The variety of school types has already been discussed. In the UK, 19.5 percent of the population are from ethnic groups other than white British (ONS, 2011), and England is the most ethnically diverse of UK's four countries, with average income inequality being above the OECD average, though decreasing since 2009. Inclusion is an important aspect of both the *National Curriculum* and the *Teachers' Standards* documents, and the SEN Code of Practice is, like the *National Curriculum*, a statutory document. All teachers have a legal duty to implement the requirements of these documents, and the Ofsted system is designed to ensure this. Both the *National Curriculum* and the *Teachers' Standards* have statements concerned the teaching of democracy and democratic values. But with the number of schools being able to set their own curricula increasing, how is adherence to the teaching of democracy and democratic values to be maintained? The role of Ofsted becomes very significant indeed, but at the time of writing, inspects most but not all schools.

Also affecting educating for democracy in England is curriculum focus on English, mathematics and science. Fifty-six of the 105 pages of the *National Curriculum: secondary education* document are dedicated to these three subjects; 25 pages are dedicated to the remaining nine subjects, with three to citizenship which contain statements on the teaching of democracy and democratic values, politics, law and justice, and four to history. If, as argued in various chapters of this book, our democratic principles and practices arise from cultural sociopolitical conditions, all of which have historical roots, and that education has a significant part in passing on those principles and practices, will the English curriculum's emphasis on English, mathematics and science undermine educating for democracy?

One other worrying aspect to be considered for the future of educating for democracy in England is the move of ITE away from universities into schools that are deemed to be high-performing by Ofsted and the impact of this on student and practicing teachers' knowledge and understanding of theory. In his speech to the First Education Reform Summit (DfE, 2014a: online), Michael Gove said:

> Instead of a faddish adherence to quack theories about multiple intelligences or kinaesthetic learners, we have had the solidly grounded research into how children actually learn of leading academic . . .

Here the ex-Minister for Education shows his lack of understanding of educational theory and its role. Empirical research takes place with defined samples, thus locking findings into place and time. Theory concerns a bigger world, or ontological and epistemological perspective, in which the findings of empirical research can be located so that tensions, contradictions and congruencies can be identified and investigated. We support a principal finding of the British Education Research Association's *Research and the Teaching Profession; Building the capacity for a self-improving education system* (2014) that teachers should be involved with research so that teachers themselves, who are the practicing experts in the field of education, can work towards a dynamic, democratically driven system.

Perhaps the constant flow of reforms endured by teachers and learners over the last three decades has been in part caused by the under-theorized, over-reactive 'solidly grounded research' advocated by successive Ministers of Education who are not themselves educationalists.

So, what answers do the deliberations in this book suggest to the two key questions raised in Chapter 1? What are the similarities and differences in educating for democracy in England and Finland that could be used as a basis for developing shared understanding and an agreed direction for Europe and beyond? What are the key elements in developing democratic practices and how might this be achieved?

Each member state of European Union is strongly committed to education through its national decision-making system and the policies produced by it. However, it is clear from the discussions in this book that there are significant differences as well as similarities between England and Finland and the wider educational community. To suggest that a particular pedagogy or resource used successfully in one country can be uprooted and replanted successfully in another is clearly simplistic and shows lack of knowledge of the cultures underpinning the principles directing societies. Nevertheless, we can learn from each other and, through primary and secondary research, discover the most effective and empathetic ways of establishing EU-wide shared practices. This being the case, the EU has an important role to play in developing knowledge and understanding of the policies, principles, processes and practices underpinning education throughout its area of influence, for example, *via* exchange programs for teachers and students from all phases. The EU is also stressing the importance of and supporting member states to engage with developmental work in education *via* different programs. Key common themes appearing in these programs are active citizenship and education for democracy. However, this book and its comparative approach between two EU countries points to reasons why national aspects will remain at the heart of a country's educational policies. Firstly, education has had an extremely important role in establishing the community building of nations and their individual identities. Educational systems reflect these national aims and thus demonstrate differences when compared with each other. Secondly, education has strong historical and cultural roots, which creates bases for policies and practice that are both explicit and implicit. A third major issue is the political spirit of a nation's society. This can be seen in our two countries' attitudes to private schools. In England, they are a long-established and important part of the educational system, producing the majority of senior politicians and underpinning elitism. Instead, in Finland, private schools have been and are seen as a threat to equality. Even so, the chapters in this book demonstrate that both countries stress the same democratic principles and are trying to promote the well-being of all citizens.

It is clear that history and politics are creating frameworks for everyday life in schools in both countries, but in England, innovation is implemented with speed. For example, after the Salamanca Statement was published, England reacted quickly to ensure its requirements were enacted throughout the education system; in Finland, 'inclusion' was debated rather than actioned. However, preventing exclusion has always been emphasized in Finnish educational policy; in England, because of the diverse nature of class society, the greater population and the stronger tradition of neo-liberalism, it has been more difficult to attain. Such comparisons are instructive but in a sense the differences they reveal are superficial, covering the complex phenomenon of education, the focus of this book. Josephine Moate described her experiences and reflections in Chapter 2: the more she has been reflecting and studying, the more she has become aware of the complex relationships between history, culture, politics and education. The chapters in this book go some way in understanding these complex relationships which, we suggest, provide the most important starting points for developing the future of educating for democracy.

The teacher's role in educating for democracy is of the greatest importance. Even if their work is structured by different frameworks (for example, tradition in Finland and political supervision in England), teachers are the cornerstones of their societies because of their fundamental role of constructing, transferring and interpreting the knowledge and understanding that their societies deem to be essential for life and fulfillment, for self/employment and for citizenship. In this, it appears that teachers share similar principles internationally, not only because of the emphasis they place on high standards of professionalism, which in some countries like Finland is awarded with high status, but also because teachers want a 'good life' for their pupils. Fairness and altruism are characteristics typically found in teachers in England, Finland and all over the world. These characteristics and the values they share create a kinship between them, a kinship revealed through opportunities such as this book to establish relationships to communicate, to deliberate and to learn. The universal endeavor of teachers to create good lives for our children, as Aristotle would have understood, is the basis for developing education for democracy.

The central idea for this book was John Dewey's idea that schools should be constructed as miniature societies reflecting the greater external society whose activities are directed by democratic principles. As we have argued, his aim is still relevant and could be advanced further in both Finland and England. According to Dewey, the key elements in developing democratic practices are teachers who are willing to study and act together in exploring different solutions to emphasize education for democracy. Such an intellectual community also encourages both teachers and students to be innovative and carry out research to achieve greater democracy in schooling and education. In other words, a key element in educating for democracy is to give space and time for innovation and research to become part of everyday life in schools. Such a basic idea for development is very simple and brings us back to the fundamental ontological question- what is it to be human? The philosopher and political theorist Hannah Arendt formulated this basic question in her famous study *The Human Condition* in the following way: 'What I propose, therefore, is very simple: it is nothing more than to think what we are doing' (Arendt, 1958:5).

Towards the future 161

Arendt's question has also been fundamental to this book. As we described in Chapter 1, we started our work by having discussions together around the topic in which both sets of academics were interested – education for democracy. This led towards an idea that we would study the topic from different perspectives with researchers from both countries. This was an innovation in practice and a research opportunity in the sense described in the paragraphs above. The research involved created an intellectual community; so began this study of the phenomenon of education for democracy as articulated in two main research questions. So the question to be asked now is: how did the community of authors experience the process, and what did they learn?

Even if the comparative approach is common in educational research, it is rare that chapters or articles in a book are written together with authors from two different cultures to the extent demonstrated in this volume. Authors were asked for their experiences and thoughts on the collaborative approach taken for this volume. Their responses were remarkably similar. Interaction was emphasized as a core phenomenon in this project. Some authors talked with each other *via* video seminars, and later, they used different ICT tools for communication. Nevertheless, they missed face-to-face meetings for deepening thinking and understanding of the concepts of democracy and education for democracy. However, discussions and shared curiosity made the process very democratic, which was one of the key themes authors stressed in their learning processes.

Two perspectives were frequently voiced by authors. Firstly, stereotypes were questioned. England and Finland are different in their democracies as well as in their school systems, which reflect the general state of society. The more they studied their phenomena from their own and each other's perspectives, the more they became conscious of complexity. Secondly, authors described how the comparative aspect had helped them to understand their own system, principles and culture: '... it made me think of Finnish education from different perspective. There are more nuances after this project'.

The identification of factors experienced while collaborating for this book, like curiosity, discussion and the construction of shared understanding, are fundamental to educating for democracy. They reflect John Dewey's thinking on education for democracy; however, this book makes it clear that we are still some distance from realizing Dewey's ideals even if they are seen as educational objective in many Western societies. Thus, we have to ask again and again the same question Arendt set up in her book *The Human Condition*: what are we doing? One very important way to develop democracies is based on research into innovative, democratically driven class and seminar room practice, practice which will become regarded and generally adopted as 'best practices' if they work well and are acceptable to the wider society. In the context of education for democracy this could be done through interventions in schools based on action research (see Chapters 10 and 11). The principles behind action research are appropriate for exploring educating for democracy because it is an approach where individuals working in their own locality can involve the whole school

162 *Matti Rautiainen & Andrea Raiker*

community and engage it in their commitment innovative intervention. These interventions should also resonate strongly with the technologies of our time. This book has used technology to enable the democratic attributes of curiosity, discussion and the construction of shared understanding to create and shape it. If we ask from ourselves, 'what is the future of education for democracy' in Europe, we can also ask: what is the future of education for digital democracy in Europe?

References

Arendt, H. (1958) *The Human Condition*. Chicago: The University of Chicago Press.
British Educational Research Association. (2014) *Research and the Teaching Profession; Building the Capacity for a Self-Improving Education System*. Available at: https://www.bera.ac.uk/wp-content/uploads/2013/12/BERA-RSA-Research-Teaching-Profession-FULL-REPORT-for-web.pdf?noredirect=1 [accessed 1 February 2016].
Department for Education. (2014a) *Speech: Michael Gove Speaks About the Future of Education Reform*. Available at: www.gov.uk/government/speeches/michael-gove-speaks-about-the-future-of-education-reform [accessed 1 February 2016].
Department for Education. (2014b) *The National Curriculum: Secondary Curriculum*. Available at: http://www.gov.uk/dfe/nationalcurriculum [accessed 1 February 2016].
Office for National Statistics (2012) *Ethnicity and Identity in England and Wales 2011*. Available at http://www.ons.gov.uk/ons/dcp171776_290558.pdf [accessed 22 January 2016]
Oukrim-Soivio, N., Rinkinen, A. & Karjalainen, T. (2015) Tulevaisuuden peruskoulu. *Opetus- ja kulttuuriministeriön julkaisuja 8/2015*.

Index

Academies UK 14, 38, 71, 72, 94–5, 98, 131, 156
accountability 14, 31, 77, 110, 116–17; Anglo-Saxon tradition 75; democratic 73; perspectives on 93–108
Acts of the Finnish Parliament: *1866 Primary School 111; 1921 Compulsory Education 111, 120; 1958 Primary School 111; 1968 Comprehensive School 112; 1996 Amendment to Comprehensive School 111; 1998 Basic Education 27, 74, 111–13, 118; 2014 Child and Families 114*
Acts of the UK Parliament: *1870 Foster 111; 1886 Idiots 111; 1893 Blind and Deaf Children 111; 1944 Education 6, 7, 48, 94, 111; 1981 Education 112; 1988 Education 7, 94, 96; 1992 Education 97; 1994 Education 7; 2001 Special Educational Needs and Disability 113; 2006 Education and Inspection 99; 2011 Education 45; Representation of the People (Equal Franchise) 6*
Ahlman, E. 142
Alppila School 83–91
Alternative Education Resource Organization 82
Arendt, H. 160–1
Aristotle 4, 43, 160
assessment 8, 33, 96, 99, 100, 131; Assessment Reform Group 33; and constructivism 50; learner involvement 38; for learning 33, 39, 74, 75; of learning 11, 33, 74, 76; Learning difficulties 112–18; marking 22; and normalisation 74, 77; Pearson analysis 2; PISA (Programme for International Student Assessment) 2, 9, 29–30, 52; Research 133, 136; teacher assessment 14, 75, 85

austerity 150; anti-austerity policies 4; Syriza 11
Australia 102–3, 115
authenticity 13, 44, 58, 60, 61, 76
authoritarianism 119
autonomy 2, 44, 75; English teachers 3, 10, 33, 48, 98; Finnish teacher 34–5, 45, 49, 51, 74, 75, 85, 154; local authority 74, 103, 105, 112; political 10; schools 39, 95, 99, 100; student 76; teacher educators 10, 50, 135

Blair, A. (Tony) 8, 17
Bourdieu, P. 83
British Education Research Association (BERA) 148, 158

Calvin, J. 150
Cameron, D. 8, 64
centralisation 71; of the curriculum 17, 70–3; of school management 73–4
China 29, 30, 31
citizenship 1, 4, 11, 12, 42, 78, 96, 109, 128, 158–60; citizenship education 27, 43, 63, 54, 72; democratic citizenship 12, 36, 52, 56, 154
classroom displays 10, 17, 18, 24
class system 6–7, 52; aristocracy 5, 10; elite 5, 28, 37, 77; middle class 55, 56, 64; working class 7
collaboration 47, 50, 57, 59, 69, 75, 86, 91, 113, 121, 131, 133, 147; in learning 32, 54
community 1, 13, 58, 59, 78, 82, 90, 99, 101, 105, 127, 136, 147, 162; curriculum 73; dialogic 67; intellectual 159–61; local 56, 72, 116; as representative democracy 5, 109; school 46, 51, 78, 83, 85, 87–8, 91, 110, 119, 155–56; students' conceptions of 46

164   *Index*

comprehensive education 10, 11, 47, 73
Conservative Party UK 7, 47, 48, 94–6, 117, 145
Critical Integrative Teacher Education (CITE) 130
critical pedagogy 45, 57, 76, 143, 149
critical thinking 4, 42, 52, 55–6, 63, 128, 145
Cygnaeus, U. 10, 143, 156

decision making 9, 10, 55, 67, 74, 82, 86, 159; pupil involvement in 2, 4, 11, 36, 52, 155; within school communities 46, 54, 76, 78, 90
deliberation 39, 127, 137, 154, 159
Denmark 78, 115, 118
Dewey, J. 8, 17, 25, 46, 127, 154; aims of education 1; conceptions of social being 13, 43, 44; critical debate 42; development of communal life 5; education and democracy 2, 4–5, 10, 47, 55, 161; individuality 1, 5, 42, 43, 55; schools as miniature democratic societies 5, 8, 160
dialogue 7, 33, 38, 55–7, 62, 65; and creativity 28, 31; and democratic education; 13, 29, 55, 67; and listening 28, 36, 64, 66; and problem-posing 66; and teacher education 67; between theory and practice 51; using art to promote 64; and voice 28, 36
Diet for Estates (Swedish parliament) 9
differentiation 101, 113
diversity 60, 61, 65–6, 75, 77, 111, 136, 157; and democratic education 12, 55; of practice 51; of schools 47; of students 52, 109–10

Economist Intelligence Unit metrics 9, 11
employability 69; in Denmark 78
empowerment 13, 54, 59, 60, 67
Engeström, Y. 140
Enlightenment 4, 32, 39, 146
equality 11, 14, 27, 58, 64, 75, 82, 84, 91, 109, 112, 135–6, 159; and authenticity 13, 60–1; and democracy 33, 67; and inequality 5, 54, 65, 105, 131, 158; Nordic society 52
European Union 2, 11, 42, 52, 159

Finnish Education Evaluation Center 99–100
Finnish Institute for Educational Research 100

Foucault, M. 2, 24, 83
freedom 4, 5, 14, 24, 76; and authority 33, 39; and curriculum 69, 73; education as the practice of 66; pedagogical freedom 2, 33, 44, 51; power of 83; of speech 3; and teacher education 34
free schools UK 38, 70, 71, 72, 78
Freire, P. 12, 27, 30–1, 33, 54, 64, 143, 147; and affection 31–2; on authenticity 61; on 'banking' 28, 57; on 'competent technicians' 13; on constructing world views 28, 33, 36; on 'cultural workers' 13; developing 'conscious' beings 55; on dialogue 28, 31, 56, 62, 63, 66; on freedom and authority 33, 39; giving students voice 28, 56; on progressive teaching 27–8, 31; teacher as facilitator 28–9; on teacher attributes 27–8, 33, 36; on teacher training 30

global education reform movement 104
Gove, M. 98, 157–8
grammar schools 7, 11, 47, 94
Greece 3, 4, 11
group work 32, 38, 59–62, 64–5, 70, 76, 84, 155; impact of classroom design on 46–7

Habermas, J. 75, 146, 154
hard power 82–3
Heidegger, M. 32
holistic pedagogy 90
Hollo, J.A. 142
hooks, B. 13, 54, 64, 143; changing selves 56; and dialogue 56, 61; importance of background 65; and teacher education 66; and transgression 61, 67
Horkheimer, M. 44–5
humanism 32, 145

inclusion 14, 52, 69, 78, 109–21, 142, 158, 160
International Civic and Citizenship Education Study 2, 36, 54

knowledge 1, 4, 12, 32, 46, 76, 103, 113, 130, 137, 154–7, 159–60; civic 54; as commodity 2, 3; and control 69; curriculum 30, 31, 72, 105; and democracy 11, 35, 43, 151; lack of 60, 64; of students 28, 36, 56, 66; subject 29–30, 31, 34, 36; theoretical 142, 145–8, 150, 158

Index   165

Labour Party 7, 8, 47, 70
Local Education Authorities (LEAs) 7, 35, 48, 70, 75, 85, 111
Locke, J. 4, 150

Magna Carta 6, 7, 9
Milton, J. 150
multiculturalism 55, 63

National Core Curriculum for Basic Education 2, 10, 27, 50, 74, 108, 111, 114, 119, 154; *and democracy* 27, 35, 36
National Curriculum 13, 29, 48, 51, 63, 71–2, 77, 79, 93, 95, 98, 103, 156–8
Neill, A.S. 87, 89
neo-liberalism: and bio-power 2; and centralisation 71; and competition, compliance and political control 8, 69; and educator professionalism 3, 150; and employability 78; and the EU 2; and inclusion policy 14, 110, 160; as knowledge as commodity 1, 2; and liberalism 5–6, 39; and performativity 7; and research 14; teachers as instruments 2; teacher tension 37
Norway 34. 102–3

OECD 52, 93, 99, 102, 158
Office of Standards in Education (Ofsted) 7, 31, 44, 48, 87–90, 96–8, 158; and dissemination of classroom practice 35, 147; and subject knowledge 31

Parent Council 99
Parliament: England 6, 7, 9, 95; Finland 9, 10, 74
Pedagogical progressivism 82
PedArt 55–9, 62, 65, 66
phenomenon-based curriculum 84, 91, 143
PISA (Programme for International Students Assessment) 2, 9, 29, 31, 34, 38, 52, 93, 98–105, 116, 120, 154–5
Practice of architectures 137
professionalism 47, 48, 78, 98, 105, 143. 145, 160; deprofessionalisation in England 8; development in England 48; development in Finland 37; and neo-liberalism 3; pre-service teachers' conceptions of 12; as responsibility 50; uninformed 33, 48
progressive education 7, 47, 81–2; embodied in teachers 27, 28, 31; in schools 13, 14
public schools UK 47, 95

Rights of the Child convention 89
role of teacher 19, 44, 55–6; 61, 64, 77, 113; in art education 73–4; in China 29; in England 29–37, 38; as facilitator 28, 47; in Finland 34–7, 39, 45, 64; in promoting democratic values 27, 36; 39, 73–4; in USA 29

Salamanca Statement 14, 113, 115, 118–19, 121, 159
Salomaa, J.E. 142
School Council 11, 73, 88–90, 98–100
Snellman, J.V. 142
Social Democratic Party Finland 10
Socio-constructivism 31, 38, 50
Socratic ontology 154
soft power 82–3, 90
Stenhouse, L. 145, 147
suffrage 154: in England 6; in Finland 10
Summerhill 83, 87–91
Sweden 9, 10, 34

teacher status 48, 50, 93, 98; as a profession 34, 37, 47, 51; Qualified Teacher Status (QTS) 30, 31, 98, 146, 156
teacher study books 35, 36
testing 93, 96, 102, 104, 115–18; in Finland 14, 21–2, 34, 77, 100; General Certificate in Secondary Education (GCSE) 14; Standardized Assessment Tests (SATs) 14, 48, 70, 96; Teachers' Standards 31
textbooks 19–21, 22, 25, 84
Thatcher, M. 7, 8, 32, 145
Topelius, Z. 10
tradition 9, 10, 49, 50, 54, 84, 86, 90–1, 119, 135, 160; of accountability effects of on Finnish education 45–6, 142–3; traditional classrooms 47, 87, 100–1; traditional teacher 28, 51, 75–6, 63

United Nations 1, 9, 89–90
United States of America (USA) 29, 30, 31, 32, 63, 116, 118

voice 12, 36, 74–6, 113, 136, 145, 154–6; and citizenship 1, 42; curriculum 69; and decision-making 36, 76; decrease in 71; finding 56, 58, 63–7; in planning curricula 73; and questioning 28, 33; as a reflective process 44; student voice and governance 78, 120, 131

166   Index

Warnock Report 112, 118
Weber, M. 3, 141
White Papers UK 105; *The Content of Initial Training* 7; *The Importance of Teaching* 8, 45, 93

Wilenius, R. 142
Winnicott, D. 81, 88–9
Woodhead, C. 97
Wright Mills, C. 144